"Gregory Gourdet takes us on an emotional journey from his Haitian family and roots to his not-so-pretty bout with drugs to his obsession with running and health. A journey that eventually places us all around *Everyone's Table*. Gregory brings us modern healthy food that's unprocessed, dairy-free, bright, and beautiful with just as much ingredient diversity and elegance. This may become my number one go-to cookbook."
—CARLA HALL, chef and TV host

"*Everyone's Table* celebrates the rich culture of Gregory Gourdet's heritage with seriously good cooking and a global pantry of healthy ingredients. His food is fresh, inventive, and bursting with flavor, and every dish is free of gluten, dairy, soy, and refined sugar. Gregory's life experiences have transformed his approach to eating and living, and now his delicious journey is documented in these exciting recipes."
—STEVEN SATTERFIELD, author of *Root to Leaf* and chef at Miller Union

Everyone's Table

Everyone's Table

GLOBAL RECIPES
for MODERN HEALTH

Gregory Gourdet
and JJ Goode

HARPER WAVE
An Imprint of HarperCollinsPublishers

Contents

A Recipe for Change

When I woke up, I was upside down.

It was New Year's Eve, 2007, and, to mark the occasion, I had spent the past twelve hours with my lips glued to a bottle. On my drive home, I blinked and next thing I knew, my Nissan Altima was in midair, and then the ceiling was the floor. Everyone's journey to health takes a different route. That car crash wasn't even the turning point of mine. Still, here I am.

I was the first in my family to be born in America. Five years before, my parents moved from Port-au-Prince to Brooklyn, and into a new world full of high-rises, underground trains, and frozen water that fell from the sky.

Even though we lived far from Haiti, our world was, for the most part, Haitian. When I was born, we moved to Queens and our neighborhood, way past the last stop on the E train, was full of people from lakay—Haitian Creole for "home." Our house was a hub of roving relatives, a blur of grandparents, aunts, uncles, cousins, and cousins of cousins coming and going from back home. And thank goodness, because the constant stream of family minded me and my sister while my mom and dad juggled multiple jobs and school. On weekends, we ping-ponged between friends and relatives in our neighborhood as well as Haitian enclaves in Brooklyn and New Jersey, attending endless church services, communions, and, more to my taste, meals.

Each woman in my family—every tante (auntie) and each mémère (grandma)—had a fragrance.

When I saw Tante Cecile, I swear I could smell her diri ak pwa, a fluffy rice-and-bean pilaf scented with garlic and clove, even when we weren't at her tiny Queens walk-up. When I think of Mémère Mane, my father's mother, I can smell her poul nan sòs: chicken legs marinated in Scotch bonnet chiles, thyme, and citrus and then stewed with tomato and peppers. It's as vivid as the sound of her broken English and the feel of her soft cheeks.

My mother smells like Sundays. When we'd get home from Mass each week, she'd always have a lavish spread awaiting us. As my mother decked out the table with various pots and platters, we'd snack on patties—buttery, flaky dough with fiery fillings like spicy beef and salt cod—my father had purchased from Madame George, a friend who ran the nearby Haitian bakery, knowing that soon, the proper meal would begin. My mother would grate and fry taro root to make craggy, golden brown fritters, slipping in slivers of Scotch bonnets to set our tongues aflame, and simmer rice with scallions, garlic, and thyme for pilaf that was tinted black from the addition of djon-djon mushrooms smuggled from Port-au-Prince. There would be legumes of all sorts—red and black and white beans, as well as split peas; makawoni au graten, a delightfully rich macaroni baked with evaporated milk, mayonnaise, and Kraft-brand Parmesan; fried green plantains and griyo, chunks of pork shoulder marinated with citrus, stewed until tender, then roasted until crispy and fatty and irresistible; and of course, to enliven each bite, there was a jar of pikliz, Haiti's condiment of choice, a fiercely tart and spicy jumble of pickled cabbage, carrots, shallots, and lots of Scotch bonnets.

Of course, we occasionally embraced the exotic cuisine of our adopted home as well. We dabbled in Spam and mayo-slathered Wonder Bread, bowls of Hamburger Helper, takeout containers of beef and broccoli, and Betty Crocker cake mixes enriched with extra eggs, freshly grated cinnamon, and Haitian vanilla.

When I was four, my parents sent me to Haiti to live with my maternal grandparents. They wanted a good life in America for me and my sister, who was just one at the time. To provide it, they needed to make enough money—my mom as a hospital microbiologist, my dad as a hospital chemist—to gain a foothold. To earn it, they needed me out of their hair. They also wanted me to experience their home country, which was not technically mine.

I remember my time there in snatches. The air, thick and hot. The tidy single-story house with a big porch. The heavy wood door and its rusty iron key. Whacking skinny, bumpy pods from the branches of zanmann trees, ripping away the flesh with our fingers, and cracking the seed between two rocks to extract the tender tropical almond inside. Yanking Scotch bonnets from the overgrown plants in the yard with my cousin Frederick and competing over who could endure the biggest bite. Running to my grandfather's sewing table to scour the pain from our tongues with the scraps of fabric on the floor.

Once we returned to New York, visits from relatives brought a new kind of excitement. When Tante Michou came to comb Manhattan's Garment District to stock her clothing store in Port-au-Prince or Tante Mona came to visit her sons in college, they brought suitcases overflowing with bags of cashew brittle and condensed-milk fudge and cassava crackers, jars of guava jelly and spicy peanut butter and pikliz, all straight from the source, and our mouths watered in a way they hadn't before. When I was older, bottles of Haitian rum provided a peculiar thrill. But we will get to that.

I was a latecomer to the cooking game. By the time I went to culinary school, I had already been a premed student at NYU, a failed attempt to follow in my parents' footsteps, and studied wildlife biology at the University of Montana, in Missoula. All I had to show for it was the knowledge that I didn't want to do either. Well, that and a newfound commitment to recreational drug use. In high school, my first dalliance with alcohol—40s of Olde English snuck into a Manhattan movie theater for a showing of *New Jack City*—produced an electrifying sense of lightness, a bodily freedom I had never felt before. I chased that freedom for years, sneaking slugs of my parents' Barbancourt straight from the bottle after they had gone to bed, then graduating to smoking weed and dropping acid to snorting ketamine, small-town meth, and cocaine and cocaine and cocaine.

These were still the good times. In Missoula, I managed to do decently in school, juggle two restaurant jobs, *and* hang with my crew of townies and kids from the coasts who bonded over partying. This was the mid-'90s, so we rented out warehouses and commandeered commuter train cars in our platform Pumas, JNCO Jeans, and Polo visors for raves fueled by Techno and ecstasy. When I wasn't high, I was cooking. At first, I cooked with my roommate, Dave, in the tiny bungalow we rented, feeding ourselves for the first time with scrambled eggs and treating the inevitable comedowns with fettuccine Alfredo, scalloped potatoes, and heaps of other cheap, fatty carbs. Later, once I realized that making food and feeding others gave me pleasure, I cooked at a bookstore slash vegetarian deli called Freddy's Feed and Read, where a patient, gracious Dead Head named Celeste taught me to make glossy, colorful pasta salads and sandwiches. I delighted in building them, meticulously stacking tempeh and sauerkraut, spreading pesto or sun-dried tomato mayo to the very edges of sprouted grain bread. I also worked at the Hob Nob, a cafe in town where the chef, Charles, saw potential in my dishwashing and prep skills, letting me griddle veggie burgers during lulls in service. The key, I learned, was to get the patties of ground chickpeas and rice perfectly crisp on the outside before dosing them with Brie. He suggested I consider culinary school.

Endlessly supportive, my parents agreed to help, as long as I cobbled together enough credits for a degree from U of M. Once I did, I set off for the Culinary Institute of America. There, for the first time, I inhaled my classes. I watched Chef Tonelli tournée turnips. I furiously scribbled notes as Chef Brunet made French onion soup. For my exams, I obsessed over the evenness of my carrot dice, the clarity of my consommé, and the amount of saffron in my risotto alla Milanese.

Still, I kept partying. I giggled through a lesson on making cedar-planked salmon with blueberry sauce, still loopy from an acid trip the night before. I did well enough in my program that I was asked to speak at graduation, and I did, stammering and sweating through an intense hangover. Yet from a distance, I was thriving, my habit like the bubbles in a barely simmering stock—visible only to those close enough to see.

When I graduated, I lucked out and got a job working for Jean-Georges Vongerichten at his

four-star flagship, Jean-Georges. I spent almost seven years absorbing his deft reimagining of French food. He blazed the Asian-fusion trail, helping to ignite a movement whose effects we see on the tables of virtually every exciting restaurant to open in the past two decades. Shallots, rosemary, and peppercorns shared plates with mango, ginger, and chile. Instead of butter and demi-glace, he deployed vegetable juices and herb oils. His goal was redefining flavor, not making healthy food, yet the two often went hand in hand. His food felt light and vibrant, and the entire culinary world took notice.

As you've probably guessed by now, when I like something, I go hard. I quickly climbed the ranks in the kitchen, in just five years going from line cook to sous chef to chef de cuisine. At twenty-nine, I was running Jean-Georges's modern Chinese restaurant, 66, creating dishes and menus for one of the best chefs in the world. But as my career accelerated, so did my habit. Cooking and drugs provided a similar thrill because they were both a tightrope walk—at the end was elation, but below were flames and failure in the kitchen and death in the bottle or bag.

In these pursuits, I had comrades, a crew of cooks who shared my work-hard–play-hard priorities. In the City That Never Sleeps, we barely slept. After work, we drank until the clubs got popping, around 2 a.m. At Twilo, Pacha, and Cielo, powders and pills had us dancing through the night and, if we had the next day off, into the morning and afternoon. After-parties led to after-after-parties, and I'd often wake up, sick and disoriented, at a friend's place deep in Harlem or Brooklyn or on the F train in Coney Island, even though I lived in a windowless basement apartment in Queens. Then, that evening, we'd all reunite in the kitchen, comparing war wounds and then busting ass to make caper-raisin emulsion and float frog legs in young garlic soup.

These were good times, too, until they weren't. When the balance tipped, my life sped up, like all trips downhill. I started hanging with a crew who went as hard as I did. Soon I was drinking at work and freebasing at night. Inevitably, I got fired. I did stints at various shitty restaurants around town until a friend insisted I try rehab. But I drank during my outpatient program. My best friend took back his apartment keys. Seeking change or escape, I moved to San Diego and joined a gym. I would stop drinking for weeks, in an attempt to keep the demons at bay and to keep them secret from my new community, only to relapse spectacularly, as I did on that fateful New Year's Eve, when after twelve hours of drinking I decided to drive home. Somehow, I escaped the shell of bent metal and broken glass with just a small scratch above my left eye. I was lucky that I spent the night in jail and not the ICU.

In a movie about an addict, this would be the moment everything changed, when the protagonist checks himself into rehab and emerges a new man. But this isn't a movie. A couple of weeks later, I was blackout drunk again. Six months after that, I was back on cocaine. It took another year for me to quit drinking and doing drugs. There was no new humiliation or accident or tearful conversation with a friend. I'd already had so many of those. Instead, it was a day like any other. I met my friend Richard, himself an alcoholic in recovery, in an Ikea parking lot to go shopping. It was 8 a.m. He was starting his day and, thanks to plenty of cocaine, I hadn't yet finished the one before. We talked, we shopped, and then I said it for the first time: I needed help. I was ready for a change.

A few days later, at his suggestion, I walked into my first AA meeting. I introduced myself as an alcoholic and addict, my voice breaking from the weight of hearing myself say those words aloud for the first time. With the support of my family, friends, and AA, I've been sober for 4,416 days. But hey, who's counting?

MY JOURNEY TO MODERN HEALTH

When I finally got sober, I took stock of the years I'd spent battering my body and decided on a revolutionary course of action—to care for it instead. If I'm honest, though, I also needed to fill the time

I had been spending on less wholesome stuff. And like I once did with partying, I went all in. I did yoga, I became a gym rat, I got way into CrossFit, and I ran. I had tried running once before, when I was staying with my parents during that unsuccessful stint in outpatient rehab. I would make it two miles, then hobble home in extreme pain. Now I ran after my shifts in the kitchen, I ran during the hours when I would have been drunk and high, I ran until I had done fifty marathons and ultramarathons, including two fifty-mile races, several of which were up mountains. They say getting sober can feel like climbing a mountain. And here I was, literally bounding up to the summit.

I also changed my diet. At the time, CrossFit training went hand in hand with a regimen called the Paleo diet. My coach suggested I try it. As you've probably heard, going Paleo essentially means eating how humans supposedly did during the Paleolithic era, when we were hunters and gatherers and before agriculture emerged. On the table are lean meats and wild fish, vegetables and fruits, nuts and seeds. Off-limits were grains, legumes, dairy, and anything processed, foods that modern methods enabled us to consume readily and in abundance but not always in a form that worked for our bodies.

This wouldn't be my first time changing the way I ate. While in college, a documentary on factory farming and an Easter ham that struck me as a little too pink turned me vegetarian for the four years I was there. After a drunken carnivorous relapse during graduation—I accidentally ate a chicken burrito—I magically turned back into an omnivore, just in time for culinary school, where many lessons required tasting duck, short ribs, veal stock, and bacon, and I was ravenous to learn. In other words, sure, if my coach wanted me to go Paleo, I'd ditch my Clif Bars and move that block of cheddar to the freezer. But I didn't expect I'd last.

Yet as I purged my fridge and pantry according to the Paleo dictates, I felt good about what went and what stayed. Everything highly processed went, and with it, preservatives, nitrates, food coloring, and other additives as well as a lot of grains and soy and refined sugars. I wasn't eager to get rid of the dairy, which is why I stowed the cheddar, but when I looked at the balance of all that milk, butter, cheese, and yogurt, I realized I'd be better off without the bad cholesterol and glut of saturated fat.

As I dug into this new lifestyle, I liked what I was eating. I also liked how I felt. For a while, I was Paleo except during the monthslong run-up to a race, when I carbo-loaded with the best of them, leaning on gluten in the process. At some point, I decided I felt so good without gluten that I committed to try running my next race fueled by sweet potatoes and beets and protein-sourced fat. It worked.

I'm not a doctor or a nutritionist, so I'll leave to the professionals any discussion of the anti-nutrient properties of the phytic acid in legumes and the impact of gluten on the immune system. But I can say that going Paleo made me question a notion that had long guided my eating: If something came from nature, it must be good for you. I realized this wasn't always true. And this made me change the way I ate. Dairy wasn't the devil, but its mostly saturated fats weren't as good for you as those mono- and polyunsaturated fats found in nuts and seeds. Soybeans and canola seeds, avocados and olives all grow from the ground, but only the latter two are truly nourishing and turned into oil by processes that retain that nourishment. No vegetables and fruits were off-limits, but I started to focus more on the dark, sexy, nutrient-dense ones—beets, carrots, sweet potatoes, and leafy greens.

While it was Paleo that started me down this path, this way of eating is at the core of so many of the best eating regimens, old and new, from the Mediterranean Diet to Whole30: whole, natural foods, plenty of good fats, nutrient-rich carbs, and meat and seafood raised and harvested by thoughtful farmers and fishers. It's a durable consensus that I like to think of as modern health—not a crash diet but a sustainable lifestyle, not a calorie-counting scheme that equates skinny with healthy but a way of eating that has the health of your body in mind. It's about curtailing the bad stuff and going all in on the good.

I still eat Paleo, more or less. I'm not Draconian about it. I can't pass up my mom's rice and beans (that and her chicken in creole sauce would be my pick for my last supper). I occasionally add corn to my summer salads, because those sweet kernels, just kissed with char from the grill, are so good. And while for true believers, the only Paleo desserts are fresh fruit, I have fun with sweets that are gluten, grain, and refined-sugar free (though I promise you, they don't taste like it).

But ever since I changed my diet, I often pay the price when I deviate. Buttered rice at a friend's wedding had me writhing on the floor in a back room. A pizza from the hyped-up place in town made me look and feel like I had swallowed a volleyball. These are clear signs that those foods aren't good for me. And that's why I stick to foods that are.

Of course, some experiences are worth a little pain. When I'm traveling, I can't *not* have bites of buttery tortelli in Tuscany, sample chewy ramen in Tokyo, or nibble my way through half the case at a Parisian patisserie. The experience of learning and tasting food, particularly at its culinary source, is too important for me, as a chef, to renounce altogether. So is accepting the gesture of hospitality feeding people embodies. To turn down homemade tortillas offered by friends in Mexico City or the rice porridge served by a host in Vietnam would bring another sort of pain.

Then, when I return from those trips, exhilarated and inspired, I make my own accommodations, recreating the flavors I love with the ingredients I choose. I want it all—to feel good, to eat well. And I want the same for everyone.

EVERYONE'S TABLE

The recipes you'll find in this book reflect the food I cook for friends and for myself.

Unless I told you, you probably wouldn't notice that all two hundred recipes are free of gluten, dairy, soy, refined sugar, and legumes. You wouldn't notice that I made them Paleo-friendly, and even more important, that I designed them to focus on superfoods—ingredients with the highest nutrient density; the best fats; and the most minerals, vitamins, and antioxidants. You wouldn't no-

tice, and that's the point. All you'd see is food you want to make. That's one reason I call this book *Everyone's Table*. I want *everyone* to be able to eat great food.

While my home city of Portland, Oregon, might be the butt of jokes for its famously fastidious diners—yes, that was me on that *Portlandia* episode!—it's far from the epicenter of "dietary distinctions," as we call them around here. Millions of Americans adhere to some health-related eating program. They're bloated by beans and suspicious of soy. They're intolerant of gluten and lactose, or they're simply avoiding pasta, bread, butter, and cheese in an effort to slim down or feel better. And you can serve all of them the food in this book. The gluten-free moms and dairy-free dads and the Paleo friends and pizza-loving, pasta-praising ones, too.

Another reason I call the book *Everyone's Table* is that the recipes feature an entire world of flavor and ingredients. For me, food has always been about connection—the stews in my mom's pot, the spices ferried to Queens by my aunts and cousins, the first grilled fish I ate on a Haitian beach all brought me closer to the place I'm from but didn't really know. This became particularly apparent after I got sober, when I had the mental space and time to explore the idea. As I started to travel, every revelatory curry and clafoutis drew me toward an understanding: that there are stories behind everything delicious, and while they can be joyous and inspiring, they can also be tragic and violent. The truth is, brutal colonialism forged the global cuisine we love. Slavery and indentured servitude forced so much culinary fusion. In Haiti, to name just one example, Spanish invaders brought disease that nearly killed the entire native population. From the ashes, a new cuisine emerged, shaped by the Spanish colonizers and later those from France, and by the enslaved Africans who overthrew their masters and made Haiti the first country to abolish the immoral practice. Cooking the food of Haiti connects me not just to my family but to my ancestors, to the complicated history behind the food on my table. When I cook food from cultures other than my own, I hope to deepen my connection to other people, but this only works if we embrace the good and confront the bad.

Today, my cooking reflects a pidgin cuisine informed by the cuisines I love and featuring the flavors I crave. You'll taste the bright acidity and chile-forward dishes inspired both by my Haitian upbringing and my deep affection for Southeast Asian food. You'll enjoy the deep, complex character wrought by unhurried cooking—from the French approach of my formal culinary education, as well as the equally worthy but often slighted techniques from North Africa, Asia, and the Caribbean—balanced by the practical considerations of a busy, normal life.

My hope is for this book to be front and center in your kitchen for a long time. To that end, it aims to be rather comprehensive. It contains close to two hundred recipes, organized into what I think are useful categories. There are, for example, vegetable dishes galore—cold, room temp, and warm, each recipe bringing a dressing, easy pickle, or unexpected cooking technique that will become part of your repertoire and up your vegetable game. There are chapters devoted to my favorite animal proteins: birds; meats; seafood; and even eggs, one of the most economical, quick-cooking, and healthiest protein sources out there. There is one on morning meals; another on drinks, from zero-proof coolers and shrubs to compelling, nutrient-packed smoothies; and of course, desserts, which are healthier thanks to delicious alternative milks and flours and minimally processed sugars but with no sacrifice of the indulgent flavors and textures we all long for. And there are sauces, oils, dressings, fermentations, and condiments that I hope will find their way into your pantry, enlivening your everyday cooking whether you choose to cook through this entire book, my dream of dreams, or not.

How to Use This Book

Like the recipes in most cookbooks, mine, too, require a little extra information to explain why they are the way they are. Read on to find out why you'll see maple syrup and honey and palm sugar and coconut sugar, but not brown and white sugar or agave. Why there's no canola or grapeseed oil, just avocado, olive, and coconut oil. You'll also find my guidance for buying and deploying ingredients that might not be familiar to everyone, as well as my take on selecting meat and seafood, so you can be sure the dishes you make are good for you and good for the world—and also really good to eat.

I hope you'll follow my lead and make certain pantry items, like harissa and red curry paste and preserved lemons and cashew butter, even though store-bought options abound. If you don't, buy the best-quality products you can find that are made without preservatives, inscrutable additives, added sugars, and unhealthy oils.

It deserves note that most ingredients in this book can be purchased from well-stocked natural supermarkets like Whole Foods. The balance can be found at Latin markets, Caribbean markets, and Asian markets, particularly those with a Southeast Asian focus. Ingredients here tend to be less expensive as well, so they're great places to stock up. And of course, you can order practically anything online.

EQUIPMENT

I tried to limit the various pots, pans, baking dishes, and gadgets to those that are relatively standard in a well-stocked kitchen. There are a few inexpensive specialized tools, though, that you may not have that do deserve your attention. A mandoline, a tool common in professional kitchens but not so much at home, allows you to quickly and evenly cut vegetables and fruits. (But please watch those fingers!) A Microplane grater makes it easy to zest citrus and grate cinnamon. A kitchen scale is helpful for any recipe, but essential for making my ice creams (page 347) and especially useful for ingredients that are best measured by weight, such as chocolate and palm sugar.

A spice grinder (a brand new coffee grinder or high-wattage blender works, too) grinds whole spices with the touch of a button. One of my goals for this book is to convince home cooks to use vibrant whole spices, not stale pre-ground powders (see page 12).

A mortar and pestle is also great for pulverizing small amounts of spices and bruising and pounding aromatics. It's also the instrument preferred by many cooks in Thailand and throughout Southeast Asia for making curry pastes, in Mexico for making certain salsas and sauces, and in Haiti for Epis (page 296). I admit to choosing a blender shortcut, both in this book and when time is limited at home. Every recipe in this book that requires a blender works with a standard-issue machine. That said, your life gets easier (and if you ask me, more delicious) with a high-wattage blender (1,000-plus), so consider splurging.

SALT

With its near magical power to enhance flavor, salt is the most important tool in your culinary arsenal. It makes food taste more like its best self. How you use salt is at least as important as what type you use. I start seasoning my food at the beginning of the cooking process, so each component reaps its effect and those components taste that much better, building on one another. A braise made with unsalted sweated onions, for example, might have a well-flavored liquid, but the onions will lack the savory sweetness and roundness that a liberal sprinkle of salt brings out and the dish will be worse for it, a missed opportunity from the jump that lowers its trajectory. I even salt aromatics, like garlic, ginger, and chile, to amplify them early so they flavor the fat they are cooking in, which then flavors the dish.

I also use salt to mellow raw garlic and onions; to draw out liquid before pickling and fermenting; and to season meat, giving it time to penetrate the flesh and break down proteins and muscle fibers so that the meat tastes better and is more tender.

When you season fish and meat, keep in mind that evenly seasoning a fillet or steak isn't always best. You must consider the ratio of the surface, which gets direct seasoning, to the interior, which does not. So as you sprinkle on a piece of salmon or skirt steak, go a bit heavier on the thicker portions and lighter on the thinner portions so each bite has more or less the same saltiness.

The amounts of salt provided in this book come as specific measurements, not pinches. You also might notice that there are no instances of the typical "season to taste" advice. That's not because you shouldn't always season to your own taste (some of us enjoy foods more seasoned than others do and some of us have good reasons to reduce our salt intake). My goal, however, is for readers to make food that tastes the way I intend it to—fully seasoned and at its best. The surest way to achieve that and achieve it consistently is, as my mentors taught me, to measure, measure, measure.

Flaky Sea Salt

I prefer flaky sea salt for finishing, gently crumbling on the flakes just before serving, and for seasoning really fresh things, like raw vegetables and fruits. The flakes have a lovely light crunch and, since the process by which they're made leaves them more or less free of trace mineral content, a bold, clean salty taste. I love the stuff from Jacobsen Salt Co., hand-harvested from Netarts Bay, about fifty miles due west of Portland. It tastes bright and brisk and oceanic. The Maldon brand is good, too.

Kosher Salt

It's familiar enough, but deserves mention here, because the kosher salt amounts in this book were measured using the Diamond Crystal brand. The grains are larger, so they feel good when you grab them, and they're hollow, which means they're less salty than the same amount of Morton, the other common brand, and therefore a bit more forgiving. If you do use Morton for the recipes in this book, take care to use about half the amount I call for.

And while I like and use kosher salt in my kitchen, I also love and use fine sea salt, which is made by the same process as flaky sea salt but is closer to the size and shape of kosher salt. If you use fine sea salt for the recipes in this book, use one third less than the amount I call for—that is, for every 1 tablespoon of kosher salt, use 2 teaspoons of fine sea salt.

OILS

We know some cooking fats are better than others and the recipes in this book reflect that truth. I call for avocado oil, which has a relatively neutral flavor and responds well to high heat, as well as several other oils that I choose for the flavors they offer—olive, coconut, and toasted sesame, to name a few. You won't, however, see any canola, soybean, grapeseed, or blended "vegetable oil." In general, they have a low-nutrient content—because of the particular ingredient from which they're made, the process used to make them, or both—and some are extracted using toxic chemical solvents. Some produce harmful substances when subjected to high heat. Fortunately, there are better choices.

Avocado Oil

This is my pick for high-heat cooking—searing steaks, crisping fish skin, and grilling—as well as for any dressings, flavored oils, or cold preparations that call for a fat with a relatively neutral flavor that lets other flavors shine. Like olive oil, it's stable when subjected to heat, but avocado oil has an even higher smoke point. Also like olive oil, avocado oil is one of the least processed oils, in part because its extraction is easy—it's pressed from the fruit's oil-rich flesh, not the seeds.

Look for avocado oil that's "unrefined" and "extra virgin," the two designations that are regulated. (Other claims like "raw" and "cold pressed" aren't, so take them with a grain of sea salt.) Extra-virgin indicates that the oil is extracted without nutrition-sapping heat and unrefined assures you that the extracted oil isn't then treated with chemicals to bleach or deodorize it. In extra-virgin, unrefined oil, the color, flavor, and nutrient content are preserved, including its very good fat—the monounsaturated oleic acid.

Avocado oil is typically more expensive than grapeseed, canola, and other neutral oils, so this is an especially good product to buy in bulk.

Coconut Oil

You'll find two main kinds of coconut oil in stores: unrefined (often referred to as virgin) and refined. I prefer the former, which is made from cold-pressed fresh coconuts, has a lower smoke point (350°F), and retains the fruit's warm tropical flavor and aroma. (Refined coconut oil is made from steam-processed dried coconuts and has a higher smoke point and a more neutral flavor.)

Coconut oil is great anytime this flavor is welcome, whether for a vegetable sauté or curry. It's wonderful for baking—while it can't quite stand in for butter, in part because of its low melting point, it does give baked goods great body and a lovely fragrance. It compares favorably to animal fats like butter (but not to olive oil) in its effect on cardiovascular health.

For baking recipes, I call for it to be melted, or used in its liquid form. Its low melting point (78°F) means this doesn't necessarily require a pan or microwave. Just let it hang out in a warm place.

Olive Oil

Extra-virgin olive oil is my go-to for everyday

cooking—for sautéing, panfrying, roasting meat and fish, dressing salads, and other preparations that require relatively low heat and benefit from the oil's fruity, grassy, peppery flavor. It's also a great finishing oil, and I even love how its fruitiness vibes with some Asian flavors, something I picked up from Jean-Georges Vongerichten.

Made from unprocessed, cold-treated olives, extra-virgin olive oil is high in antioxidants, and because it has lots of monounsaturated (aka good) fats, too, the oil is stable at relatively high heat. It not only retains its nutritional value when exposed to heat better than other oils, such as sunflower oil, but its low polyunsaturated fat content makes it resistant to the heat-induced damage that can produce harmful compounds. At home I keep two types on hand—a mild, inexpensive olive oil for cooking and another bolder-flavored, sometimes splurgy oil for finishing.

Toasted Sesame Oil

Not to be confused with plain sesame oil, this is the oil pressed from toasted sesame seeds. While plain sesame oil is neutral in flavor and has a high smoke point, toasted sesame oil has a rather bold, nutty complexity and shouldn't be heated for an extended period of time, because it can take on a burnt flavor. I generally treat it as a finishing oil or use it in dressings, though I also occasionally add it toward the end of the cooking process—to an already reduced sauce or during the final tossings of a sauté. I use it primarily for its exceptional flavor, but it doesn't hurt that it's minimally processed and high in antioxidants and unsaturated fats.

SPICES

I'm a big believer in buying whole spices. Switching from the powdered stuff—don't get me started on pre-ground cinnamon!—will instantly make the food you cook taste better. Once spices are ground, the clock on their flavor and fragrance starts ticking, as their volatile oils escape and degrade. And when you buy them from the supermarket, who knows how long ago that was. The best way to control that clock is to start it yourself.

For the most part, recipes in this book call for toasting whole spices in a dry skillet to release those oils (a move that would burn pre-ground spices), invigorating the spices' flavor and delighting the cook and anyone who passes the stove. After they're toasted, let them cool slightly and grind them in an inexpensive spice grinder. I like to grind a little more than I need for a dish, so I've got some handy for the next few days. Occasionally, to create a brighter flavor, I bloom spices in hot oil. This can be done with both whole and ground spices, though, again, if the spices are freshly ground, your food will be better for it.

Ground or whole, spices should be stored in an airtight container away from heat, light, and moisture. Whole spices keep far longer. Still, the sooner you use them, the more vibrant they'll be.

CHILES

Born in the Americas, chiles have made their way around the globe, ingratiating themselves with cooks in Thailand and Spain, the Caribbean and Korea, and Ethiopia and Ghana and becoming a vital part of the world's cuisines. The heat provided by these diverse little fruits comes from the capsaicin contained in their flesh and concentrated in their veins. The compound, technically an irritant but actually a delight, brings a new dimension to food—if umami is the fifth taste (page 23), then to me, heat is the sixth. This heat awakens the palate, stimulates the appetite, and literally makes your mouth water. It increases body heat, boosting blood circulation, lowering blood sugar, and making you sweat, thus ultimately cooling you off.

I use chiles in so much of my food—raw and roasted, simmered and sautéed—whether it's to provide a small spark or set a raging fire. In my recipes, you'll find chiles where you'd expect to, like in Thai soups, Jamaican jerk, and Mexican mole, and also where you might not, like in clam chowder, pineapple smoothies, and chocolate desserts. Chiles, of course, provide more than just heat. They have a vast array of flavors—from grassy serrano chiles and fruity Scotch bonnets to nutty chiles de arbol and smoky gochugaru.

Of course, everyone has different tolerance for the heat of chiles, so if you're particularly sensitive, feel free to use less than I call for.

Dried Chiles

Ancho Chiles: These are dried ripe poblano chiles, and like their fresh counterparts, they're fleshy, earthy in flavor, and mild in heat. Yet they also take on a slightly smoky quality and dried-fruit sweetness.

Chipotle Chiles: Chipotles are ripe jalapeño chiles that have been dried and smoked. In this book, I call for the small reddish-purple variety most popular in the United States, known as chipotle morita, not the larger tan chipotle meco. Not that both aren't lovely—sweet and fiery with a bold smokiness.

Gochugaru: Ground from deseeded sun-dried Korean chiles called gochu, the flakes of gochugaru are spicy, smoky, and slightly sweet—a must for making red kimchi (page 279) and a delicious way to step up your chile game.

Guajillo Chiles: Slightly hotter than pasillas and anchos, guajillos are dried marisol chiles and bring a bright acidity that balances their sweet, fruity flavor.

Pasilla Chiles: The dried version of chilaca chiles, pasillas are mild in heat, earthy, and raisin-y (their name means "little raisin"), but without the sweetness.

Small Dried Red Chiles: Many recipes call for these, and you've got options that provide the bold, sharp heat you're after. You can use chiles de arbol, which have a nutty, slightly acidic flavor. You can use dried Thai chiles, which taste slightly smoky and have an especially high heat level. Or Tianjin chiles, often called Chinese chiles, which have a slightly musty, smoky quality. Whichever I pick, I typically crumble them between my fingers before using.

Occasionally, I offer red chile flakes as an option when their straightforward heat fits the bill.

Fresh Chiles

Fresno Chiles: These sweet, slightly fruity red chiles have a vibrant heat that's a bit milder than jalapeños. Red (ripe) jalapeños make a fine substitute.

Scotch Bonnet and Habanero Chiles: These two cousins share a lantern shape, fruity flavor, and fiery heat. While they're essentially interchangeable for the purposes of this book, they each have their own distinct character. Habanero chiles are more widely available in the United States, but Scotch bonnets are worth seeking out, particularly for the Caribbean- and African-inspired dishes, which were designed with their slightly sweet, especially fruity quality in mind. Any color—orange, green, red—will do. Buy extra—they freeze well.

Serrano and Jalapeño Chiles: These two chiles, popular with Mexican cooks, have a similar bright, grassy flavor and heat, with the slimmer serranos delivering a bit more fire.

Thai Chiles: Also called bird or bird's eye chiles, these chiles are small and slim, 2 to 3 inches long and about ¼ inch wide and can be found at Chinese and Southeast Asian markets and, relatively recently, supermarkets like Whole Foods. They're nearly as fiery as habaneros and Scotch bonnets, with a direct heat and sharp flavor. Red (ripe) chiles are a bit sweeter and fruitier, while green (unripe) ones are grassier. For this book, the two can be used interchangeably. Like habaneros and Scotch bonnets, they also freeze well.

Yuzu Kosho: This fermented product, a specialty of Kyushu, Japan, is a coarse paste made from salt, fresh chiles, and yuzu, an especially fragrant variety of citrus popular in Japan. It comes in two varieties, red and green, depending on the color (that is, the ripeness) of the chiles used. Often sold in small, narrow jars, it's potent stuff: salty, spicy, and highly aromatic from the citrus zest.

HERBS

Fresh herbs figure heavily in my recipes because they're integral to the cuisines that inspire me—the thyme and parsley in Haitian stews and marinades; the cilantro, mint, and dill in Southeast Asian soups and salads. I use them exclusively for flavor, though I take comfort in their polyphenol content, plant compounds with potent antioxidant and anti-inflammatory effects.

I often leave tender herbs unchopped, simply tearing mint and basil leaves in half if they're large and plucking cilantro, dill, and parsley into small sprigs (pluches is what I learned to call them in fancy French kitchens), because their tender stems have flavor, too, not just the leaves. Their delicate flavor is best preserved by sparing these herbs from heat, so I often add them at the last moments of cooking or to finish a dish before serving. I don't treat them as garnish, though. They're stars in their own right, whether they're used judiciously—a little cilantro delivering flashes of brightness between bites of dark gingery glazed chicken—or liberally, in handfuls, for an explosion of freshness and herbaceousness.

Woodsy, hardier herbs like rosemary, oregano, and thyme can be used for finishing a dish as well, though their stronger flavor does oblige restraint. They're especially welcome in roasts, soups, and stews and take well to drying, retaining their essence better than delicate herbs. To substitute dried for fresh, use about half the amount called for and cook them thoroughly, so they have a chance to infuse their flavor into liquids and fats.

Makrut Lime Leaves

If you're unfamiliar, it's time to get familiar, because the glossy, deep-green leaves of the makrut lime tree are remarkable. Primarily used in Southeast Asian cooking, they have a bold, intoxicating aroma that is citrus distilled, the essence of lime without the mild bitterness or acidity that we associate with limes and lemons. With the center ribs removed, the leaves flavor broths and curries or are very thinly sliced and added to salads.

Buy them—online or in markets with a Southeast Asian focus—and freeze any you don't use within a few days. They freeze exceptionally well and thaw in moments. Skip the dried version, which is no substitute for fresh.

Note that these leaves were once commonly referred to by the k-word, a slur that deserves to be banished but one that still lingers on some packaging.

AROMATICS

There is a dish in this book called Eggs and Greens (page 106). It is, at its essence, what the title promises: wilted hearty greens briefly baked with eggs. But taste it and it's so much more. It's complex and fragrant and slightly spicy. And that's because of a heavy dose of aromatics—ginger, garlic, and chiles sautéed in oil and seasoned with plenty of salt.

So many of the dishes I cook begin like this, with some manner of aromatics cooked in fat or simmered in liquid to release their flavors and fragrances, creating the foundations for soups, stews, sauces, and more. This might be as simple as garlic briefly toasted in olive oil or as complex as a curry paste slowly sweated in coconut fat. The aromatics infuse the fat, and that fat, which carries flavor so well, seasons the dish, ensuring those flavors reach far and wide.

For the most part, the aromatics I call for will be familiar to most readers—garlic and onions, shallots and scallions, ginger and chile. Yet a few deserve a little explanation, in case you haven't come across or cooked with them before. They're all, it deserves mentioning, not just good for your food but also good for your body, delivering vitamins, minerals, phytochemicals, and antioxidants.

Galangal

Sometimes referred to as Thai ginger because its appearance so closely resembles the more widely used rhizome, galangal is quite distinct. Common to Thai, Indonesian, and Malaysian cooking, it has smoother, lighter skin, a bolder flavor—more astringent and earthy, herbal and citrusy—and paler, firmer flesh than ginger. It has no substitute. Look for it fresh and frozen at markets that specialize in Southeast Asian ingredients and some major supermarkets. If you're buying frozen, thaw before using.

Lemongrass

Native to South and Southeast Asia, lemongrass is a long, sturdy grass with a fragrant heart. Accessing it requires some trimming, but the effort pays off. Sliced or pounded, bruised or blended, the heart delivers an irreplaceable flavor and aroma, similar to lemon peel but more potent, with a hint of sweetness and gingery zing. Look for it in the produce section, often near the herbs, at supermarkets, though keep in mind that it tends to be both fresher and less expensive at Asian supermarkets.

To get the most from my lemongrass, I use as much of it as possible, trimming off just enough of the tough top and bottom and removing just enough layers of the husk as necessary. This varies slightly depending on the application—lemongrass meant to be eaten raw requires a little more trimming than lemongrass meant to be pounded or blended or dodged by your spoon, as in Thai-inspired soups. After it's trimmed, I call for it to be bruised (whacked with the back of a knife blade, just to release some of those fragrant oils) then thinly sliced against the grain. In general, after trimming, each large stalk should yield 3 to 4 tablespoons of thinly sliced lemongrass.

Trimming Lemongrass: Cut off and discard the brittle dark-green tops and the tough nub at the bottom, about ¾-inch from the base of each stalk. Remove the tough outer layers (two should do it for lemongrass to be blended; three is more like it for lemongrass to be eaten raw) until the remaining stalk feels smooth and looks pale green. You'll be left with approximately 5 to 6 inches of lemongrass.

Turmeric Root

I use this root (okay, technically, it's a rhizome) often for the striking yellow color it imparts but also for its earthy, mustardy qualities and slightly peppery flavor. In the past, many Americans only knew turmeric in its dried, powdered form, but now that the root's anti-inflammatory properties and status as an antioxidant powerhouse have gained traction in the United States, the fresh product has become much easier to find. Look for it in health food shops and Whole Foods, not just in South and Southeast Asian markets. In the Middle East as well as South and Southeast Asia, turmeric's benefits have been known for centuries, and the root is used for both medicinal and culinary purposes. Studies show our bodies reap more nutrients from the fresh version than the dried. So when you find some, buy it and keep it in the fridge, where it keeps for several weeks.

FRUITS AND VEGETABLES

Most of the vegetables in this book will be familiar to you. A few may not, so I'll tell you a bit about them here. In general, in-season produce tastes better and is less expensive than out-of-season stuff. If you can, buy local and shop at your local farmers market, both to support small-scale local agriculture and to access the most delicious stuff. That said, I tried hard to fill this book with recipes for fruits and vegetables that are readily available at supermarkets year-round, rather than leaning hard on the hyper-seasonal stuff chefs like me tend to fuss over. That's why you won't find morels, sugar snap peas, apriums, or spigarello. My thinking is, I want to make sure as many people cook these recipes as possible, to eat more fruits and vegetables no matter the season. When a recipe is dependent on high-season produce, I let you know. And of course, anytime you opt for top-notch ingredients, your food will be better for it.

Always wash fruits and vegetables before you cook with them, even when they have peels and skins that you ultimately discard. I say that at the risk of stating the obvious. But it deserves mention, because most cookbook recipes don't include washing instructions. Washing is especially important in the age of boxed greens and spotless carrots, when a shopper could easily be convinced that it's all good to go. Even these, respectively, warrant a plunge in cold water and a scrub under the spray of the faucet. This is to rinse away anything harmful, which is rare but real, and also to ensure that an awesome meal isn't spoiled by a salad full of grit or a grubby beet.

Carrots, potatoes, and other sturdy vegetables that you're eating unpeeled—either for ease, nutrition, looks, or all three—should be scrubbed well (with a clean brush or sponge or the back of a knife blade) to dislodge dirt, then rinsed. Leafy greens, hearty and tender, should be bathed in cold water and agitated for the same reason. Any grit should settle to the bottom, so use your hands to lift the greens from the water, leaving the unwelcome matter behind. More delicate vegetables, like mushrooms and berries, should be briefly and gently rinsed and left to dry on kitchen towels. And do dry those vegetables afterward: the greens in a salad spinner and the delicate and sturdy vegetables with kitchen towels. And do it well. Lingering water dilutes flavor, inhibits browning, and causes spatter.

Plantains

Plantains are a staple food in the tropical regions of the world, especially throughout the Caribbean, Africa, and Latin America. They're related to the bananas we eat ripe and raw but have thicker skin and starchier, firmer flesh that must be cooked. In this book, I call for plantains in more or less four stages of ripeness: unripe, ripe, very ripe, and damn-that's-ripe. Because identifying these stages is a bit different than assessing the ripeness of common bananas (and because I love looking at plantains), I've included this handy spectrum to represent each one.

You can find them at varying levels of ripeness at the supermarket and let them ripen further at home, keeping them in a paper bag to encourage them. Still, they ripen slowly—starting from unripe, they can take three weeks or more to reach the very ripe stage.

Unripe plantains (1 and 2) range from completely green to yellow with a green hue. Properly cooking them unlocks a fantastic texture: satisfyingly starchy but not crumbly, with a mild tropical savoriness. To peel them, trim off the stem and bottom of each plantain to expose the flesh, then use the tip of a sharp knife to make three evenly spaced lengthwise cuts from one end to the other, cutting through the peel but stopping at the flesh. Remove and discard the peel. Sometimes, very green plantains need a little soak to help the peel separate from the flesh. If so, add the plantains to a large bowl, cover with cool water, and soak for 10 minutes to loosen the peel. Drain them, then pull off the peels.

Ripe plantains (3 and 4) resemble ripe bananas— they're fully and vividly yellow, perhaps with some brown spots.

Very ripe plantains (5): Remember—black is beautiful. While you'd probably chuck a banana

that was almost completely black with just a patch or two of yellow, that's exactly what you want in order to bring out those caramel notes for sweet plantains (page 84).

Damn-that's-ripe plantains (6) are fully black and slightly shriveled, perfect for Plantain Bread (page 130) and mole (page 313). At this point, they can be stored in the fridge for a week or so.

Taro

Popular in Asia, Africa, Latin America, the Pacific Islands, and the Caribbean, taro is eaten for its root and its leaves. In this book, I call for the root, technically a corm, which is roundish with brown hairy-looking skin. Inside, the flesh is white with little pinkish flecks and packed with fiber, vitamins, and minerals, but is relatively low in calories. Cooked taro root is starchy, nutty, and slightly sweet. Peel away its tough skin with a sharp knife.

Yuca

Also known as cassava or manioc, yuca is a large tuberous root that resembles a long sweet potato with thick brown waxy skin. A hardy crop with lovely dense, starchy flesh, it's a major staple throughout South America, Africa, and the Caribbean. Its starch is often extracted to make tapioca flour (see page 27) as well as those little pearls used in tapioca pudding and boba tea. Before cooking, carve off the brown skin as well as the thin, fibrous white layer underneath with a sharp knife.

FISH AND OTHER SEAFOOD

You'll see plenty of seafood in this book, because it tastes great and it's great for you—high in protein and full of vitamins, minerals, and good fats, including abundant omega-3s, which our bodies don't produce themselves. The subject of much fanfare, omega-3s deserve every bit of it. Fish and seafood contain the most beneficial forms, known as DHA and EPA. A diet rich in these fats does so much good—it improves heart health, reduces inflammation, combats certain autoimmune diseases,

and enhances brain function. Fish skin, by the way, has an especially high concentration of omega-3s, which is one of two reasons you'll find several recipes in these pages that show you how to get that skin really crispy. (The other? It's really delicious.)

Your task as a consumer is to make sure the fish and seafood you buy are farmed or caught using sustainable methods—those with minimal greenhouse gas emissions and those that don't harm the planet in other ways. That means avoiding anything that's overfished or poorly farmed (like bluefin tuna and hamachi), caught with methods that damage habitats or other fish populations (bottom trawling and longlining, for instance), or raised via irresponsible aquaculture (many catfish and tilapia farms generate as many GHGs as operations that produce beef).

With that in mind, I chose fish and shellfish for this book—sea bass and salmon, black cod and halibut, scallops and clams, mussels and lobster—with readily available sustainable options. While both farmed and wild seafood can have low ecological impact, and all else equal, my preference is for wild, which tends to have more omega-3s than farmed. When you can, look for local options or even domestically caught seafood, because shipping fish around the globe puts its own stress on the environment.

Determining what's sustainable requires some diligence on your part. You must buy from markets that provide information about where their fish and seafood come from and how they were caught. If the fishmonger or labeling doesn't answer these questions, shop somewhere else. Look for the blue MSC (Marine Stewardship Council) label when you shop, which indicates seafood is harvested in a way that minimally impacts the species and environment, or download the Monterey Bay Aquarium's Seafood Watch app.

And finally, note that a few recipes call for tuna (sustainable yellowfin or albacore) to be very briefly seared and essentially eaten raw. For those dishes, I offer the same advice for buying tuna as I would for buying any other fish. Visit a fishmonger you trust and buy tuna that's good and fresh. If you're still unsure, ask whether they'd eat that tuna raw and follow their lead.

POULTRY AND MEAT

Animals raised on pasture—not in feedlots—eat the food they're meant to eat. They're happier, have better flavor, and are healthier for the people who eat them—higher in vitamins, minerals, and omega-3s, though lower in total fat. Even better, buy meat from farms that practice regenerative agriculture, an old-school method of raising animals for meat that doesn't use feeds or chemical fertilizers, improves soil health, and encourages plant growth through grazing, which can actually offset greenhouse gases produced by animal agriculture.

At minimum, look for meat that's labeled organic and raised without antibiotics. Both claims are reasonably well regulated, and both practices have benefits for you and the planet. But note that labels can be deceptive. Not all claims on packaging are well regulated. "Free-range" chickens, for instance, aren't necessarily raised outdoors and on pasture, with all the benefits that come with it. To be sure, it's best to shop at markets that go beyond typical labeling and use their own verification process, or at butcher shops that sell meat from small farms and provide information on how it was raised.

When I'm ready to cook, I rinse any poultry that came in a package containing juices, blood, and other liquids, as well as any that releases liquid after hanging out in the fridge for a couple of days. Recently, the USDA has retracted their recommendation of rinsing meat, arguing that the resulting splatter could spread bacteria rather than rinsing it away. My take is that a mindful home cook can rinse a chicken without sending raw particles flying. Just a quick rinse will do. And of course, be aware that a powerful sink spray can spread bacteria, so make sure to clean your kitchen accordingly.

ACIDITY

Ask any chef or passionate home cook and they'll tell you: acidity is a vital component of dynamic food. One of the five basic flavors, it's often underutilized, and one of my hopes is that my recipes reveal what food can be when you apply acidity generously.

Sometimes, it's there to deliver a pop of tartness. Other times, it provides a quiet brightness that elevates and balances other flavors, like sweetness and saltiness. Each source of acidity has its own affinities—lime with tropical flavors, wine vinegars with European ones—born from centuries of culinary evolution. Here are the sources you'll find in this book.

Apple Cider Vinegar

Fermenting the sugar from apples turns them into this tangy vinegar with subtle apple aroma and flavors. Look for an unfiltered organic brand for extra nutrients.

Citrus

I often look to the bright acidity of limes and lemons, and occasionally to oranges. Sometimes I use the three together to approximate the flavor of the sour oranges common in Haiti, which cooks use to marinate fish and meat. Always use lemon and lime juice freshly squeezed from the fruits. (Limes and lemons with smooth, glossy skin tend to be especially juicy.) For orange juice, however, I'm not shy about using the freshly squeezed stuff sold in the cold-pressed juice section of supermarkets like Whole Foods.

Coconut Vinegar

Coconut vinegar is made from coconut sap fermented for 8 to 12 months until it naturally turns into vinegar. A staple in South and Southeast Asian cooking, it has bright acidity and a warm, pronounced coconut flavor.

Distilled Vinegar

High in acidity but neutral in flavor, distilled vinegar is just the thing when you want clean, crisp flavor that lets other ingredients shine. Keep in mind that using another type of vinegar for pikliz (page 285) would earn you a very stern look from my mother.

Rice Vinegar

Rice vinegar, sometimes called rice wine vinegar, is one of very few exceptions to this book's "no grains" rule. It, indeed, comes from rice, which like all grains, contains a certain amount of antinutrients—the compounds that inhibit the body's absorption of certain nutrients. Yet it's made through fermentation, lessening the anti-nutrient effects, and its mellow acidity and mild sweetness is just right for several of the dishes in this book. Avoid the "seasoned" kind, which contains sugar and salt as well as vinegar.

Tamarind

Native to Africa and a common sight in the cooking of South and Southeast Asia, the Middle East, and South America, the tamarind fruit grows in pods, each one containing sticky brown pulp clinging to hard, shiny seeds. (Those seeds are technically legumes, which I generally avoid because of their lectin and phytate content, but you ditch them for the pulp.) The pulp offers a big punch of complex, warm acidity and a tang with a sweet edge that hints at dates and lemons.

For the purposes of this book, purchase the seedless pulp (sometimes also labeled tamarind paste) in blocks at markets. Look for Vietnamese and Thai brands, which provide the flavor I'm after when I cook. (You can buy the whole dried pods, but extracting the pulp is a rather laborious process.) Sold on shelves, not in the refrigerated case, these blocks are made up of the fruit's fibrous pulp, without the pods and seeds. It requires a soak in hot water, some vigorous stirring and a little bashing, and straining (see page 327) to extract a flavorful liquid to be used in recipes. The pulp keeps for up to a year in the pantry and up to six months in the fridge after the package is opened.

Note that products called tamarind concentrate and many products sold as tamarind paste contain preservatives or have been pasteurized to be shelf stable, dulling the fruit's flavor. You'll get a far better result when you extract the liquid from the blocks of pulp.

Wine Vinegars

These vinegars are made using a two-step fermentation—the first turns grape juice to wine, and the next turns that wine to vinegar. Both white and red bring a lovely mild acidity. Red wine vinegar also adds color and a bit of fruitiness, so I usually pair it with foods with fruitier flavor and a pink or red hue. Sherry vinegar has a darker, more complex flavor profile with lovely caramel notes.

UMAMI

As you might have heard, the crew of four basic tastes we learned about as kids has a new member. To the quartet of salty, sour, sweet, and bitter, we now include umami, a Japanese word with only decent English equivalents—something akin to "savoriness" or "deliciousness." It's not some product of the former foursome but a distinct taste of its own, with receptors on the tongue and all. The best way to describe it is to imagine eating ingredients known to provide it. Think of how a grilled steak, seared scallops, or long roasted tomatoes provides more than just saltiness or sweetness or acidity, how the flavor fills your mouth and makes it water—how you want more.

At the turn of the twentieth century, Kikunae Ikeda, a Japanese chemist, identified the source of this intangible deliciousness as glutamic acid, which is found in fish, beef, and cheese, as well as in tomatoes, mushrooms, seaweed, and fermented foods, just to name a few. A year later, he began mass-producing a crystalline version—glutamic acid stabilized with one molecule of sodium. The chemical name was monosodium glutamate, best known as MSG.

I know health freaks who tell you MSG gives you instant brain damage. I know chefs who keep it in their back pocket. The FDA says its safe, but I don't use it. Looking to ingredients that contain high levels of naturally cultivated glutamates and coaxing out umami from foods through cooking and fermentation is way more fun. Below are my favorite sources of added umami.

Coconut Aminos

Made from the sap tapped from blossoms on the coconut tree, this savory dark brown liquid has tons of umami and way less salt than soy sauce. It's also free of common allergens, including gluten and soy. It has a mild, complex sweetness, too, and only a whisper of coconut flavor, so it recedes into the background, providing that umami roundness to dishes. I use it lavishly, particularly in sauces and marinades. I love the Coconut Secret brand, which is made from just sap and sea salt.

Dried Shrimp

Like so many sea creatures, shrimp are loaded with umami and drying them only intensifies this quality. They're used extensively in China and Southeast Asia, West Africa, and Central and South America. For the XO Sauce (page 299) in this book, look for dried shrimp made without preservatives or anything but shrimp and maybe salt at Asian markets. They're better for you and taste better, too.

Fish Sauce

Fish sauce is the iconic condiment of Southeast Asia, an umami powerhouse that's a big reason why the flavors of Thai and Vietnamese food, for instance, are so vivid and inviting. Made by fermenting small fish, often anchovies, with salt for up to two years, the resulting liquid is salty and funky, though notably not "fishy." Fish sauce pairs so well with tartness, sweetness, and heat, and it's incredibly versatile as I hope you'll see as you cook through this book, where it supercharges marinades for meat and dressings for salads featuring chilled fruit; sticky sauces for chicken; and deep, complex curries. My favorite brands are Megachef and Red Boat. The Squid brand is more economical and still quite good.

Katsuobushi

One of two main components of the Japanese stock called dashi and a common ingredient in Japanese cooking, katsuobushi is skipjack tuna (katsuo in Japanese) that's been cooked, smoked, dried, and fermented until it's as hard as wood. It's typically sold as papery shavings and commonly called bonito flakes, young bonito being a less expensive substitute for the traditional skipjack tuna. In dashi, it provides a deep, smoky, almost meaty flavor.

Kombu

Kombu is an edible kelp, a member of the brown algae family but colloquially referred to as "seaweed." Primarily harvested in the waters around the Japanese Island of Hokkaido, the kelp is dried in the sun and is one of two components, along with katsuobushi (see above), in dashi, the indispensable Japanese stock. Kombu is an excellent source of glutamic acid, the amino acid responsible for umami, and in fact, the Japanese chemist who first identified umami did so by studying kombu. In this book, I use it primarily for making dashi. After making the stock, I suggest reserving the kombu to add to pickling liquids because it still has umami left to give.

Look for "dashi kombu" at Japanese markets, major supermarkets, and online. Also, don't wipe off the white substance you may see on the surface of kombu—it's flavorsome stuff.

Mushroom Powder

Drying and grinding mushrooms, which are high in glutamic acid, makes for an excellent umami-boosting powder. It's easy to make yourself (see page 326), but there are some great commercial options. I prefer all-natural brands made without MSG and additives like autolyzed yeast extract. A good tell that a brand will be high quality is that the ingredients lists the types of mushrooms used. I love, for instance, Nom Nom Paleo's Magic Mushroom Powder, made from porcini mushrooms and a hint of chile. Note that many brands contain salt—glutamic acid often buddies up with sodium to achieve its full effect—in varying levels, so use care when cooking, adding the powder gradually.

Stock

Whether it's made from beef, chicken, fish bones, crustacean shells, or mushrooms, stock is a great source of umami and flavor in soups, stews, and braises.

Yet, unlike most books written by chefs, this one doesn't include a proper recipe for stock. That's because at home, I don't often make stock. Sure, if I find myself with a chicken carcass after carving a roasted bird (see page 231), I'll toss it in a pot with plenty of water and bits and pieces of whatever vegetables and aromatics I've been messing with—lemongrass peelings, leek tops, herbs stems, ginger hunks, or tomatoes and carrots that are blemished but still lovely—and let it simmer away. (Okay, there's a recipe!) But I don't always have the time or the bones, and, anyway, most butcher shops sell their own, typically in the freezer section, and those shelf-stable cartons in the supermarket work just fine. If you can only find unsalted stock, be sure to season to taste.

Sun-Dried Tomatoes

Now that we've fully recovered from '90s sun-dried tomato overload, we can re-embrace their glories. Drying tomatoes increases the concentration of glutamates, turning them into an umami dynamo. Look for supple dried tomatoes sold in bags from brands made without artificial preservatives.

NUTS AND SEEDS

Nuts and seeds are an excellent source of good fat, fiber, and protein. They lower "bad" cholesterol and blood pressure, and they're packed with vitamins, minerals, and antioxidants. But I use them for their myriad flavors, varied crunchy textures, and flavor-forwarding fats.

Yes, I toast and scatter them on salads, but in this book I also explore their incredible versatility. So you'll also find them soaked and pureed to make rich nut milks and creams, briefly fermented to make tangy Caesar-like dressing, baked into crispy crackers and crumbly tart crusts, and slowly simmered in stews.

To roast nuts or sunflower seeds, preheat the oven to 350°F, spread them on a sheet pan and cook until toasty and golden, 13 to 15 minutes.

To toast sesame seeds, put them in a small skillet, set over high heat, and toast, stirring constantly, until golden brown, about 2 minutes.

DAIRY ALTERNATIVES

The alternatives in this book don't just stand in for dairy. They bring their own flavors that make dishes even better.

Alternative Yogurts

While their composition varies by brand, these "yogurts" are typically made from various dairy-free products—typically coconut milk or cream, cashew milk, almond milk, and, not relevant in this book, soy milk—mixed with starter cultures (usually probiotic bacteria) designed to activate fermentation in products that don't contain lactose. Some recipes call for specific yogurts—grilled carrots (page 58) go great with coconut yogurt—but for the most part, any plain, unsweetened one will do, as I primarily use them for their tang and creamy texture.

There are lots of great brands out there, and some not so great ones, so I'll share my picks here. The COYO brand makes wonderfully thick, creamy coconut yogurt; Forager makes a nice cashew yogurt; and 365 makes a pleasant almond yogurt. Quality varies by brand, so if you're not using one of my recommendations, taste it first to be sure it's thick, tangy, and delicious.

Coconut Milk and Cream

Coconut milk and cream are made by the same process—the firm white flesh of mature coconuts is shredded, mixed with hot water, then pressed to extract the fatty, milky liquid. Coconut cream has a higher ratio of coconut flesh to water than coconut milk, so it's thicker with a higher fat con-

tent. Both coconut milk and cream are extremely versatile ingredients and replace dairy milk and cream, cup for cup, throughout this book. Sometimes, I use them expressly for their sweet, aromatic coconut flavor, and other times I let the flavor take a back seat, leaning on them instead for their richness and flavor-carrying fat.

Look for brands, like Aroy-D, that have no stabilizers. Even better, look for Aroy-D brand cartons, which not only contain no stabilizers or thickeners but are also "ultra heat treated" (subjected to brief, high heat) to make the milk and cream shelf stable without losing as much flavor as canned. If you can't find Aroy-D, 365 makes a good, inexpensive option that's organic. It does contain guar gum, which in small amounts is just fine for you, though strict Paleo folks avoid it because it's made from a legume. While it probably goes without saying, avoid coconut milk "beverages," which is a different product, and "light" coconut milk, which is watery and not ideal for the recipes in this book.

I've found that Asian supermarkets tend to offer a better selection and better prices, so when I'm there I like to buy big cartons by the half dozen.

Nut and Seed Milks and Butters

In my recipes, you'll find lots of nondairy milks and butters to provide fat, flavor, and nutrition. Making them is easy (see pages 317–321) and often gives you a better tasting product. Store-bought nut and seed milks (often labeled "beverages") typically contain multiple emulsifiers and stabilizers, and those that don't tend to be so expensive that you save money whipping them up yourself.

ALTERNATIVE FLOURS

The flours you see in this book don't taste or work quite like wheat flour, so I understand if the prospect of cooking with them is a bit daunting. Yet they each have special powers and, made from nuts, fruits, and roots, they offer far more nutrition and far less allergen risks than wheat. More good news: they're easier to find than ever, as the appetite for the world's cuisines grows and as special diets gain traction.

Almond Flour

Almond flour is just finely ground almonds. For the recipes in this book, look for flour labeled "superfine" and made from almonds that have been blanched to remove the skin. It's part of my Paleo-Friendly Flour Blend (page 327), but because it often works as a one-to-one replacement for wheat flour, you'll see plenty of cakes that use it exclusively.

Arrowroot Starch

I use arrowroot starch to thicken sauces to a velvety sheen. It's a grain-free alternative to cornstarch, and an easily digestible starch that's minimally processed when extracted from the arrowroot plant. Cornstarch, on the other hand, is extracted through an aggressive chemical process.

Coconut Flour

Coconut meat left over from the process of making coconut milk is dried then ground to make this flour, which has a slightly sweet nuttiness but no discernible coconut flavor. It's high in fiber, heart-healthy fats, and iron, but low in carbs and doesn't spike your blood sugar like wheat flour. Because coconut flour is dense and dry, it's almost always combined with other flours in baked goods.

When buying nut and seed butters, skip those made with added sugars, palm or vegetable oil, and additives.

Plantain Flour

Plantain flour is the product of dried, pulverized slices of green plantains. It can be substituted, cup for cup, for wheat flour in many recipes, plus it's lower in calories and rich in iron, vitamin C, carotene, and other vitamins. When cooked, it imparts a mild banana flavor, perfect for Plantain Bread (page 130).

Tapioca Flour

Tapioca flour, also known as tapioca starch, is made from the starch extracted from the cassava plant. It has a high starch content, a slight sweetness, and when used alone in baked goods, produces a chewy, almost gelatinous texture that defines many iconic Asian desserts. In baking, I typically use it alongside other flours, where it balances coarser ones to give cakes and bread just the right crumb. I also use it to dust chicken (page 226), because it fries to an incredible crisp.

SWEETENERS

This is far from a sugar-free cookbook. (Sorry, Keto friends!) While I do avoid adding sugars when coaxing out the natural sweetness from fruits and vegetables does the trick, sometimes only sweeteners will do—to balance the lovely bitterness of grilled foods, to tame the acidity of limes or the heat of chiles, and to offer the sweet comfort that only sugar can provide. No doubt a diet free of added sugars is the healthiest, but here I prefer moderation to abstinence. In other words, do make my Haitian Spiced Pineapple Upside-Down Cake (page 375), but with its 3 cups of sweet stuff, you might not want to make it once a week. In general, the compromise I make is to insist on using *healthier* sources of sugar, knowing that you'll eat more fruits, vegetables, fish, and healthful meat when they taste great.

The sweeteners in this book are minimally processed. They contain some nutrients (though notably, not enough to make them healthy or cancel out the effect of that sugar) and fall relatively low on the glycemic index, meaning they're absorbed more slowly by your body and cause minimal spikes in your blood sugar. Sweeteners high on the glycemic index (GI), like corn syrup and white sugar, put a ton of stress on the body. Too much can lead not just to diabetes, but to heart disease, liver issues, and some cancers, not to mention loss of energy from all those blood sugar spikes and crashes.

Glycemic index, however, isn't the only metric for gauging the effects of sweeteners. Agave nectar and syrup, once considered a relatively healthy sweetener because they have very low GI, have been reassessed for their high fructose content, which when eaten in excess puts strain on the liver and gets converted to bad cholesterol, among other bad stuff.

Bottom line: Sugar isn't good for you. But sugar tastes good. And these options are a little better than the others.

Coconut Sugar

I love granulated coconut sugar for its toasty, caramel-y flavor, which is especially great in baked goods. Made from sap extract from the flower of the coconut palm tree and cooked to evaporate the water, it retains some nutrients and fiber, though not nearly as much as whole foods.

Date Syrup

Popular in North African and Middle Eastern cuisine, date syrup has made its way to the supermarket shelf, in particular those stores with an eye on health foods. That's because date syrup is far more nutritious than other sweeteners, with higher levels of potassium, magnesium, and hella antioxidants. The product is simple, just dates simmered in water and strained to produce a luscious, molasses-like syrup. Just Date Syrup makes a great one. I use it when making dark and sexy sauces and drizzle it on foods at the last minute for a little final sweetness.

Honey

One of the least processed sweeteners there is— okay, if you don't include the processing done by the bees who produce it—honey is an incredible product that only seems ordinary because it's so commonplace. And because it begins as flower nectar—the complex sugars broken down by the bees' digestive systems and concentrated via the collective flapping of their wings—its flavor varies based on the plants the bees dine on. This isn't true of industrial honey, so look for local honeys that speak to a region.

Besides its floral flavor, honey has a relatively low glycemic index and contains an enzyme that helps our body digest it without stressing the liver.

Maple Syrup

Made from reducing the sap of maple trees, the resulting syrup has a fantastic caramel-y flavor and contains plenty of minerals and antioxidants, as well as plenty of sugar. It's my go-to all-purpose sweetener, because unlike honey, it can either headline a dish or recede into the background, letting other flavors take center stage. Like so many good things, maple syrup isn't cheap, but it keeps forever, so buy in bulk to save money. Look for syrup grades with amber to dark color and rich or robust flavor, which tend to be made with later-season syrup. Most important, make sure you buy pure maple syrup. If you don't burn through it like I do, be sure to store it in the fridge.

Palm Sugar

Like coconut sugar, palm sugar is made from the sap from a type of palm tree, though not the coconut palm. The sap is then heated to concentrate it and caramelize the sugars. It has a slightly fruitier, brighter flavor than coconut sugar, and contains some minerals, inulin (which is good for your gut), and phytonutrients with antioxidant properties, though again, it's no health food.

In the United States, it's typically sold in two forms—discs and small tubs. While those tubs are supposed to contain soft palm sugar, the sugar inside has often hardened and is difficult to extract. That's why I prefer the discs. They're still quite firm and require pounding in a mortar or a fine chopping with a sturdy knife to be measured for the recipes in this book.

AND A WORD ABOUT PLASTICS

One thing you won't see in my pantry are single-use plastic products. You won't see them in my recipes either—I don't wrap leftover baked goods in plastic wrap or marinate in resealable bags. They're bad for us and bad for the world, plain and simple. Resisting their convenience is just one small way to make a positive impact. I hope you'll give it a shot. When I need an airtight seal, I use reusable containers with tight-fitting lids. Instead of pressing plastic to the surface of fermenting vegetables, I look to parchment or wax paper. I wrap vegetables, herbs, and fruits with reusable material, such as the amazing Bee's Wrap.

1

Raw and Cold Plants

CRUNCHY CUCUMBER SALAD WITH CHILES, SESAME, AND CILANTRO

Serves 6 to 8

A brief marination and an aromatic chile paste add brightness and complexity to a simple salad of cold, crunchy cucumbers.

3 pounds Asian or Persian cucumbers, quartered and cut into 2-inch pieces
1 tablespoon kosher salt
1 cup unseasoned rice vinegar

½ cup Aromatic Chile Paste (page 298)
¼ cup coconut aminos
¼ cup toasted sesame oil

4 medium garlic cloves, very finely chopped
Big handful small cilantro sprigs
¼ cup raw sesame seeds, toasted (see page 26)

MAKE THE DISH

Combine the cucumbers and salt in a large mixing bowl, toss well, and let them sit for 15 minutes.

In the meantime, combine the vinegar, chile paste, coconut aminos, sesame oil, and garlic in a medium mixing bowl and stir well. After the 15 minutes are up, drain the cucumbers, discarding the liquid in the bowl. Add the cucumbers to the dressing, toss well, and let them marinate in the fridge for 15 minutes or so. Stir in the cilantro.

Transfer to a serving bowl, sprinkle on the sesame seeds, and serve.

ROMAINE HEARTS, AVOCADO, AND RADISHES WITH CASHEW GREEN GODDESS

Serves 6

Perfect for radish and spring onion season but easy to make year-round, this knife-and-fork salad is all about the interplay of textures: crunchy romaine, crisp radishes, and fatty, creamy avocado. The tangy, herb-packed cashew dressing takes it to the next level. The secret: a ferment of the cashews for an umami boost.

For the Dressing

1 cup Soured Cashew Cream (page 269)

3 tablespoons white wine vinegar

1 teaspoon kosher salt

1 medium garlic clove, peeled

½ cup lightly packed small parsley sprigs

½ cup lightly packed small cilantro sprigs

½ cup lightly packed small dill sprigs

½ cup lightly packed mint leaves

3 slender spring onions or scallions, trimmed, thinly sliced, whites separated and reserved for the salad

1-inch piece jalapeño chile

For the Salad

2 bunches small radishes, some halved, some thinly sliced

3 heads romaine hearts, bases trimmed, leaves separated

1 large bunch mature spinach, bottoms trimmed

3 large ripe Hass avocados, pitted, peeled, and cut into bite-size chunks

3 tablespoons extra-virgin olive oil

1½ teaspoons flaky sea salt

Two large handfuls mixed herbs, like basil and mint leaves and small dill sprigs

MAKE THE DRESSING

Combine all the dressing ingredients in a blender and puree on high until creamy, pale green, and as smooth as possible, about 2 minutes. It keeps in an airtight container in the fridge for up to 1 week.

MAKE THE SALAD

Ten minutes or so before you plan to serve, fill a large mixing bowl with ice water, add the radishes, and let them hang out. Right before serving, drain them well and pat them completely dry with clean kitchen towels.

Spread the thick dressing on a platter, then layer on the romaine heart leaves and spinach, then the avocados, radishes, and spring onion whites. Drizzle with the olive oil, sprinkle on the flaky salt, then scatter on the herbs. Serve right away.

WATERMELON-BERRY SALAD WITH CHILE DRESSING AND LOTS OF HERBS

Serves 6 to 8

A thrilling way to treat high-summer fruit, this gorgeous jumble of flavors and textures is explosively good. The Thai-inspired, blend-and-go dressing—tart and spicy and salty—plays up the sweetness of watermelon and berries, such as blueberries, raspberries, and hulled and halved strawberries, while keeping the fruit salad firmly in savory territory. A flurry of herbs adds even more freshness and dimension.

For the Dressing

⅓ cup lime juice (from about 3 juicy limes)

⅓ cup fish sauce

3 tablespoons thinly sliced cilantro stems

3 tablespoons finely chopped palm sugar or coconut sugar

½-inch knob fresh galangal, peeled and roughly sliced against the grain

1 large garlic clove, peeled

1 small moderately hot fresh red chile, such as Fresno or ripe red jalapeño, stemmed and roughly chopped

1 fresh red Thai chile, stemmed

For the Salad

2 pounds peeled watermelon

1 small red onion, halved and thinly sliced

1 teaspoon flaky sea salt

2 large lemongrass stalks, trimmed (see page 15), bruised, then very thinly sliced

½ cup extra-virgin olive oil

2 big handfuls very lightly packed mixed herbs, such as mint leaves, Thai or Italian basil leaves, and small cilantro sprigs

MAKE THE DRESSING

Combine all the dressing ingredients in a blender and blend on high speed until smooth, about 2 minutes. It keeps in an airtight container in the fridge for up to 3 days. Shake well before using.

MAKE THE SALAD

Cut the watermelon into 3 x 1 x 1-inch sticks, flicking out seeds as you go. You will have about 6 cups. Chill the watermelon in the fridge for at least an hour.

Combine the chilled watermelon and onion in a large mixing bowl and season all over with the flaky salt. Add the berries, lemongrass, and dressing, then toss gently but well. Drizzle on the olive oil, add the herbs, and gently toss once more. Transfer to a platter to serve.

CREAMY ASPARAGUS SALAD WITH SUNFLOWER SEED FURIKAKE

Serves 6

Sunflower and sesame seeds team up for a creamy, gingery dressing for asparagus that is snappy and juicy from a quick sauté. The textures just multiply from there—crunchy, punchy pickled onions; rich chunks of avocado; and a shower of furikake made with nori seaweed, crispy garlic, and more nutty sunflower seeds.

For the Dressing
¼ cup plus 2 tablespoons unseasoned rice vinegar
¼ cup raw sunflower seeds
¼ cup raw sesame seeds, toasted (see page 26)
1 small shallot, roughly chopped
1 medium garlic clove, peeled

2-inch knob ginger, peeled and sliced against the grain
½ small jalapeño chile
2 teaspoons kosher salt
1 teaspoon toasted sesame oil
¼ cup extra-virgin olive oil

For the Salad
2 bunches asparagus
1 tablespoon avocado oil

1 teaspoon kosher salt
2 large Persian cucumbers, cut into ¾-inch pieces
2 ripe Hass avocados, pitted, peeled, and cut into ½-inch pieces
½ cup drained Quick-Pickled Red Onions (page 286)
½ cup Sunflower Seed Furikake (page 324)

MAKE THE DRESSING

Combine all the dressing ingredients but the olive oil in a blender and blend on high speed until as smooth as possible, about 2 minutes. Add the olive oil, then blend again until the dressing is creamy and smooth, about 30 seconds. Reserve about ¼ cup for this recipe. The rest is great for any hearty salad.

It keeps in an airtight container in the fridge for up to 5 days.

MAKE THE SALAD

One by one, bend each asparagus spear to break off the tough bottoms and discard them. Cut the asparagus into 2-inch pieces. Heat the avocado oil in a wide, heavy skillet over high heat until shimmery and, working in two batches to avoid crowding, cook the asparagus until bright green and just slightly charred but still crisp, about 2 minutes. Season with the salt, transfer to a sheet pan in a single layer, and let cool to room temperature.

Combine the asparagus, cucumbers, and dressing in a large mixing bowl and toss really well to coat. Add the avocado and toss gently to coat without smashing the avocado. Transfer the mixture to a platter, then sprinkle with the pickled onions and the furikake. Serve right away.

POWER GREENS AND HERBS WITH CAESAR-STYLE PINE NUT DRESSING

Serves 4

Bold greens deserve bold dressing. That's why I dress hearty, nutrient-dense greens with a thick, creamy concoction of lemon, garlic, and pine nuts. Briefly fermented so they develop a little tang and umami, the pine nuts supercharge the dressing—think Caesar, without the cheese.

You'll notice I suggest that you spoon the thick dressing onto the sides of the bowl, not directly onto the greens, then use tongs and gently toss to coat the greens in the dressing. It's a day-one trick I learned at culinary school and ensures that the dressing doesn't weigh down the salad.

10 cups lightly packed mixed dark leafy greens, such as mature spinach, collards, chard, and kale (thick stems removed)

1 cup Creamy Fermented Pine Nut Dressing (page 268)

2 tablespoons extra-virgin olive oil

2 teaspoons flaky sea salt

2 cups lightly packed mixed herbs, such as basil, shiso, dill, and cilantro

MAKE THE DISH

Put the greens in a large mixing bowl. Spoon the dressing onto the sides of the bowl, just above the greens. Use salad tongs to gently toss the salad so the greens are well coated by the dressing.

When the greens are just about evenly dressed, drizzle in the olive oil, sprinkle in the salt, and toss again briefly. Add the herbs and give it all a final, gentle toss. Serve right away.

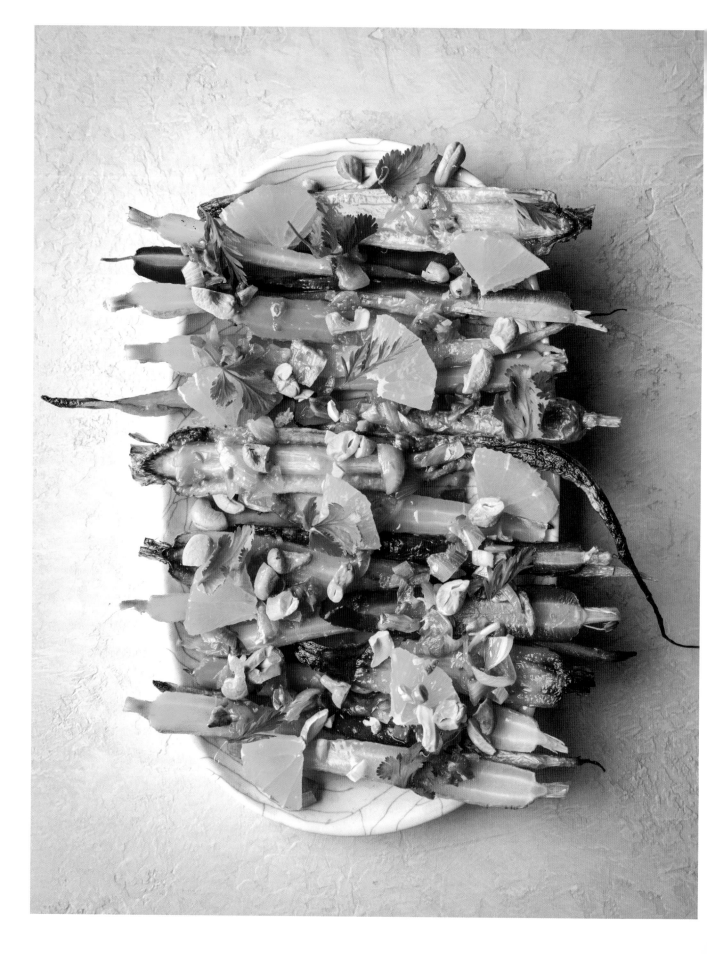

CARROT SALAD WITH ORANGES, CASHEWS, AND CHARRED CHILE DRESSING

Serves 4

I love how sweet carrots get in a hot oven, becoming this perfect creamy foil for tart dressing and crispy, crunchy textures. I don't even peel them here, for the extra nutrients—give me *all* the beta carotene and vitamin A—and okay, because it's easier that way.

While I roast the carrots, I char a couple of chiles on the stovetop burner, which add extra flavor and some heat to the simple dressing of fish sauce, lime, and the garlic and shallots plucked from the pan of carrots. Juicy oranges cool things down and cashews provide crunch and a little lovely fat.

For the Carrots
1½ pounds trimmed medium carrots, scrubbed well

3 medium shallots, quartered

8 large garlic cloves, peeled

2 tablespoons extra-virgin olive oil

¾ teaspoon kosher salt

For the Dressing
2 moderately spicy fresh red chiles, such as Fresnos or ripe jalapeños

¼ cup lime juice (from about 2 juicy limes)

2 tablespoons fish sauce

1 tablespoon finely chopped palm sugar or coconut sugar

For the Dish
1 medium orange

2 tablespoons extra-virgin olive oil

½ cup unsalted roasted cashews, very roughly chopped

Handful small cilantro sprigs

COOK THE CARROTS
Preheat the oven to 450°F. If any carrots are especially fat, halve them lengthwise so they're about the same size as the rest.

Combine the carrots, shallots, and garlic on a sheet pan in a single layer, then evenly drizzle with the oil and sprinkle on the salt. Roast until the carrots are very tender (a knife tip inserted into the thickest one should meet no resistance), 15 to 20 minutes. Remove the shallots if they get too charred and the garlic cloves if they turn any darker than deep golden brown before the carrots are done. Let it all cool completely.

MAKE THE DRESSING
Turn on a gas burner, lay the chiles on the stove rack, and char them over the flames, flipping them occasionally, until their skins are blistered and black all over, about 3 minutes. Let cool briefly, then scrape off the skins with a small knife.

Chop the garlic, shallots, and chiles into a chunky mince. In a small bowl, combine the lime juice, fish sauce, and sugar and stir until the sugar dissolves. Add the garlic, shallots, and chiles and stir.

MAKE THE DISH
Halve the carrots lengthwise then again crosswise. Put them in a large bowl, add the dressing, and toss well. Set them aside to marinate for 5 minutes or so. While they marinate, trim just enough off the top and bottom of the orange to reveal the flesh, then stand it up and carve off the peel and white pith. Quarter the orange, then cut it into ¼-inch-thick slices.

Transfer the carrots to a platter, spoon on the dressing, drizzle with the olive oil, and garnish with the cashews and orange slices. Top with the cilantro and serve.

COLLARDS AND CABBAGE SALAD WITH MAKRUT LIME, HAZELNUTS, AND SPICY CASHEW DRESSING

Serves 6

Ribbons of vitamin-packed collards join crunchy red cabbage and carrots for this stunner of a cold-weather salad that eats great all year round. The magic is in the dressing, comfortingly creamy from cashews but full of surprises, like coconut milk, ginger, and curry paste. Makrut lime leaves—fresh or frozen but not dried, please—add an incredible perfume, but if you can't find them, grate on the zest of a lime.

6 cups stemmed and sliced (¼ inch wide) collard greens (1 medium bunch)

6 cups very thinly sliced red cabbage (a mandoline helps)

4 cups long, thin carrot matchsticks (a mandoline helps)

1 small red onion, thinly sliced

¾ cup Spicy Cashew Dressing (page 301)

2 tablespoons extra-virgin olive oil

2 teaspoons flaky sea salt

Handful mixed small cilantro sprigs and mint leaves

1 cup roughly chopped unsalted roasted hazelnuts

8 fresh or frozen makrut lime leaves, center ribs removed and very thinly sliced

MAKE THE DISH

Combine the collards, cabbage, carrots, and red onion in a large serving bowl. Pour the dressing onto the sides of the bowl, just above the vegetables. Use tongs to toss the salad so the greens are well coated in the dressing.

When the greens are just about evenly dressed, drizzle in the olive oil, sprinkle in the salt, and toss again, briefly. Add the cilantro and mint and give it all a final, gentle toss. Transfer to a platter, then sprinkle with the hazelnuts and makrut lime leaves and serve.

TOMATOES ON TOMATOES WITH SHALLOT-CHILE DRESSING

Serves 4 to 6

When you get your hands on late-summer tomatoes, heavy and nearly bursting with juice, celebrating the star of the season is as easy as slicing them. Yet a little prep does wonders. The first thing you do is pop some cherry tomatoes in the oven. While their flavor intensifies and their sugars caramelize, you douse sliced shallots and a little chile in vinegar to make a quick pickle. Assembling the salad is a breeze, your new condiments playing up the sweetness and acidity of tomatoes without distracting from their glory.

For the Shallot-Chile Pickle
3 medium shallots, halved and thinly sliced
2 fresh red Thai chiles, very thinly sliced
1½ teaspoons kosher salt
½ cup red wine vinegar

For the Salad
2 pounds mixed ripe tomatoes (such as heirloom, beefsteak, and cherry), cored if necessary and cut into bite-size pieces
1 teaspoon flaky sea salt

1 cup Slow-Roasted Cherry Tomatoes (page 307)
3 tablespoons extra-virgin olive oil
Large handful mixed herbs, such as basil, cilantro, sage leaves, and dill

MAKE THE SHALLOT-CHILE PICKLE
Combine the shallots and chiles in a medium bowl, sprinkle on the kosher salt, and toss well. Let sit for 5 minutes so the salt can begin to soften the shallots. Add the vinegar, stir well, and let sit for another 15 minutes. Stir once more.

MAKE THE SALAD
Put the raw tomatoes on a platter, cut-sides up, and season with the flaky salt. Scatter on the roasted cherry tomatoes, then the shallot-chile pickle, including the liquid. Drizzle with the olive oil, then sprinkle on the herbs and serve right away.

HIGH-SUMMER SALAD WITH COCONUT DRESSING AND LOTS OF HERBS

Serves 4 to 6

By August, the tomatoes are fat, the stone fruit is juicy, and the time is right for this summer showcase of a salad. A coconut milk dressing keeps all that natural sweetness squarely in the savory realm, with tartness from lime, heat from fresh chiles, and a punch of green from a shower of herbs. The result is exciting enough to turn the simplest grilled chicken or fish into a satisfying meal.

My grain-free friends will immediately notice the corn in the list of ingredients. While it's technically a grain, I'll admit to being a sucker for the sweet, smoky pops of charred kernels. By all means, leave it out if you like!

For the Dressing

¼ cup lime juice (from about 2 juicy limes)

2 tablespoons coconut milk

2 tablespoons extra-virgin olive oil

2 tablespoons coconut sugar or finely chopped palm sugar

1 small garlic clove, very finely chopped

1 very hot fresh chile, such as Thai or small serrano, thinly sliced

2 fresh or frozen makrut lime leaves, center ribs removed, very thinly sliced

½ teaspoon kosher salt

For the Salad

1 large ear corn, shucked

½ teaspoon avocado oil

¼ teaspoon kosher salt

3 large ripe tomatoes (whatever looks best), cored and cut into ¾-inch-thick wedges

1 tablespoon flaky sea salt

2 ripe nectarines, pitted and thinly sliced

1½ cups mixed summer berries, halved if you want

1 cup Slow-Roasted Cherry Tomatoes (page 307)

1½ tablespoons extra-virgin olive oil

Handful mixed herbs, such as basil and mint leaves and small cilantro sprigs

MAKE THE DRESSING

Combine all the dressing ingredients in a small mixing bowl and stir to completely dissolve the sugar. It keeps in an airtight container in the fridge for up to 4 days.

MAKE THE SALAD

Fire up a grill to cook with high heat or preheat the broiler and set an oven rack close to the heat source. Rub the corn with the avocado oil, season with the kosher salt, and grill (or broil on a sheet pan), turning occasionally, just until the kernels are barely cooked and slightly charred, 3 to 5 minutes. Let the corn cool slightly, then use a sharp knife to cut off the kernels, discarding the cob.

Arrange the tomato wedges on a platter, cut-sides up, and sprinkle on the flaky salt. Arrange the nectarines, berries, corn, and roasted cherry tomatoes on top, then spoon on the coconut dressing. Drizzle with the olive oil, garnish with the herbs, and serve.

RAW BUTTERNUT SQUASH SALAD WITH SMOKY CHILES, POMEGRANATE, AND LOTS OF SEEDS

Serves 4 to 6

If you've never tried butternut squash raw, prepare to retire your sheet pan. While it's typically served roasted, the fall staple is delicious uncooked, earthy and sweet with a delicate crunch. I toss it with crisp apples and Asian pears; dress it with a smoky, tangy vinaigrette; then pile on the texture with pomegranate, pumpkin, and hemp seeds. A mandoline slicer, a fancy one or a cheap one, makes the prep a breeze.

Note that the solid top of butternut squash is far easier to julienne on the mandoline than the hollow base. So I tend to use the top for this preparation and save the bottom for soup.

For the Dressing
2 dried chipotle chiles, stemmed
1 medium garlic clove, minced
1 teaspoon kosher salt
½ cup white wine vinegar
½ cup extra-virgin olive oil

For the Salad
¼ cup hulled raw hemp seeds
4 cups julienned (2½ x ⅛ inch) peeled butternut squash
2 large apples, cored and julienned (2½ x ⅛ inch)
2 large Asian pears, cored and julienned (2½ x ⅛ inch)

3 scallion whites, thinly sliced
2 teaspoons flaky sea salt
¼ cup pomegranate seeds
¼ cup unsalted roasted pepitas (hulled pumpkin seeds)
Large handful basil leaves

MAKE THE DRESSING
In a small bowl, soak the chipotles in hot tap water until softened, about 20 minutes. In the meantime, put the garlic in a small bowl, sprinkle on the kosher salt, and set aside while the chipotles soak. Once the chipotles are soft, drain them (discarding the water), mince them, and scrape them into the bowl with the garlic. Add the vinegar and oil and give it a good whisk.

It keeps in an airtight container in the fridge for up to 2 weeks. Whisk well before using.

MAKE THE SALAD
Put the hemp seeds in a small skillet, set it over high heat, and toast, stirring every 30 seconds or so, until golden, about 3 minutes. Set aside to cool.

Combine the squash, apples, pears, scallion whites, and flaky salt in a large mixing bowl. Give the dressing another good whisk, then pour it into the bowl and toss really well to coat the ingredients in the dressing. Transfer to a serving platter, sprinkle on the hemp seeds, pomegranate seeds, pepitas, and basil. Serve right away.

ROASTED GOLDEN BEETS WITH ACHAR AND PICKLED RHUBARB

Serves 4 to 6

Proof that a couple of pantry items can make a simple dish spectacular, these roasted beets are next level thanks to the spicy, tangy South Asian pickle called achar and a sour, crisp rhubarb pickle. Each bite is a wallop of acid and earth, sweet and heat.

I recommend golden beets here because purple ones turn the achar red, but that's a small problem in a world of big ones. Oh, and if your beets are babies, you can get away with leaving on their tender skins.

2 pounds trimmed medium golden beets

6 garlic cloves, peeled

2 tablespoons extra-virgin olive oil

2 teaspoons kosher salt

½ cup Achar (page 273), solids and oil

Flaky sea salt

½ cup drained Chile and Lime–Pickled Rhubarb (page 287)

Handful mint leaves

MAKE THE DISH

Preheat the oven to 425°F. In a large bowl, combine the beets, garlic, and olive oil and toss to coat well. Sprinkle in the kosher salt and toss again. Transfer the mixture to a large baking pan (deep enough so the beets don't reach the rim), pour in 3 tablespoons of water, and cover tightly with foil.

Roast the beets until you can pierce them with a sharp knife with just a touch of pressure, 45 minutes to 1 hour. Remove the foil and let the beets sit until they're cool enough to handle but still warm. Use a paper towel to rub the beets to remove their skins (they should slip off easily). Discard the skins and cut the beets into bite-size pieces. Chop the garlic, too, discarding any cloves that got too dark.

Give the large bowl a quick rinse and wipe, then toss together the beets, roasted garlic, achar, and a good sprinkle of the flaky salt in the bowl. Arrange on a platter, garnish with the pickled rhubarb and mint, and serve warm or cool.

2

Cooked and Hot Plants

SWEET AND SAVORY GLAZED CARROTS

Serves 2 to 4

A new style of old-school glazed carrots, these get cooked in orange juice, maple syrup, chile, and a little fish sauce, so they're sweet and salty, bright, and a bit funky. It's a quick side dish that may out-flavor everything else on the table.

In the first step, I take you through cutting the carrots into obliques, also known as roll cut—an easy way to make the dish look fancy, but better yet, a way to maximize surface area and get the most flavor from that glaze.

2 pounds trimmed medium carrots, peeled

3 tablespoons virgin coconut oil

1 tablespoon finely chopped ginger

1 tablespoon fish sauce

1½ cups freshly squeezed orange juice

2 teaspoons maple syrup

1 moderately spicy red chile, such as Fresno, thinly sliced

½ juicy lime

MAKE THE DISH

Cut off the top and bottom of each carrot. Now, you're going to cut the carrots, one by one, into obliques. Starting from the bottom of a carrot, hold your knife at a 45-degree angle and make a 1-inch-long cut. Roll the carrot just a quarter turn toward you, so the cut side faces you, then make a similar angled cut. Roll again and cut again until you've cut the entire carrot. As the carrots get fatter at the top, shorten the cut slightly, so the pieces are approximately the same size, even if they're slightly different shapes.

Heat the coconut oil in a wide, heavy skillet over medium-low heat until it's fragrant. Add the carrots and ginger and cook, stirring occasionally, until the carrots brighten in color, about 2 minutes. Add the fish sauce, stir well, then add the orange juice, maple syrup, and chile.

Increase the heat to medium-high, bring the liquid to a strong simmer, and cook, stirring often, until the liquid reduces to a syrupy glaze that coats the carrots and the carrots are fully tender with just a slight bite in the center, about 20 minutes. If the liquid looks like it'll get syrupy before the carrots are done, reduce the heat slightly.

Take it off the heat, squeeze on the lime, and stir well. Transfer to a serving bowl and serve.

GRILLED CARROTS WITH HERBY COCONUT YOGURT AND SPICY BEET VINAIGRETTE

Serves 4 to 6

Don't ask me why, but you don't often spot people grilling carrots alongside peppers, zucchini, and eggplant. It's a shame, because they also grill beautifully, developing a char that balances out their sweetness. Herby coconut yogurt helps, too, tipping the scale with tang and freshness, while quickly pickled beets contribute crunch, acidity, and a different dimension of sweetness.

For the Beet Vinaigrette
1 large beet (about 4 inches in diameter, any color), peeled and cut into ¼-inch cubes
½ teaspoon kosher salt
¼ cup plus 2 tablespoons red wine vinegar
2 medium garlic cloves, thinly sliced
2 fresh Thai chiles, thinly sliced

¼ cup plus 2 tablespoons extra-virgin olive oil

For the Herby Coconut Yogurt
Handful mixed herbs, such as basil, mint, dill, and cilantro
1 cup plain coconut yogurt
1 scallion, trimmed and thinly sliced

½ teaspoon kosher salt
1 juicy lime

For the Carrots
2 pounds trimmed medium carrots, halved lengthwise if thicker than 1 inch
1 tablespoon avocado oil
½ teaspoon kosher salt

MAKE THE BEET VINAIGRETTE
Put the beet in a small mixing bowl, season with the salt, stir, and set aside for 10 minutes to soften and season the beet. Combine the vinegar, garlic, and chile in a small saucepan, bring all to a boil over high heat, then lower heat to gently simmer for 1 minute, just to cook off the garlic's raw flavor. Pour the hot mixture over the beets, stir, and let sit at room temperature for 1 hour. Stir in the olive oil.

MAKE THE HERBY COCONUT YOGURT
Roughly chop the herbs. In a small bowl, combine the yogurt, most of the herbs, the scallion, and the salt. Use a Microplane to grate the lime zest into the bowl, then halve the lime and squeeze in the juice. Stir well.

GRILL THE CARROTS AND MAKE THE DISH
Fire up a grill to cook with medium-high heat. On a plate, rub the carrots with the avocado oil to just barely coat them (excess oil will lead to flare-ups and unpleasant flavor). Season the carrots with the salt, toss, and grill, turning them occasionally and moving them to a cooler part of the grill if they get dark before they're tender, until lightly charred and fully tender, 6 to 8 minutes. Let them cool for a couple of minutes.

Spread the yogurt on a platter and top with the carrots. Spoon on the pickle-y beets first, then drizzle on about 2 tablespoons of the vinaigrette. Sprinkle with the remaining herbs and serve.

GRILLED BROCCOLI WITH GINGER-SCALLION SAUCE AND CHILE PASTE

Serves 4

Broccoli is a marvel when you cook it on scalding-hot grill grates, the stems turning tender and crisp and the florets crackly. From there, I spoon into its nooks an aromatic chile paste and a wildly delicious Chinese condiment made from ginger and scallions doused in hot oil to mellow their harshness and bloom their flavors.

I like grilling broccoli in smallish pieces, so it gets more char and cooks more evenly. Plus, you don't need to cut it again after it comes off the grill.

1½ pounds broccoli	1 teaspoon kosher salt	3 tablespoons Aromatic Chile
1 tablespoon avocado oil	½ cup Ginger-Scallion Sauce	Paste (page 298)
	(page 303)	Handful cilantro sprigs

MAKE THE DISH

Fire up a grill to cook with medium-high heat or preheat the broiler with an oven rack in the top position. Cut the broccoli florets off the stalks and cut them into 2½-inch pieces. Trim the bottom of the stalks by about ½ inch, peel the stalks if the outer layer is thick and tough, then cut them into similar-size pieces.

Combine the broccoli in a large mixing bowl with the oil and salt and toss to coat well. If you're broiling, spread it in a single layer on a sheet pan. Grill or broil the broccoli, occasionally flipping and rotating it for even cooking, until it's bright green, charred at the edges, and tender but still crisp, 5 to 8 minutes.

Transfer the broccoli to a platter, add the ginger-scallion sauce and chile paste, and sprinkle on the cilantro. Serve warm or room temperature.

BRUSSELS SPROUTS WITH CHILES, LIME, AND MINT

Serves 6

The secret to Brussels sprouts is cooking them hot and quick. That's why, in a restaurant setting, I take the time to separate the leaves and char them in a screaming hot wok. At home, I spare myself the tedium and slice them thin instead. This way, they take just minutes to develop charred, crispy edges and they stay sweet enough to convert even the most stubborn sprout skeptics. A super-simple sauce enlivens them with the Southeast Asian trifecta of tart, funky, and sweet.

For the Sauce

¼ cup fish sauce

¼ cup lime juice (from about 2 juicy limes)

2 tablespoons finely chopped palm sugar or coconut sugar

3 fresh Thai chiles, thinly sliced

2 large garlic cloves, finely chopped

For the Dish

1½ pounds Brussels sprouts, bottoms and outer leaves trimmed

3 tablespoons avocado oil

1½ teaspoons kosher salt

Large handful mint leaves

Healthy drizzle of extra-virgin olive oil

MAKE THE SAUCE

In a medium serving bowl, combine the fish sauce, lime juice, palm sugar, chiles, and garlic and stir well, breaking up any chunks of palm sugar until it has completely dissolved.

MAKE THE DISH

Cut the Brussels sprouts lengthwise into ⅛-inch-thick slices. Loose pieces are just fine—they'll get crispy in the pan later. Heat a large, heavy skillet over high heat until it's good and hot. Work in three batches to cook the Brussels sprouts, so you don't crowd the skillet and to get nice color. Wipe out the skillet in between batches.

For each batch, add 1 tablespoon of the avocado oil to the skillet, give it a swirl, and heat until smoking hot. Add about one third of the Brussels sprouts, spreading them in a single layer. Cook, without stirring, until the bottoms char, about 3 minutes, then flip the slices and char the other side, about 2 minutes more. Transfer each batch of Brussels sprouts to a sheet pan (put it near the stove to keep warm), spread them out so they don't stack and steam, then sprinkle on ½ teaspoon of the salt.

Transfer the charred Brussels sprouts to the bowl with the sauce, toss well, and let them sit for 15 minutes (they get even better as they soak up the dressing). Just before serving, stir in the mint and olive oil.

MUSHROOMS WITH CHILES, LIME, AND MINT

Serves 2 to 4

The same vivid sauce that I use on Brussels sprouts (page 62) goes great with earthy mushrooms. I like to use a mix of shiitake, oyster, cremini, and maitake for some awesome textural variety, but feel free to use whatever looks good at the market that day.

For the Sauce
2 tablespoons fish sauce
2 tablespoons lime juice (from 1 juicy lime)
1 tablespoon finely chopped palm sugar or coconut sugar

2 small fresh Thai chiles, thinly sliced
1 large garlic clove, finely chopped

For the Dish
3 tablespoons avocado oil

2 pounds mixed mushrooms, trimmed and cut into large but still bite-size pieces
1 teaspoon kosher salt
Healthy drizzle of extra-virgin olive oil
Large handful mint leaves

MAKE THE SAUCE
In a medium serving bowl, combine the fish sauce, lime juice, palm sugar, chiles, and garlic and stir well, breaking up any chunks of palm sugar until it has completely dissolved.

MAKE THE DISH
Heat a large, heavy skillet over medium-high heat until it's good and hot. Add the avocado oil to the hot skillet, give it a swirl, and let the oil get shimmery.

Add the mushrooms to the pan (it's fine that they're crowded in a few layers), stir well, and then spread them out into an even layer as best you can. Cook, stirring every minute or so, until the mushrooms begin to turn golden and shrink to more or less a single layer, 4 to 5 minutes. Raise the heat to high and keep cooking, stirring occasionally, until the mushrooms are a deep golden brown, 5 to 7 minutes more. Stir in the salt and cook for another minute or so.

Transfer the mushrooms to the serving bowl with the sauce, and give them a toss. Drizzle with the olive oil, scatter on the mint, and serve warm.

BRUSSELS SPROUTS ROASTED WITH KIMCHI AND SCALLIONS

Serves 4 to 6

Remember the first time you tasted sweet, crisp-edged roasted Brussels sprouts? I felt that same thrill when I tasted what a quick trip in a hot oven does to kimchi. High heat works a similar magic on Korean fermented cabbage, intensifying its tangy, salty, spicy qualities. By roasting them together, you double down on all this deliciousness and, with just 10 minutes of effort, you get one of the best things you've put on your table in a long time.

1½ pounds medium-size Brussels sprouts

2 cups well-drained spicy cabbage kimchi, cut into roughly 2-inch pieces if necessary

6 medium scallions, trimmed and cut into 2-inch pieces, whites halved lengthwise

½ cup avocado or extra-virgin olive oil

2 teaspoons kosher salt

1½ teaspoons toasted sesame oil

MAKE THE DISH

Preheat the oven to 500°F.

Trim off the bottoms of the Brussels sprouts. If the outer leaves are wilted or yellowed, remove and discard them. Cut the sprouts in half lengthwise (or into quarters, if they're bigger than an inch in diameter).

Combine them in a large mixing bowl with the kimchi, scallions, avocado oil, and salt and toss well. Spread the mixture in a single layer on a large sheet pan and roast in the oven (there's no need to stir) until the Brussels sprouts are slightly charred at the edges and tender but not mushy, 15 to 20 minutes.

Drizzle with the sesame oil, toss well, and serve.

SAUTÉED SPINACH WITH GOLDEN RAISINS AND PINE NUTS

Serves 4 to 6

If this one seems simple, that's because it is. Inspired by a classic Catalan dish, spinach gets a toss in a pan with garlic, toasty pine nuts, and plump raisins. The not-so-secret secret is cooking the nutritious green as quickly as possible, so the spinach doesn't give up its water and stays silky and emerald green.

2 tablespoons extra-virgin olive oil

1 cup pine nuts

3 medium garlic cloves, thinly sliced

2 small dried red chiles, crumbled, or ½ teaspoon red chile flakes

1 teaspoon kosher salt

1 cup golden raisins

2 pounds mature spinach (about 3 bunches), bottoms trimmed

MAKE THE DISH

Heat a large Dutch oven over medium-high heat for a minute or so, then add the oil. When it's shimmery, add the pine nuts and garlic and cook, stirring frequently, until the garlic is lightly golden and fragrant and the pine nuts are golden, about 2 minutes. Add the chiles and about half the salt and stir well.

Add the raisins, and cook, stirring occasionally, until they begin to plump and brighten in color, about 1 minute. Increase the heat to high, wait a minute, then add the spinach and quickly mix and toss so the spinach mingles with the pine nuts and raisins as it wilts. As soon as the spinach has wilted and gone from dull to bright green, stir in the remaining salt, transfer to a large plate, and serve right away.

COCONUT-CREAMED COLLARDS

Serves 2 to 4

I adore long-cooked collard greens, but I also love simply wilting them, especially in this luscious sauce of coconut milk cooked with ginger and garlic until it thickens. As you might imagine, you can swap out kale or Swiss chard for collards. If you're using chard, thinly slice its tender stems and throw them in with the greens.

1 tablespoon extra-virgin olive oil

3 garlic cloves, thinly sliced

1-inch knob ginger, peeled, halved lengthwise, and thinly sliced against the grain

1 teaspoon kosher salt

1¾ cups well-shaken coconut milk

2 tablespoons coconut aminos

10 cups lightly packed stemmed collard greens (about 3 small bunches)

MAKE THE DISH

Heat the oil in a large Dutch oven over medium heat until shimmery. Stir in the garlic, ginger, and salt, and cook, stirring occasionally, until the garlic turns golden at the edges, about 1 to 2 minutes. Pour in the coconut milk and coconut aminos (they may splatter a bit), increase the heat to bring to a boil, then lower the heat to simmer until the liquid has reduced to about ½ cup (it'll have the texture of melted ice cream and the bubbles will go from small to big), about 12 minutes.

While it's simmering, cut the collard greens into long, 1-inch-wide strips (I like to stack a few leaves, roll them up, and slice).

When the coconut milk has reduced, stir in the collard greens, increase the heat to medium-high, and cook, stirring and tossing frequently, until the collards are just wilted and bright green, about 3 minutes. Serve hot.

CRISPY SMASHED BEETS WITH GARLIC, SCALLIONS, AND CHILE

Serves 4 to 6

Potatoes often get the cook-smash-and-cook treatment, but I'm here to show you that beets deserve it, too. Roasted in the oven and then smashed, the skin-on beets get panfried in olive oil until they're dark and sexy, with a mixture of tender, slightly crisp, and crackly textures. Then they're lavished with olive oil fragrant from garlic, chiles, and scallions to complete this super-savory beet hash.

2 pounds trimmed small to medium beets, scrubbed well

12 garlic cloves, peeled

2 moderately spicy red chiles, such as Fresnos, cut into ½-inch-wide slices

1 tablespoon extra-virgin olive oil, plus ⅓ cup for panfrying

1½ teaspoons kosher salt

6 scallions, trimmed and cut into 2-inch pieces

Flaky sea salt, for finishing

MAKE THE DISH

Preheat the oven to 425°F. In a large bowl, combine the beets, garlic, chiles, and the 1 tablespoon of olive oil and toss to coat well. Season with the kosher salt. Transfer the mixture to a large Dutch oven or baking dish (deep enough so the beets don't go over the rim), pour in 3 tablespoons of water, and cover tightly with foil.

Roast until the beets are very tender (a sharp knife should go in with barely any pressure), 45 minutes to 1 hour. Remove the foil and let the beets sit until they're cool enough to handle but still warm.

Reserve the garlic and chiles, discarding any that got too dark. Transfer the beets to a cutting board (lined with parchment paper, to avoid staining the board), then use a small plate to, one by one, gently crush the beets to a relatively even thickness of ½ to ¾ inch. Try to keep them mostly in one piece.

Heat the remaining ⅓ cup of olive oil in a large, heavy skillet over medium-high heat until shimmery. Cook the beets, in batches if necessary to avoid crowding, flipping once, until charred and crisp at the edges, about 3 minutes per side. It's okay if they fall apart a bit—any little pieces will get extra crispy. As they're done, use a slotted spoon to transfer them to a platter, leaving the oil behind.

When all the beets are ready, add the scallions and the reserved garlic and chiles to the pan and cook, stirring, just until fragrant, 1 to 2 minutes. Scatter the mixture over the beets, season with flaky salt, and serve.

CHARRED RED CABBAGE WITH XO SAUCE

Serves 6

Cabbage isn't usually a showstopper, but bring these crispy-edged wedges to the table, a psychedelic spectacle of black char, purple, and blue, and conversation will indeed come to a halt. This alchemy requires just a quick trip under the broiler and a generous dose of XO sauce, a spicy, chewy, funky, pricey condiment born in Hong Kong and reimagined by this Haitian guy in Portland.

1 large head red cabbage (about 3 pounds), blemished outer leaves removed

½ cup extra-virgin olive oil
1 tablespoon kosher salt
¾ cup XO Sauce (page 299), at room temperature

Small handful basil leaves, preferably Thai

MAKE THE DISH

Preheat the oven to 450°F and set an oven rack in the top position. Cut the cabbage through the core into 12 wedges (about 1½ inches thick), so the layers in each wedge remain intact. Evenly drizzle 1 tablespoon of the oil onto a large sheet pan, then arrange the wedges flat on the pan in a single layer with a little space between them. Evenly sprinkle on the salt and drizzle on the remaining oil.

Roast the cabbage on the top rack until the white parts have turned purple, the leaves look soft and supple, and the wedges turn brown at the edges, about 10 minutes. Remove the cabbage, preheat the broiler, then broil the cabbage on the top rack until the edges are black and crispy and the insides are tender with a slight bite, about 5 minutes. Use a spatula to flip each piece, then broil again for 5 minutes more, to char the other sides.

Transfer to a serving platter, spoon on the XO Sauce, and serve hot or warm. Just before serving, sprinkle on the basil.

ROASTED EGGPLANT WITH DRIED TOMATO RELISH

Serves 4 to 6

You've got to try creamy roasted eggplant topped with this deeply flavored, wonderfully chewy relish made from dried tomatoes, ginger, and chiles, a sort of vegan version of Chinese XO sauce.

For the Tomato Relish

2 cups sun-dried tomatoes, finely chopped

½ cup extra-virgin olive oil

2 teaspoons kosher salt

15 large garlic cloves, thinly sliced

5 small dried red chiles, crumbled, or 1½ teaspoons red chile flakes

2 large shallots, cut into ⅛-inch dice

3-inch knob ginger, peeled and finely chopped

2 tablespoons coconut aminos

2 tablespoons date syrup or honey

For the Dish

2 pounds Chinese or Japanese eggplant (4 or 5), tops trimmed and halved lengthwise

2 teaspoons kosher salt

5 tablespoons extra-virgin olive oil

Small handful mixed herbs, such as basil leaves and small cilantro sprigs

MAKE THE TOMATO RELISH

Combine the tomatoes, olive oil, salt, garlic, chiles, shallots, and ginger in a medium, heavy skillet set over medium heat and give it a stir. Before you stir again, wait until the oil gets hot and the aromatics start giving off liquid, causing the mixture to bubble rapidly. Stirring frequently now, cook until the ingredients have softened and browned a bit at the edges, 8 to 10 minutes.

Stir in the coconut aminos and date syrup and reduce the heat to gently simmer until they have evaporated and everything is several shades darker, shriveled, and a little chewy, about 5 minutes more.

Cooled, it keeps in an airtight container in the fridge for up to 3 months.

MAKE THE DISH

Cut a crisscross pattern into the flesh of the eggplants, cutting all the way down to but not through the skin. Season the eggplants all over with the salt, going heavier on the flesh sides than the skin sides. Let the eggplants sit and soften at room temperature for at least an hour or in the fridge for up to 24 hours.

Preheat the oven to 350°F. Once the eggplants have softened, give them a few gentle squeezes to remove some of the liquid and pat them dry with a kitchen towel. Working in three batches, heat 1½ tablespoons of the oil in a large, heavy skillet over medium-high heat until shimmery. Add one third of the eggplant, flesh-sides down, and cook, flipping when the first sides are deep golden brown, until you can easily pierce the thickest parts with the tip of a knife, 8 to 10 minutes total.

Transfer the eggplants, flesh-sides up, to a baking dish or sheet pan rubbed with the remaining ½ tablespoon of oil, spread the relish on the eggplants in an even layer, and bake for 10 minutes so the flavors can meld.

Serve the eggplants—hot, warm, or at room temperature. Sprinkle on the herbs just before serving.

CAULIFLOWER PUTTANESCA

Serves 4 to 6

I have always loved puttanesca, the promiscuously salty team of flavors that sauced one of my favorite pasta dishes before I went gluten free. I channel that same boldness, warming olives, capers, chiles, and jarred roasted tomatoes (or sun-dried, in a pinch) and spooning them all over simply roasted cauliflower.

1 large head cauliflower (about 3 pounds), leaves removed, cut into bite-size florets

¾ cup extra-virgin olive oil

2 teaspoons kosher salt, plus a pinch

10 large cloves garlic, finely chopped

1 cup drained oil-packed roasted or sun-dried tomatoes, halved

¾ cup pitted mixed olives, large ones halved

¼ cup drained capers

1½ teaspoons red chile flakes

Large handful basil leaves, torn

Small handful small parsley sprigs

1 juicy lemon

MAKE THE DISH

Preheat the oven to 450°F. On a sheet pan, combine the cauliflower, ¼ cup of the oil, and 2 teaspoons of the salt, then give it all a toss to coat. Spread the cauliflower in a single layer and roast, without stirring, until deep golden, roasty, and tender but with a soft crunch to the stems, 10 to 15 minutes.

In the meantime, heat the remaining ½ cup of olive oil in a medium skillet over medium heat until shimmery. Add the garlic and the remaining pinch of salt and cook until the garlic is golden, about 3 minutes. Add the tomatoes, olives, capers, and chile flakes and cook, stirring occasionally, just until it's all warmed through, 2 to 3 minutes.

When everything is ready, put the cauliflower in a big bowl and pour in the contents of the skillet, including the flavorful oil. Add the basil and parsley, use a Microplane to grate in the lemon zest, then halve the lemon and squeeze in the juice. Stir really well and transfer to a platter to serve. Serve warm or at room temperature.

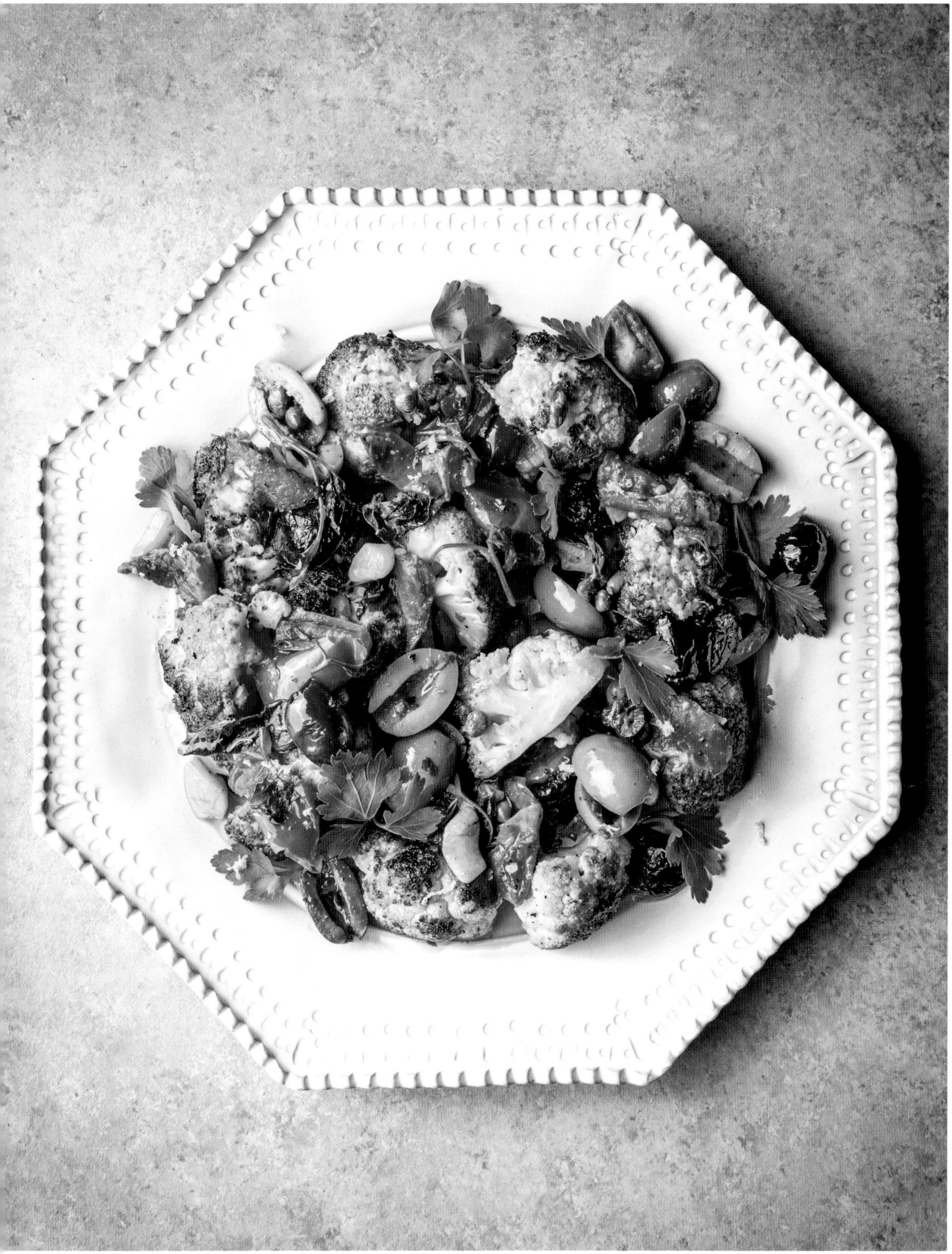

WHOLE ROASTED JERK CAULIFLOWER

Serves 3 to 4

Here, I give cauliflower the royal treatment to take it from side dish to table centerpiece, long-cooking until it's fork tender and finishing it with a fiery, blend-and-go glaze inspired by jerk. A specialty of Jamaica, jerk is a prime example of a delicious food with a brutal history—the preparation likely born from either Arawaks, who were enslaved by Spanish conquistadors, or Maroons, African slaves brought by the British who escaped into the Blue Mountains.

I tame its Scotch bonnet–fueled heat with a bit of coconut sugar, so the complexity of allspice, nutmeg, and ginger can shine through. The coconut aminos stand in for soy sauce, a common ingredient in jerk brought to Jamaica by Chinese immigrants.

For the Cauliflower
1 large head cauliflower (about 3 pounds), leaves removed
3 tablespoons extra-virgin olive oil
1 tablespoon kosher salt

For the Jerk Glaze
¼ cup coconut aminos
2 tablespoons extra-virgin olive oil

¼ cup chile oil, homemade (page 306) or store-bought
2 tablespoons coconut sugar
1 tablespoon fresh thyme leaves, or ½ tablespoon dried
½ teaspoon black peppercorns
½ teaspoon allspice berries
2 dried or fresh bay leaves
1 moderately spicy fresh red chile, like Fresno, stemmed
1 scallion, trimmed and roughly chopped

1 large garlic clove, peeled
1 small shallot, roughly chopped
½ Scotch bonnet or habanero chile, stemmed
1-inch knob ginger, peeled and thinly sliced against the grain
¼ nutmeg, or ⅛ teaspoon ground
1 juicy lime

ROAST THE CAULIFLOWER
Set an oven rack 10 inches or so from the broiler. Preheat the oven to 375°F.

Trim the base of the cauliflower so it can sit flat. Flip the cauliflower base-side up and cut a deep "X" into the base, stopping when you reach the stems of the florets. This helps the core and base cook at the same rate as the rest of the head.

Rub the cauliflower all over with the olive oil, then season the cauliflower all over with the salt. Sit the cauliflower in a large, heavy ovenproof skillet (11- to 13-inch works best) and roast to soften up the cauliflower (it'll go from white to cream in color), 30 to 35 minutes. Pour ½ cup of water directly into the skillet and keep roasting until the water has evaporated and the cauliflower has patches of light golden brown and is just tender enough to easily be pierced with the tip of a sharp knife, 20 to 25 minutes more.

MAKE THE JERK GLAZE
While the cauliflower is roasting, combine the glaze ingredients, including the finely grated zest and the juice of the lime, in the blender and blend on high speed until completely smooth, about 1 minute.

MAKE THE DISH
When the cauliflower is tender, remove it from the oven and preheat the broiler. Use a flexible spatula to rub the top and sides of the cauliflower (don't neglect those lower sides!) with the blended mixture.

Broil the cauliflower, basting it after 5 minutes with the juices that have accumulated in the skillet and trying your best to get that flavorful liquid in all of its nooks and crannies, until the top has spots of black char, 10 to 12 minutes. Serve hot or warm.

BANNANN PEZE

Serves 4

No fruit says Haitian cuisine like the plantain. We eat this dense, high-nutrient food, a rich source of both fiber and complex carbs, every which way—boiled and steamed and fried, green and ripe and super ripe, any time of day from breakfast to dinner. Here, the fruit is unripe (see page 17 to help you buy the right ones), smashed to expose the inner flesh, and twice-fried for the Haitian staple bannann peze, virtually the same as the dish many Spanish-speaking, plantain-loving cultures call tostones, petacones, and platanos fritos.

The finest versions of bannann peze achieve their exalted crispness by a simple, counterintuitive trick. After their first trip in hot oil, they take a dip in salted water, absorbing a little seasoning to flavor them and a little liquid that steams during the second fry, producing a lacy interior structure that fries crisp. Be sure to serve them with plenty of pikliz (page 285), the tart, spicy Haitian cabbage pickle, to balance that lovely crackle, salt, and fat.

3 unripe plantains
Extra-virgin olive oil for
  shallow frying (about 1 cup)

2 tablespoons kosher salt
Flaky sea salt

Pikliz (page 285)

MAKE THE DISH

Remove and discard the peel of the plantains (see page 17). Cut the plantains into 1-inch-thick rounds. Line a sheet pan with paper towels. Pour enough oil in a large skillet to reach a ¼-inch depth and heat over medium-low heat until shimmery. Working in batches to avoid crowding, cook the plantains, flipping once and standing the rounds up to cook the sides as well, until light golden brown all over and slightly crumbly and gummy inside, 6 to 8 minutes total. Transfer the plantains to the lined sheet pan as they're fried, adding more oil if necessary to maintain the depth. Turn off the heat but keep the oil in the skillet.

Fill a large bowl with 4 cups of water, add the kosher salt, and stir until the salt has completely dissolved. One by one, put the plantain rounds on a cutting board and use a small plate to firmly press them so they flatten to a bit less than ¼ inch thick. Put them back on the sheet pan, using a spatula if they stick to the cutting board. When they're all flattened, transfer them to the salted water, making sure they're all submerged, and soak for about 10 seconds. Drain and pat dry with kitchen towels to prepare for the second frying.

Prepare a fresh layer of paper towels on the sheet pan. Reheat the oil, adding more if necessary to reach the same depth as before, over medium heat until shimmery. Fry the plantains again, in batches, flipping once, until they're light golden brown and crisp all the way through, 1 to 2 minutes per side. As they're done, transfer them to the sheet pan and immediately season lightly with flaky salt.

Transfer to a platter and serve hot with lots of pikliz.

PAN ROASTED SWEET PLANTAINS WITH ONION AND THYME

Serves 2 to 4

At home, Mom always had plantains in our fruit bowl, and I'd get excited when after a week or two, a few had turned black and slightly shriveled. That's when they were ripe enough for her to fry them up in oil, with no seasonings at all, not even salt. Still, to taste them, you'd think that someone snuck in maple syrup or honey, so complex and caramel-y was their sweetness. While you, too, could certainly stop this recipe right after frying the plantains, the addition of onion and thyme brings some unexpected savoriness to the dish. Even my mom would like it.

3 very ripe large plantains (see page 18)

¼ cup extra-virgin olive oil

1 medium yellow onion, cut into ⅛-inch-thick half-moon slices

3 garlic cloves, cut into ⅛-inch-thick slices

½ teaspoon kosher salt

1 tablespoon fresh thyme leaves

MAKE THE DISH

Peel the plantains by trimming about ½ inch off each end, cutting a lengthwise slit through the peel, and removing it. Discard the peel and cut the plantains crosswise into 1-inch-thick rounds.

Heat 2 tablespoons of the olive oil in a large, heavy skillet over medium heat until shimmery. Add the plantains flat-sides down in a single layer and cook, flipping once and reducing the heat slightly if they get dark too quickly, until deep golden brown on both sides, 4 to 5 minutes per side. Tip the pieces onto their sides and cook, rolling them around occasionally, until they're browned all over and fully soft inside, about 3 minutes more. Use a slotted spoon to transfer the plantains to a plate.

Add the remaining 2 tablespoons of oil to the skillet and heat over medium until shimmery. Add the onion and cook, stirring occasionally, until the onion turns light brown around the edges, 3 to 5 minutes. Reduce the heat to medium-low, add the garlic, and continue cooking until the onion is tender and deep golden with brown edges, 10 to 15 minutes more. Stir in the salt.

Return the plantains to the pan, add the thyme, and stir occasionally so the thyme flavor blooms and all the flavors have a chance to come together, about 2 minutes. Transfer to a platter and serve.

AKRA

Serves 4 (makes about 20 fritters)

If you've never had this classic Haitian snack, you need to make it right away. The fritters are made from taro root, a knobby brown root vegetable common in the Caribbean and throughout Asia, and seasoned with parsley, thyme, garlic, and fragrant fresh chile. Grating the taro releases its starch, so the fritters can bind without the addition of flour—great for grain-free folks and also anyone who loves a light fritter—and they fry up to create a crisp crust encasing a creamy, fluffy center. I serve them as soon as they leave the pan, though they're still great warm.

You occasionally see people recommend using gloves to handle taro to avoid the slightly sticky substance released when you peel it (similar to butternut squash). If you're afraid it might irritate your hands, go ahead and use gloves or look for it pre-peeled in Asian markets.

1 pound taro root, peeled

4 scallions, trimmed and very thinly sliced

3 large garlic cloves, finely chopped

1 Scotch bonnet or habanero chile, finely chopped

1 large egg, lightly beaten

Large handful parsley, finely chopped

1 tablespoon fresh thyme leaves

2 teaspoons kosher salt

½ teaspoon ground black pepper

Extra-virgin olive oil, for shallow frying

1 juicy lime, halved, or pikliz (page 285), for serving

MAKE THE DISH

Using a metal box grater, grate the taro on the side with the smallest holes. You should get about 2 cups of pulp. Scrape the pulp into a medium bowl, add the scallions, garlic, chile, egg, parsley, thyme, salt, and pepper, and stir really well. The batter keeps in an airtight container in the fridge for up to 3 days.

Fill a large, heavy skillet with ¼ inch of olive oil and heat over medium heat until shimmery. Line a plate with paper towels and put it near the stove.

Next, form the fritters one at a time, adding them to the oil as they're formed. Using a dinner knife, scoop out a blade full of batter, gently patting the batter so it stays put, to create a long, skinny fritter that's about 4 inches long and ¾ inch high. Transfer it to the oil by holding the knife right above the oil and slowly letting the batter slide off the knife, giving it a little nudge if it sticks. Repeat with the remaining batter, but work in several batches to avoid crowding the pan and leave about ½ inch between each fritter.

Fry over medium heat, carefully flipping the fritters so each side gets a turn in the hot oil, until crispy and golden brown all over and tender and creamy in the center, about 3 minutes per side. Transfer them to the prepared plate as they're done.

Eat right away with a squeeze of lime or some pikliz.

TAMARIND-MAPLE–GLAZED ACORN SQUASH WITH CHILE YOGURT

Serves 6

Fruity, tangy tamarind joins forces with maple syrup to heighten the earthy sweetness of roasted squash. Crunchy, salty pumpkin seeds and cool yogurt spiked with smoky chiles add more layers of flavor and texture.

For the Chile Yogurt
1 dried ancho chile
1 dried chipotle chile
2 cups plain almond or coconut yogurt
1 teaspoon kosher salt

For the Glazed Squash
2 medium acorn squashes, seeded and each cut into 8 wedges
1 teaspoon kosher salt
3 tablespoons extra-virgin olive oil
¾ cup maple syrup
¾ cup Tamarind Water (page 327)

For the Dish
¼ cup salted roasted pepitas (hulled pumpkin seeds)
1 lime, for zesting
Small handful small cilantro sprigs

MAKE THE CHILE YOGURT

Put the ancho and chipotle chiles in a small skillet, set it over high heat, and cook, flipping them frequently, until fragrant, 1 to 2 minutes. Stem the chiles, combine them in a small bowl, and cover with hot tap water. Let them soak until softened, about 20 minutes.

Drain, discarding the water, and finely chop the chiles. Scrape the chiles and their seeds back into the bowl, add the yogurt and salt, and stir really well.

It keeps in an airtight container in the fridge for up to 3 days.

COOK AND GLAZE THE SQUASH

Preheat the oven to 375°F. Divide the squash, skin-side down, between two large, heavy skillets—using skillets, rather than a large sheet pan, will help you when basting. Evenly season the flesh with the salt, then drizzle with the olive oil, and roast until a knife meets with no resistance when inserted into the thickest part of the squash, about 30 minutes.

In the meantime, combine the maple syrup and tamarind water in a small saucepan, set it over medium heat, and bring to a boil. Cook, stirring frequently, until reduced by about half (it'll be glossy and molasses-thick), 5 to 7 minutes.

Once the squash is roasted, drizzle the maple glaze onto the flesh and return the skillets to the oven. Cook for 5 minutes to give the glaze a chance to thicken a bit, then remove the skillets from the oven and baste the squash with the syrupy liquid, tilting the skillets and using a large metal spoon to scoop the liquid onto the squash three or four times. Keep roasting for 5 minutes, then baste again the same way and cook until the squash is glossy, sticky, and lightly charred at the edges, about 3 minutes more. Let the squash cool slightly.

MAKE THE DISH

Spoon the chile yogurt onto a platter and top with the squash, drizzling on any glaze left in the skillets. Sprinkle with the pepitas, use a Microplane to grate on the lime zest, then sprinkle on the cilantro. Serve right away.

DAIKON WITH DASHI, JALAPEÑO, AND THYME

Serves 4

In Japan, cooks use dashi, a stock made from katsuobushi (dried, cured bonito) and kombu (dried kelp), to make flavorful stews, soups, and sauces. Compared to the myriad meat stocks of French cuisine, which rely on long-simmered bones, dashi requires almost no time at all yet offers a huge payoff in its smoky, briny qualities. Here, I unite dashi and chicken stock to make a liquid supercharged with umami that imbues simmered daikon radish with flavor. A little thyme and jalapeño provide quiet, welcome surprises.

For the Dashi

5 x 3 inches kombu (dried kelp), broken into several pieces

2 cups chicken stock, salted homemade or store-bought

⅔ cup lightly packed katsuobushi (bonito flakes)

For the Dish

3 tablespoons extra-virgin olive oil

1¼ pounds daikon radish, peeled and cut into ½-inch cubes

1½-inch knob ginger, peeled and very finely chopped

4 scallions, trimmed and thinly sliced

½ jalapeño chile, finely chopped

1 tablespoon coconut aminos

2 tablespoons fresh thyme leaves

MAKE THE DASHI

Combine the kombu and stock in a medium pot and bring to a simmer over medium heat. Reduce the heat to low and very gently simmer for 20 minutes to reduce the liquid slightly. Remove the kombu from the stock and reserve for another use (see page 25). Add the katsuobushi, stir well, then turn off the heat. Let steep for 20 minutes. Strain the liquid into a measuring cup, pressing gently on the solids and then discarding them. You should have about ¾ cup; if you don't, add a splash of water so you do. It keeps in an airtight container in the fridge for up to 3 days.

MAKE THE DISH

Heat the oil in a large, heavy skillet over medium-high heat until shimmery. Add the daikon and cook, not messing with it too much, until it browns just slightly at some of its edges, about 3 minutes. Add the ginger, scallions, jalapeño, coconut aminos, and dashi. Bring the liquid to a lively simmer, then adjust the heat to maintain the simmer and cook, stirring once or twice, until the daikon is almost tender yet still has some crunch in the center, about 3 minutes.

Stir in the thyme, and cook, again at a lively simmer, stirring every minute or so, until the liquid reduces to a thin layer of rich sauce that lightly coats the daikon and the daikon is fully tender but not mushy, 3 to 4 minutes. Transfer to a serving bowl and serve.

LOTS OF ROASTED VEGETABLES WITH GINGER AND CHILE

Serves 6 to 8

It's simple really, just a couple sheet pans of vegetables—nothing fancy, nothing you can't find year-round—roasted with olive oil until crisp-tender and caramelized at the edges. I cut them so they're rustic and pretty, leaving the tops on the beets and radishes and the thin skins on the beets and carrots, and so they're done at about the same time. To keep things fun, I toss in some garlic, ginger, and jalapeño along with the bounty.

It's great beside a bronzed turkey in the fall, grilled salmon in the spring, or on its own as the main event.

3 small red beets, skin and tops on, scrubbed and cut into 4 wedges

3 small yellow beets, skin and tops on, scrubbed and cut in 4 wedges

1 small red onion, halved and cut into 1-inch wedges

10 small radishes, tops on, halved lengthwise

1 large yellow bell pepper, stemmed and seeded, cut into long 1-inch-wide strips

2 bulbs baby fennel (stems and fronds on), halved, or 1 medium bulb fennel, quartered through the core

8 small, slim carrots, scrubbed, tops trimmed

1 medium celeriac, peeled, quartered, and cut into ¼-inch-thick slices

15 large garlic cloves, peeled

2 large jalapeño chiles, cut into ¼-inch-thick rounds

4-inch knob ginger, peeled and julienned (about 2 x ⅛ inch)

1½ tablespoons kosher salt, plus a generous pinch

1¼ cups plus 2 tablespoons extra-virgin olive oil

1 bunch kale, center stems removed, torn into big bite-size pieces

MAKE THE DISH

Preheat the oven to 450°F.

Spread the beets, red onion, and radishes on one sheet pan in more or less a single layer, and the bell pepper, fennel, carrots, celeriac, garlic, jalapeños, and ginger on another sheet pan. (I keep each type of vegetable together on the sheet pans so I can quickly pull one if it's done earlier than the others; and it helps me easily arrange them by type later for a striking way to serve.) Evenly sprinkle everything with the 1½ tablespoons of salt and drizzle with 1¼ cups of the olive oil. Roast in the oven for 10 minutes.

Pull the sheet pan with the ginger from the oven and transfer the ginger to a plate. Put the sheet pan back in the oven and continue roasting until all the vegetables are tender and slightly charred, 10 to 15 minutes more.

Keep the oven on. Transfer the vegetables to a large platter, keeping each type together, if you like. Put the kale on one of the sheet pans, drizzle with the remaining 2 tablespoons of olive oil, add the remaining generous pinch of salt, and toss well. Roast in the oven until tender and crisp at the edges, 5 to 7 minutes. Add the kale to the platter with the vegetables.

Serve hot, warm, or at room temperature.

LEGIM

Serves 4 to 6

When I feed friends Haitian food for the first time, I go big. There might be a whole fish (page 217), a lip-tingling beef stew with yucca and plantain (page 262), or griyo, chunks of citrus-marinated pork shoulder, stewed until tender and fried crisp. Then there's legim, the sleeper hit, an unassuming sidekick that ends up being everyone's favorite.

It's just a rustic stew of rather homely vegetables, really, sometimes made with beef but meatless in my family. But when you stagger the vegetable cooking a bit and apply those alluring Haitian seasonings—thyme, scallions, and fruity, fiery chiles—something special happens. When the eggplant has given up its shape to become a creamy binder, you crank up the heat and turn what is essentially vegetables steaming together in a pot into this rich, savory dish, and the epitome of ugly delicious. Eat it hot. Eat it warm. Eat it cold the next day.

2 large globe eggplants (about 1½ pounds total), cut into 1½-inch cubes

2 tablespoons kosher salt

½ cup extra-virgin olive oil

1 large onion, cut into ¾-inch pieces

10 garlic cloves, smashed

½ head napa cabbage, bottom trimmed, chopped into 1½-inch pieces

3 large carrots, peeled and cut into ¼-inch-thick rounds (about 2 cups)

1 bunch scallions, trimmed and cut into 2-inch pieces, whites halved lengthwise

2 fresh Scotch bonnet or habanero chiles, finely chopped

3 tablespoons Epis (page 296)

2 tablespoons fresh thyme leaves

1 large bunch spinach, stem bottoms trimmed

MAKE THE DISH

Combine the eggplant and 1 tablespoon of the salt in a large mixing bowl. Toss well with your hands, rubbing the salt against the eggplant. Let the eggplant sit for at least 1 hour, so the salt has time to draw out liquid from the eggplant. Remove the eggplant from the bowl, leaving the liquid behind, and give it a firm squeeze to wring out as much liquid as you can. Transfer the eggplant to another large bowl or plate.

Heat the oil in a wide, heavy pot or Dutch oven (5- to 6-quart capacity works well) over medium-high heat until shimmery. Add the eggplant (it'll fit in a few layers, which is just fine) and cook, stirring frequently, for 5 minutes to get a bit of color on the eggplant. Add the onion and garlic and cook for 4 minutes more to get a bit of color on the onion. Add the cabbage, carrots, scallions, chiles, epis, thyme, and the remaining 1 tablespoon of salt, reduce the heat to medium, and stir well.

Cook, stirring occasionally, until the vegetables start to release some of their liquid, about 5 minutes, then reduce the heat to medium-low and cook, stirring every 5 minutes or so, until the carrots are fully tender, the eggplant has broken down, and the liquid has completely evaporated, 35 to 40 minutes.

Have a taste, because next you're going to crank up the heat, not only to cook the spinach quickly but also to transform these tasty stewed vegetables into the far richer, more enticing concoction that is legim. Stir in the spinach, increase the heat to high, and wait 30 seconds or so for brown flavorful bits to appear at the bottom of the pot. Using a wooden spoon, scrape up the brown bits and stir well, then repeat the waiting, scraping, and stirring three more times, or until the eggplant thickens and goes from grayish to a rich golden hue, the spinach is wilted but still bright green, and the legim tastes deep and savory.

Serve the legim hot or warm.

HONEY-GLAZED SWEET POTATOES WITH JAPANESE CURRY SPICE

Serves 4 to 6

Simply roasted sweet potatoes get a last-minute honey glaze. But before your mind wanders to teeth-aching Thanksgiving casseroles, know that the salty umami from coconut aminos, the warm, savory spices in the curry powder, and a touch of bitter char on the honey keep these beauties from crossing over into dessert-for-dinner territory.

2 pounds medium sweet potatoes
½ cup honey
1 tablespoon coconut aminos

1 tablespoon Japanese Curry Spice (page 325)
1 teaspoon kosher salt

2 tablespoons extra-virgin olive oil
Big pinch thinly sliced scallions

MAKE THE DISH

Preheat the oven to 375°F. Pierce the sweet potatoes all over with a fork, put them on a sheet pan, and roast until they give slightly when pressed but before they're very soft, 40 to 50 minutes. In the meantime, stir together the honey, coconut aminos, curry spice, and salt in a small bowl.

When the potatoes are cooked, remove them from the oven, let cool slightly, then cut into ½-inch-thick rounds. Increase the oven temperature to 500°F. Drizzle the sheet pan with the olive oil, arrange the sweet potato rounds in a single layer, then drizzle generously with the honey mixture.

When the oven is preheated, roast the sweet potatoes again until the honey bubbles and turns golden and the edges of the potatoes char a bit, about 5 minutes. Sprinkle on the scallions and serve hot or warm.

SWEET POTATOES IN RED MOLE WITH TOASTED PUMPKIN SEEDS

Serves 8

This mole, like any good version in this vast category of Mexican sauces, takes time to prepare. The good news is that it keeps well in the fridge or freezer, so you can bust it out the next day for an impressive dinner that will seem to have taken almost no time. Frequently served to accompany meat, the sauce—with its richness, acidity, and complex flavor—goes so well with sweet potatoes. It's a vegan dinner that will thrill your most carnivorous friends.

8 medium sweet potatoes
My Red Mole (page 313)

1 teaspoon kosher salt

1 cup salted roasted pepitas
(hulled pumpkin seeds)

MAKE THE DISH

Preheat the oven to 400°F. Use a fork to prick each sweet potato several times all over. Put the sweet potatoes on a sheet pan and roast until tender at the center, about 45 minutes. Give them a poke with your finger. They're ready when they give to just a little pressure. Let them cool slightly, just until you can handle them.

In the meantime, very gently warm the mole in a medium pot (with ½ cup of chicken stock or water, if you've made the mole in advance). When the potatoes are cool enough to handle, peel them, trim the pointy ends, and cut them into 1-inch-thick rounds.

To serve, arrange the sweet potatoes in eight shallow serving bowls, season with the salt, and spoon on the mole. Sprinkle on the pepitas and serve.

DIRTY MASHED POTATOES WITH ROASTED GARLIC AND CASHEW CREAM

Serves 6

The flavor of sweet caramelized onions with loads of garlic and an easy cashew cream make these mashed skin-on potatoes as decadent as any dairy-deluged version, minus all the bad fat. A last-minute broil gives the top a little crackle as a contrast to that creamy potato.

For the Cashew Cream
1½ cups raw cashews
1 tablespoon kosher salt

For the Onions and Garlic
¾ cup extra-virgin olive oil
2 large yellow onions, cut into thin half-moon slices
1 tablespoon kosher salt
30 garlic cloves, sliced as thin as the onions

For the Dish
1½ pounds small potatoes, such as new, red bliss, or fingerling

MAKE THE CASHEW CREAM
Combine the cashews, salt, and 1½ cups of water in a small mixing bowl and let the nuts soak at room temperature for 1 hour (it's okay if they float). Transfer the mixture to a blender and blend on high speed until very smooth, about 2 minutes.

MAKE THE ONIONS AND GARLIC
While the cashews are soaking, heat the oil in a large, heavy skillet (the onions should fit in about two layers) over medium-high heat until shimmery. Add the onions and salt, stir well, and cook, stirring occasionally, until the onions start to soften and release liquid, about 3 minutes. Stir in the garlic, then reduce the heat to medium, and cook, stirring occasionally, until the onions have a slightly creamy texture and turn golden and even a little brown at the edges, about 7 minutes. Reduce the heat to medium-low and keep cooking until the onions have a very creamy and almost melting texture, 5 to 8 minutes more. Turn off the heat.

MAKE THE DISH
In a medium pot, combine the potatoes and enough water to cover by an inch or so and bring to a strong simmer over high heat. Adjust the heat and simmer until you can cut one of the potatoes in half with no resistance, about 15 minutes. Drain well, reserving 1 cup of cooking liquid.

Return the potatoes to the medium pot, add the onion mixture (including the oil), then crush and stir to make a chunky mash. Add the cashew mixture and use a whisk to incorporate the cream into the potatoes. Gradually add up to 1 cup of the reserved cooking liquid so the mixture has the texture of slightly loose, creamy mashed potatoes. You can do this up to 2 hours in advance.

Move an oven rack to the top position and preheat the broiler. Transfer the mixture to a casserole dish or another shallow ovenproof pot that'll hold it in a 3- or 4-inch layer. Broil on the top rack until the top is bubbly and golden brown, about 3 minutes. Serve hot.

JAPCHAE-STYLE NOODLES WITH VEGETABLES

Serves 6

Inspired by the Korean noodle stir-fry japchae, this dish pays homage to its glories while swapping out the soy for coconut aminos and sugar for honey. The noodles, however, stay put, because they're dangmyun, the slick, springy Korean glass noodles made from sweet potato starch. They're tossed with a pretty assortment of vegetables that you should feel free to customize, though I highly recommend what I do here: taking the time to cook them in batches so they don't sacrifice their individual character and each variety stays crisp and dynamic.

Do yourself a favor and use a mandoline to slice those sweet potato matchsticks. And skip the egg for a vegan version.

For the Sauce
3 tablespoons coconut aminos
2 tablespoons honey
2 tablespoons toasted
    sesame oil
1 tablespoon kosher salt
2 teaspoons finely chopped
    garlic
2 teaspoons raw sesame seeds,
    toasted (see page 26)
1 teaspoon ground black
    pepper

For the Eggs
2 large eggs
⅛ teaspoon kosher salt
1 teaspoon avocado oil

For the Dish
½ pound Korean sweet
    potato noodles
3 tablespoons avocado oil
¾ pound fresh shiitake
    mushrooms (about 15),
    stemmed and cut into
    ¼-inch-thick slices
1 tablespoon kosher salt

1 medium yellow onion, cut
    into ⅓-inch-thick half-moon
    slices
6 scallions, trimmed and cut
    into 2-inch pieces, whites
    halved lengthwise
1 medium sweet potato,
    peeled and cut into long,
    ⅛-inch-thick matchsticks (a
    mandoline helps)
1 red, orange, or yellow bell
    pepper, stemmed, deseeded,
    and cut into ⅓-inch-wide
    strips
1 moderately spicy green chile,
    such as jalapeño, thinly sliced

MAKE THE SAUCE
Combine the sauce ingredients, and stir really well.

MAKE THE EGGS
Crack the eggs into a small bowl, add the salt, and beat well, like you were making scrambled eggs.

Heat the oil in a medium nonstick skillet over low heat to warm it. Pour in the eggs and quickly swirl the skillet so the eggs cover the surface in a thin layer. Cook gently, without stirring, for 2 minutes, then cover the skillet and cook just until the surface of the eggs has set (it will still look shiny, but no longer wet), about 2 minutes more. Slide the eggs onto a cutting board, let cool slightly, then slice into long ¼-inch-wide strips.

MAKE THE DISH
Bring a medium pot of water to a boil over high heat. Add the noodles, let them soften slightly, then stir gently to loosen the noodle bundle. Cook until they're fully tender but still with a nice bounce and chew, about 5 minutes. Drain, then run the noodles under cool (not cold) running water, and drain again, giving the noodles an extra few shakes to make sure they're well drained. Cut the noodles roughly in half with scissors, transfer them to a large mixing bowl, and set it near the stove.

Heat 1 tablespoon of the oil in a large, heavy skillet over medium-high heat until shimmery. Add the mushrooms and cook, stirring occasionally, until golden and tender, about 5 minutes. Stir in 1 teaspoon of the salt and transfer the mushrooms to the bowl with the noodles.

Raise the heat to high, add 1 tablespoon of the oil to the skillet, and let it shimmer. Add the onion slices and cook quickly until they're translucent and golden at the edges but still slightly crisp, about 2 minutes. Stir in 1 teaspoon of the salt. Add the scallions and cook until the whites are just tender and the greens are bright green and wilted, about 1 minute more. Transfer it all to the bowl with the noodles.

Add the remaining 1 tablespoon of oil to the skillet, let it shimmer, then add the sweet potato, bell pepper, and chile. Cook on high until the pepper has softened slightly and the potato is tender with a slight crunch, about 2 minutes. Stir in the remaining 1 teaspoon of salt and transfer to the bowl with the noodles.

Add the sauce to the bowl, then toss really well with tongs, taking a little time to loosen the noodles and distribute the vegetables. If you've made the eggs, add the strips here and give everything a final toss. Serve warm or at room temperature.

3

Eggs Anytime

EGGS AND GREENS

Serves 2 to 4

A few simple steps transform ho-hum sautéed greens into this unforgettable one-pot dish—perfect for breakfast, lunch, or dinner. Packed with vitamins, fiber, and other good stuff, collards, chard, and kale can taste a little too healthy. They need a boost. So the first thing you do is sweat copious ginger, garlic, and chiles, along with a generous sprinkle of salt, to infuse olive oil that then supercharges those leafy greens. Once they're coated in the flavorful oil, you bake them with the eggs, the hot oven crisping those greens at the edges. A last-minute dose of fresh herbs cuts through the richness and refreshes your palate, so each bite is as rousing as the one before.

If you've made Jalapeño Oil (page 305)—fresh chiles briefly blistered in, then blended with, avocado oil—now is the perfect time to bust it out. These greens really sing after a drizzle of healthy, flavor-furthering fat imbued with the grassy heat of jalapeños.

1 small bunch collard greens

1 small bunch kale (any kind will do)

1 small bunch Swiss chard

½ cup extra-virgin olive oil

3-inch knob ginger, peeled and cut into very thin matchsticks

10 garlic cloves, thinly sliced

1 fairly spicy fresh red chile, such as Fresno or ripe jalapeño, thinly sliced

½ teaspoon kosher salt

6 large eggs

1 teaspoon flaky sea salt

2 small dried red chiles, crumbled

Handful mixed herbs, such as basil leaves, chopped parsley, small dill sprigs, and thinly sliced scallion

MAKE THE DISH

Preheat the oven to 450°F. Remove the stems from the collard greens, kale, and Swiss chard, reserving the chard stems, which are nice and tender. Finely chop the chard stems. Cut the greens into 1-inch-wide strips. You should have about 5 lightly packed quarts total.

Heat the olive oil in a 12-inch heavy ovenproof skillet over medium heat until shimmery. Add the ginger, garlic, fresh chiles, and ½ teaspoon of the kosher salt, and cook, stirring frequently, until the aromatics are fragrant and the edges of the garlic turn golden brown, about 2 minutes.

Add the chard stems and cook for 1 minute. Add half the greens and toss with tongs until slightly wilted, about 1 minute. Add the remaining greens and the remaining kosher salt, then mix all really well to coat them with the aromatics. Cook, tossing occasionally, just until they've all slightly wilted, about 2 minutes. Turn off the heat.

Crack the eggs onto the greens and the remaining kosher salt, leaving a couple of inches between each one. Transfer the skillet to the oven and bake until the egg whites are set and the yolks are set but still runny, 7 to 10 minutes.

Remove the pan from the oven and sprinkle the sea salt and dried chile over each egg. Sprinkle on the herbs and serve.

SOFT-BOILED EGGS AND ASPARAGUS WITH HARISSA AND PRESERVED LEMON

Serves 4 to 6

Soft-boiled eggs show off their golden yolks beside bright-green, juicy spears of asparagus. Drizzled with a two-ingredient dressing made with dusky harissa and sprinkled with salty, citrusy preserved lemon, it's just the thing for brunch, lunch, or a light dinner.

6 large eggs

1½ pounds asparagus

2 tablespoons extra-virgin olive oil

½ teaspoon kosher salt

2 tablespoons harissa, homemade (page 300) or store-bought

2 tablespoons lemon juice (from 1 juicy lemon)

1 tablespoon diced preserved lemon peel, homemade (page 288) or store-bought

Flaky sea salt

Small handful herbs, like basil or parsley leaves

MAKE THE DISH

Bring 5 cups of water to a boil in a small pot over high heat. Gently add the eggs and boil for 7 minutes (set a timer). Carefully pour off the cooking water, then cover the eggs with cold water to cool them briefly. Crack the eggs, then, one at a time, carefully peel them under cold running water. They keep in an airight container in the refrigerator for up to 1 day.

Preheat the oven to 450°F. One by one, bend each asparagus spear to break off the tough bottoms and discard them. Put the asparagus on a sheet pan in a single layer, then evenly drizzle on 1 tablespoon of the olive oil and sprinkle on the kosher salt. Roast in the oven just until the asparagus is bright green, slightly browned, and tender with a juicy crunch, about 5 minutes.

In the meantime, combine the harissa and lemon juice in a small bowl and stir well. When the asparagus is ready, transfer it to a platter. Halve the eggs and add them to the platter, then drizzle everything with the harissa dressing. Sprinkle on the preserved lemon peel, drizzle with the remaining 1 tablespoon of olive oil, and sprinkle some flaky salt on the eggs. Serve warm or at room temperature, scattering the herbs on just before serving.

CRISPY-EDGED THAI-STYLE OMELET WITH HERB SALAD AND SRIRACHA

Serves 2 to 4

In my home, no matter how bare my fridge gets, I always have eggs, fish sauce, and hot sauce. In other words, I can always make this memorable omelet—the lighter take on the delightful deep-fried Thai version—with its tender layers of egg capped with a golden brown, crispy top. The homemade sriracha-style sauce is extra credit—there are plenty of great brands out there, too. Don't skip the little shallot and herb salad; it adds freshness and crunch.

In this recipe, I take you through the omelet technique, which is simple to execute but unfamiliar enough to most Western egg buffs to deserve extra explanation. But good news: This omelet's amorphous shape (I'm looking at you, French omelet!) means it's difficult to mess up.

For the Omelet
8 large eggs
1 tablespoon plus 1 teaspoon fish sauce
3 tablespoons avocado oil

For the Dish
Small handful herbs, such as basil leaves, small parsley or cilantro sprigs, or a mix
1 small shallot, thinly sliced

A drizzle extra-virgin olive oil
A pinch flaky sea salt
Sriracha, homemade (page 271) or all-natural store-bought

MAKE THE OMELET

In a medium mixing bowl, combine the eggs and fish sauce and beat well so there are no pockets of yolks or whites and the surface is a little foamy.

Heat a 10-inch nonstick skillet over high heat until very hot. Add the avocado oil, swirl the skillet, then wait about 10 seconds so the oil is especially hot but not smoking. Pour the egg mixture into the skillet, then immediately swirl to coat the surface with an even layer of egg. Watch as the edges puff up—it's cool!

Using chopsticks or a spatula and starting at 12 o'clock, pull the edge of the omelet about 2 to 3 inches away from the skillet's edge, then tip the pan to let the liquid egg from the top rush to the edge of the skillet. Do the same at 3, 6, and 9 o'clock. Repeat the process, pulling each edge just 1 to 2 inches this time. The cooked portion will bunch up in soft folds near the center of the pan, but try to keep the omelet relatively flat.

Wait 1 to 2 minutes, without messing with the omelet, until the bottom is golden brown and the surface is covered with soft, shiny folds of cooked egg with just a bit of golden runny egg. Turn off the heat.

Grab a plate that's slightly larger than the skillet and invert the plate onto the skillet. Using oven mitts or two kitchen towels, firmly hold the skillet and plate in place and quickly flip the two together, so the omelet goes bottom-side up onto the plate. Put the plate on the counter and carefully remove the skillet.

MAKE THE DISH

Combine the herbs and shallot in a small bowl, add the olive oil and sea salt, and toss gently but well. Serve the omelet with the herb salad and the sriracha on the side.

SLOW-COOKED EGGS WITH CAULIFLOWER CONGEE AND CRISPY SHIITAKE

Serves 4

Because I do my best to eat nutritionally dense foods, I don't eat much white rice nowadays. I make exceptions, though, like when I travel and because I love me some rice porridge. Virtually every Asian country has its rendition—Thailand has jok, the Philippines has arroz caldo, Vietnam has chào, China has congee—each one warm, mellow, and as comforting as any dish out there.

Back home, I like to re-create the pleasure using so-called cauliflower rice. I treat it just like the real thing, simmering it with stock, ginger, and garlic (I even puree a bit of it once it's cooked to mimic the starchy, creamy quality of rice porridge) and topping it with slivered ginger and sliced scallion. Just before serving, I slide in eggs made in the Japanese onsen-style—carefully cooked so the whites are just barely set and the yolks are molten.

For the Cauliflower Congee

2 pounds cauliflower (about 1 medium head), leaves removed

2 tablespoons avocado oil

6 large garlic cloves, roughly sliced

2-inch knob ginger, peeled, halved, and very thinly sliced

1 tablespoon plus 1 teaspoon kosher salt

3 cups chicken or vegetable stock, salted homemade or store-bought

For the Eggs and Shiitakes

4 large eggs

2 tablespoons avocado oil

6 ounces shiitake mushrooms, stemmed and cut into ¼-inch-thick slices

½ teaspoon kosher salt

For the Dish

1-inch knob ginger, peeled and cut into very thin matchsticks

1 scallion, trimmed and thinly sliced

2 tablespoons Toasted Chile Oil (page 306)

4 teaspoons coconut aminos

MAKE THE CAULIFLOWER CONGEE

Trim off about ¼ inch of the dried-out bottom nub of the cauliflower and cut the rest into about 2-inch pieces. Working in batches, pulse the cauliflower in a food processor until it's broken into rice-size pieces.

Heat the avocado oil in a medium soup pot or Dutch oven over medium heat until shimmery. Add the garlic, ginger, and salt, and cook, stirring occasionally, until fragrant, about 1 minute. Add the cauliflower and stock, raise the heat to high, and bring to a boil. Reduce the heat to maintain a moderate simmer and cook, stirring occasionally, until the cauliflower is very tender (you'll be able to crush a piece easily under a spoon), 10 to 15 minutes.

Scoop out about half of the mixture and puree it in a blender until silky smooth. Return it to the pot and stir well. Turn off the heat and cover to keep the congee warm.

MAKE THE EGGS AND SHIITAKES

Bring 4 cups of water to a rolling boil in a small, heavy pot. Measure ½ cup of cold tap water and keep it nearby. Keep the eggs nearby, too. Once the water in the pot is at a boil, turn off the heat. Gradually add the tap water, about 2 tablespoons at a time and stirring between additions, until the water registers between 190 and 195°F on a thermometer. Immediately (but carefully) use a slotted spoon to lower the eggs into the water, making sure none crack on the way down and prodding them to space them as far apart as possible. Cover the pot and set a timer for 10 minutes. When the timer goes off, pour off the water and fill the pot with enough cold tap water to cover the eggs. Keep them in the water in a warm place while you finish the dish.

Heat the avocado oil in a medium skillet over high heat until shimmery. Add the shiitake slices and spread them out in a single layer. Lower the heat to medium and cook until the bottoms are golden and crisp to the touch, about 3 minutes. Sprinkle on the salt, then flip the shiitake slices and keep cooking until the slices are lightly crispy all the way through, about 2 minutes more.

MAKE THE DISH

Ladle the congee into four bowls. One at a time, give the eggs a short, quick tap on the edge of the pot, so as to not break the yolks, then carefully crack them into the center of each bowl. Garnish with the crispy shiitakes, ginger, and scallion. Drizzle on the toasted chile oil and coconut aminos and serve right away.

SPANISH TORTILLA WITH MELTED LEEKS AND PIMENTON AIOLI

Serves 4 to 6

When I visit Spain, I make a beeline for a tapas bar for tortilla española, one of my favorite egg dishes on earth. When I make them myself, I stick closely to the classic, using plenty of olive oil and studding the tender egg with potato. But because I love them so, I swap in creamy, sweet melted leeks for the traditional onion. Hot, warm, or cold, it's heaven any time of day, with or without the bright, smoky aioli I like to serve alongside it.

Like the Thai-style omelet (page 110), the novel-to-many technique merits some explanation, so don't be thrown off by the detail I provide.

For the Aioli
1 large egg yolk
2 tablespoons lemon juice (from 1 juicy lemon)
1 large garlic clove, very finely chopped
1 teaspoon kosher salt

1 teaspoon pimenton picante (hot smoked Spanish paprika)
½ cup extra-virgin olive oil

For the Leeks and Potatoes
¾ pound whole leeks
½ cup extra-virgin olive oil
2 teaspoons kosher salt

½ pound Yukon Gold potatoes, peeled and cut into ⅛-inch-thick half-moons

For the Tortilla
10 large eggs
2 teaspoons kosher salt
¼ cup extra-virgin olive oil

MAKE THE AIOLI

Roll a damp kitchen towel into a donut shape and set it on your work surface. Put a medium bowl on top of the towel so its base fits snugly in the hole. This will help the bowl stay in place as you whisk to make the aioli. Next, combine all the aioli ingredients except for the olive oil in the bowl. Whisk until well combined and a single color. Now, start adding the oil, drop by drop at first, while vigorously whisking to incorporate it. Once the mixture starts to look thick and creamy, you can begin to add the oil in a slow, steady stream, continuing to whisk vigorously to make sure the oil is incorporated at the same rate it's added. Keep this up until all the oil has been incorporated and the mixture is thick, creamy, and a single rosy orange color.

It keeps in an airtight container in the fridge for up to 3 days.

MAKE THE LEEKS AND POTATOES

Trim off the tough bottom from each leek, about ¼ inch from the root base. Next, trim off the tough dark-green tops, not by just lopping them off but by cutting in an upside-down "V"—this preserves the center of those tops, which is pale and tender.

Halve the leeks lengthwise, then slice them crosswise into ¼-inch-thick half-moons. You should have about 4 cups. Put the leeks in a large bowl, fill with cool water, then agitate and stir well as you separate the layers. Use your hands to transfer the leeks to a colander to drain so any dislodged dirt and grit remains in the water. Finally, shake out any excess water, drain the leeks really well, and pat dry with kitchen towels.

Heat ¼ cup of the olive oil in a 10- or 11-inch ovenproof, nonstick skillet over medium heat until shimmery. Add the leeks, evenly sprinkle with 1 teaspoon of the salt, and stir well. Cook, stirring every couple

(cont.)

of minutes, until the leeks are fully soft and creamy and turn a pale, golden color, 6 to 8 minutes. Turn off the heat and transfer the leeks to a medium bowl.

Wipe out the pan, then add the remaining ¼ cup of oil and heat over medium-low heat until warm. Add the potatoes and the remaining 1 teaspoon of salt and cook, flipping the potatoes occasionally and gently so they remain intact, until they're tender with a slight firmness, 6 to 8 minutes.

MAKE THE TORTILLA AND SERVE

Preheat the oven to 350°F. Position an oven rack in the top position. Crack the eggs into a large bowl, add the salt, and whisk until the eggs are well beaten, with no visible blobs of the whites. Add the leeks and stir well, so they're evenly dispersed (they'll want to clump) in the eggs. Add the potatoes (and any oil in the pan) and stir gently but well.

Heat the oil in the skillet over medium-low heat until just warm. Add the egg mixture and use a flexible spatula to start dragging it until some soft folds form as the bottom begins to set. Next, start pulling the egg mixture from the edges and bottom of the skillet toward the center, tipping the skillet to let the runny egg in the center spill into the edges. As the egg mixture cooks, it will continue to form more of those soft folds. Keep at it until it's half set, with edges forming and a fairly runny center, about 2 minutes.

While the egg mixture cooks, keep your eye on the edges. When a nice border of set egg has formed, use the flexible spatula to pull the edges of the egg mixture from the pan's edges so the resulting tortilla will have nice rounded sides.

Soon you're going to finish cooking the tortilla in the oven, but first you need to make sure the bottom layer (which will ultimately be the top layer) is set. While you're cooking, occasionally move the skillet around in a circular motion with it still on the stovetop. When the entire tortilla moves as one mass in the skillet, it's ready for the oven. Transfer the skillet to the top rack and cook until the surface is covered with soft, shiny folds of cooked egg with just a bit of golden runny egg at the center, 3 to 5 minutes.

Grab a plate that's slightly larger than the skillet and invert the plate onto the skillet. Using oven mitts or kitchen towels, firmly hold the skillet and plate in place and quickly flip the two together, so the tortilla goes bottom-side up onto the plate. Put the plate on the counter and carefully remove the skillet.

Let the tortilla cool for about 15 minutes, then slather on the aioli. Leftover tortilla keeps in an airtight container the fridge for up to 2 days and tastes great cold.

FRIED EGGS ON THAI-STYLE CHICKEN WITH BASIL

Serves 4

In Thailand, I must've eaten about a hundred fried eggs, cooked on high heat so the edges crisp while the yolks stay creamy and slipped onto a mound of robustly flavored ground chicken. Those mellow eggs are perfection with a stir-fry full of fire, salt, and funk. It's typically finished with peppery holy basil, which can be tough to find in the States, so I use sweet, licorice-y Thai basil. It has a decidedly different flavor but is nonetheless delightful.

2 tablespoons avocado oil, plus extra for the eggs

6 garlic cloves, thinly sliced

4 medium fresh Thai chiles, thinly sliced

1½ pounds ground dark meat chicken

2½ tablespoons fish sauce

2 tablespoons coconut aminos

1½ teaspoons coconut sugar

2 large handfuls Thai basil leaves

4 large eggs

Kosher salt

MAKE THE DISH

Heat a large, heavy skillet over high heat. When it's hot, add the oil and swirl to coat the pan. Wait a few seconds, then add the garlic and chiles and immediately start stirring and don't stop until the garlic is golden at the edges, 30 seconds to 1 minute.

Add the chicken and cook, stirring almost constantly and breaking up clumps, until the liquid the chicken releases has evaporated and the chicken is no longer pink, about 5 minutes.

Stir in the fish sauce, coconut aminos, and coconut sugar and cook, occasionally stirring and breaking up any remaining clumps, until the liquids have evaporated and the chicken is golden brown, 4 to 5 minutes. Turn off the heat, add the basil, and stir well. Divide the chicken among four plates.

Heat a medium nonstick skillet over high heat. Pour in enough oil to give you about a ⅛-inch depth and wait until it's shimmery. Carefully crack one egg into the oil, cook until the edges of the white get golden brown, then crack another egg next to it. Cook until the whites curl, brown, and crisp at the edges; the surface of the whites is fully set; and the yolks get golden and thick but are still runny. All of this happens fast, in 45 seconds to 1 minute. Sprinkle a tiny pinch of salt on each egg and use a slotted spatula to transfer the eggs to a plate while you cook the rest.

Slide the eggs on top over the chicken and serve.

SUNNY-SIDE UPS AND SAUTÉED GREENS WITH CHINESE-STYLE SAUSAGE

Serves 4 to 6

Hearty greens wilted with ginger and garlic are a treat alongside sweet and savory Chinese sausage-style patties—ground chicken seasoned with honey and five spice. Especially when you use the sausage drippings to fry sunny-side up eggs. And it all goes down in a single skillet.

If you have them handy, it's a great time for Ginger-Scallion Sauce (page 303), Toasted Chile Oil (page 306), or both—drizzled on right before serving.

For the Sausage Patties
1½ pounds ground dark meat chicken
2 teaspoons kosher salt
3 tablespoons coconut aminos
2 tablespoons honey
1 teaspoon Eight Spice (page 326) or Chinese five spice
¾ teaspoon red chile flakes
½ teaspoon white pepper

For the Greens
2 large bunches dark leafy greens, such as collards, chard, or kale
2 tablespoons extra-virgin olive oil
1½-inch knob ginger, peeled and finely chopped
4 large garlic cloves, smashed and roughly chopped

4 scallions, trimmed and cut into 2-inch pieces, whites halved lengthwise
½ teaspoon kosher salt

For the Dish
4 tablespoons extra-virgin olive oil
8 large eggs
Flaky sea salt

MAKE THE SAUSAGE PATTIES

Combine all the sausage ingredients in a medium mixing bowl and use a spoon to mix well. Once combined, keep mixing for a minute or so longer to make a smooth, slightly sticky mixture that's all one color. Form the mixture into twelve ½-inch-thick patties (use about ¼ cup for each one).

MAKE THE GREENS

Strip the leaves from stems of the greens and tear them into a few pieces (you want about 8 cups of leaves), discarding the stems for all but chard. Thinly slice the tender chard stems.

Heat the oil in a large, heavy skillet with a lid (either nonstick or well-seasoned cast iron) over medium-high heat until shimmery. Add the ginger, garlic, scallions, and salt, and cook, stirring once or twice, until the garlic browns at the edges, about 1 minute. Add the greens (and chard stems, if using) and cook, tossing every 30 seconds or so, just until the greens begin to wilt, 3 to 4 minutes. Transfer them to a serving platter (no need to clean the skillet just yet) and keep them in a warm place.

MAKE THE DISH

Heat 2 tablespoons of the oil in the same large, heavy skillet over medium-low heat until hot but not yet shimmery. Cook the sausage patties, flipping once, until both sides are golden brown and the patties are cooked through, 2 to 3 minutes per side. Transfer them to the serving platter, reserving the skillet and drippings.

Add 1 tablespoon of olive oil to the skillet with the sausage drippings, set it over medium-low heat, and let the oil get nice and warm. One at a time, crack four of the eggs into the pan, then cook, undisturbed, until the surface of the whites is fully set, about 2 minutes, then cover the skillet and let the yolks get golden and thick but still runny, about 1 minute more. As they're done, use a slotted spatula to transfer the eggs to the platter, then repeat with the remaining olive oil and eggs.

Sprinkle the eggs with flaky salt plus the ginger-scallion sauce and chile oil, if you've got them. Serve right away.

STEAK AND EGGS WITH THAI-STYLE TAMARIND-CHILE SAUCE

Serves 4

I give the classic, rich duo of steak and eggs a Thai makeover here, applying a fish sauce marinade to the meat and pairing it with cilantro, shallots, and a riff on jaew—a stunner of a dipping sauce, bright with lime and tamarind and spicy from dried chiles, that you'll make again and again. Giving soft-boiled eggs a quick roll-around in the savory bits left in the pan after cooking the steaks is a joy that ensures no flavor is left behind.

I love hanger steak for its beefy flavor and nice, tender chew, but feel free to use skirt, strip, or any quick-cooking steak you like, as long as you adjust the cooking time accordingly.

For Marinating the Steak and Making the Eggs
1½ pounds hanger steak (about 3 pieces)
1½ teaspoons kosher salt
3 tablespoons coconut aminos
3 tablespoons fish sauce
3 tablespoons finely chopped palm sugar or coconut sugar
4 large eggs

For the Tamarind-Chile Sauce
¼ cup fish sauce
¼ cup lime juice (from about 2 juicy limes)
1 tablespoon finely chopped palm sugar or coconut sugar
12 small dried red chiles
2 tablespoons Tamarind Water (page 327)

2 medium shallots, thinly sliced
Handful small cilantro sprigs, roughly chopped

For the Dish
1 tablespoon avocado oil
Toasted Chile Oil (page 306; optional)

MARINATE THE STEAK AND MAKE THE EGGS
Season the steak on both sides with the salt. In a medium mixing bowl, combine the coconut aminos, fish sauce, and palm sugar and stir until the sugar dissolves. Add the steaks to the bowl and toss to coat well. Cover and marinate in the fridge, flipping once halfway through, for at least 2 hours or up to 24 hours.

In the meantime, bring 5 cups of water to a boil in a small pot over high heat. Gently add the eggs and cook for 7 minutes (set a timer). Carefully pour off the cooking water, then cover the eggs with cold water to cool them briefly. Crack the eggs, then, one at a time, and carefully peel them under cold running water. They keep in an airtight container in the refrigerator for up to 1 day.

MAKE THE TAMARIND-CHILE SAUCE
Combine the fish sauce, lime juice, palm sugar, chiles, and tamarind water in a blender and blend until the chiles are in tiny pieces (you don't want it completely smooth). Pour the mixture into a small serving bowl, stir in most of the shallots and most of the cilantro, and let sit for 20 minutes or up to 1 hour.

MAKE THE DISH
Preheat the oven to 350°F. Remove the steaks from the marinade and pat them dry with paper towels.

Heat the avocado oil in a large, heavy ovenproof skillet over high heat until shimmery, then give it another minute or so. Add the steaks and cook, without messing with them, until the bottoms have a deep brown crust, 2 to 3 minutes. Flip the steaks, cook for 2 minutes more, then transfer the skillet to the oven. Cook until they're medium rare (a thermometer will register 120°F), 5 to 7 minutes, depending on the thickness of your steaks. Transfer the steaks to a cutting board to rest for 10 minutes or so.

While the steaks are resting, set the skillet with the steak drippings over medium-low heat, add the eggs, and let them roll around in the pan for 15 seconds or so to pick up some steak flavor without cooking the yolks any further. Transfer them to a serving platter.

Slice the steaks against the grain into approximately ⅓-inch-thick slices and arrange them on the platter. Drizzle with toasted chile oil, scatter on the remaining cilantro and shallots, and serve with a small bowl of the tamarind-chile sauce.

4

Morning Meals

GRANOLA WITH SEEDS, DRIED CHERRIES, AND COCONUT FLAKES

Makes about 6 cups

Making your own granola couldn't be easier. A big bowlful of good stuff—pecans and cashews, flax and pumpkin seeds, dried cherries and coconut flakes—gets tossed in coconut oil and maple syrup and baked in the oven to a crispy, toasty delight. Packed with protein and good fats, it's great as a grab-and-go snack or as cereal drenched in cold nut or seed milk.

¼ cup maple syrup

2 tablespoons melted virgin coconut oil

1 teaspoon vanilla extract

1 cup raw cashews

1 cup flax seeds

1 cup raw unsalted pecan halves

1 cup salted roasted pepitas (hulled pumpkin seeds)

1 cup unsweetened coconut flakes or coconut smiles

1 cup unsulphured dried cherries (tart or sweet)

MAKE THE GRANOLA

Preheat the oven to 300°F. Combine the maple syrup, coconut oil, and vanilla in a large bowl and whisk to combine. Add the remaining ingredients except for the dried cherries and stir well so they are well coated with the liquid. Transfer the mixture to a large, parchment paper-lined sheet pan and spread it into a thin, even layer. This is really important in ensuring the granola evenly dries and crisps without getting too dark.

Bake until it turns a rich mahogany color and the nuts, seeds, and coconut flakes are crisp, about 30 minutes. (Take a peek after 20 minutes and stir if the edges are darker than the center, returning it to a nice even layer.) Stir in the dried cherries and let cool completely.

It keeps in an airtight container for up to 2 weeks.

SPICED CARROT-PUMPKIN MUFFINS

Makes 12 muffins

Tender, moist, and crowned with the crunch of pumpkin seeds, these spiced, protein-packed muffins are a joy to eat. And a pleasure to make, too, since they require no more than a big bowl and a muffin pan.

Muffin game changer: Get yourself some inexpensive silicone baking cups to line the muffin pan, because then the muffins bake better and pop right out. Otherwise, paper muffins cups are just fine.

1 cup grated carrot (from about 1 large carrot)

1½ cups Paleo-Friendly Flour Blend (page 327)

¾ cup unsweetened canned pumpkin

½ cup honey, plus more for finishing

3 large eggs, lightly beaten

2 tablespoons smooth cashew, almond, or sunflower seed butter

1 tablespoon melted virgin coconut oil

1 teaspoon baking powder

1 teaspoon baking soda

1 teaspoon freshly ground cinnamon (from about two 3-inch sticks)

⅛ teaspoon kosher salt

3 tablespoons unsalted roasted pepitas (hulled pumpkin seeds)

Flaky sea salt

MAKE THE MUFFINS

Preheat the oven to 350°F and position a rack in the center of the oven. Insert paper or silicone cups into a muffin pan.

Wrap the grated carrot in a clean kitchen towel and wring it to remove some of its natural liquid. In a large mixing bowl, combine the flour blend, pumpkin, honey, eggs, nut butter, coconut oil, baking powder, baking soda, cinnamon, and kosher salt along with the grated carrot. Use a whisk or handheld electric mixer to mix everything well.

Spoon the batter evenly into the muffin cups, filling each to about ¼ inch from the rim. Evenly sprinkle on the pepitas. Bake until the muffins register 200°F in the center (temperature is the best way to tell when cakes made with my Paleo-friendly flour blend are ready), 25 to 30 minutes. Let the muffins cool in the pan for 10 minutes before you eat them. They're great warm from the oven. Otherwise, transfer them to a wire rack to cool completely and keep in an airtight container for 4 days at room temperature.

When you're ready to eat, drizzle the muffins generously with honey and sprinkle on a little flaky salt.

PLANTAIN BREAD

Makes 1 loaf

Plantain flour steps up to the plate in this better-for-you variation on banana bread, delivering sweet, toasty flavor and tons of good stuff. I encourage you to go full-plantain, using super-ripe fresh plantains in place of bananas for an especially deep flavor, but that's up to you.

The bread makes magical toast, crisp on the outside and warm and tender within, so give slices 5 minutes or so in a 350°F oven, then bring on the schmears—coconut oil and a sprinkle of sea salt, or nut butter and jam. My favorite combo: Spicy Cashew Butter (page 319) and Strawberry Jam (page 316).

Note: Easy to find online, plantain flour is made from the green (or unripe) fruit and makes a nutritious (full of vitamin A, E, and K, plus potassium and iron, if you're wondering), gluten-free substitute for wheat flour in so many preparations.

1 cup plantain flour (see Note)	½ cup coconut sugar	2 damn-that's-ripe plantains (see page 18) or 3 overripe bananas (fully brown with black patches)
½ cup extra-fine almond flour	2 large eggs	
3 tablespoons tapioca flour	⅔ cup virgin coconut oil, plus more for greasing the loaf pan	
1 teaspoon baking soda	2 tablespoons plain coconut or almond yogurt	
1-inch cinnamon stick, freshly grated	1 teaspoon vanilla extract	
½ teaspoon kosher salt		

MAKE THE BREAD

Preheat the oven to 350°F and position an oven rack in the center position. In a small mixing bowl, stir together the flours, baking soda, cinnamon, and salt.

In a large bowl, whisk the sugar and eggs together until the sugar dissolves and the mixture looks light and fluffy. Add the coconut oil, yogurt, and vanilla. Peel and mash the plantains or bananas, measure out 1½ cups of the mashed fruit, and add it to the large bowl.

Fold the flour mixture into the egg mixture until smooth, with no pockets of loose flour. Grease a 9 x 5–inch loaf pan, pour in the mixture, and bake on the center rack until a small knife inserted in the center comes out clean, about 45 minutes. Let the bread cool for 5 minutes, then invert onto a board or rack to cool completely.

It keeps in an airtight container at room temperature for up to 3 days.

COCONUT PANCAKES WITH BLUEBERRY-MAPLE SYRUP AND BASIL

Serves 6 to 8 (about 16 pancakes)

Sweet, nutty coconut flour (high in fiber and micronutrients, low in carbs) teams up with tapioca flour for pancakes with an irresistible texture, enough of a cake-like crumb to feel substantial but still light enough to have you going back for more. Sprinkled with torn basil and drizzled with maple syrup warmed with blueberries until they burst, these are my pick over standard flapjacks any day.

Besides being straight-up delicious, these pancakes are a dream to make. Instead of combining dry and wet ingredients separately, as you do with traditional pancakes, here you just combine everything and stir. And because the batter contains no gluten, it's impossible to overmix. Plus, you can make the batter up to 24 hours in advance—a no-no for standard pancakes—and they're much less likely to overcook. Breakfast just became a breeze.

For the Blueberry-Maple Syrup
1 cup maple syrup
1 cup blueberries
¼ teaspoon kosher salt

For the Batter
2 cups coconut flour

2 cups tapioca flour
4 cups well-shaken coconut milk
¼ cup honey
½ teaspoon baking soda
½ teaspoon baking powder
½ teaspoon kosher salt
4 large eggs

For the Dish
⅔ cup virgin coconut oil
Small handful Thai or Italian basil leaves, torn at the last minute
¼ cup unsweetened toasted coconut flakes

MAKE THE BLUEBERRY-MAPLE SYRUP

Combine the maple syrup and blueberries in a small saucepan, set it over low heat, and cook, stirring occasionally, until the berries plump and the syrup looks purplish, about 5 minutes. Turn off the heat, stir in the salt, and cover to keep warm.

MAKE THE BATTER

In a large mixing bowl, combine the coconut flour, tapioca flour, coconut milk, honey, baking soda, baking powder, salt, eggs, and ½ cup water and whisk well to make a thick, scoopable batter. It will keep, covered, in the fridge for up to 24 hours.

MAKE THE DISH

Preheat the oven to 200°F.

Heat a large cast-iron or nonstick skillet over low heat for a minute or two to get it nice and warm. Make one big pancake at a time. For each pancake, add about a teaspoon of coconut oil to the skillet, swirling to coat the surface. Add ⅓ cup of batter and use the back of a spoon to gently spread it into a 4- to 5-inch circle. Cook until the bottom is golden, about 3 minutes. Flip the pancake and cook until the second side is golden and the inside has a moist cake-like crumb, about 3 minutes.

Spread or drizzle about 1 teaspoon of coconut oil on the surface of each pancake, then transfer the pancake to an ovenproof plate and keep it in the oven while you cook the rest, transferring the pancakes to the plate as they're cooked. To serve, stack the pancakes, spoon on the syrup, and sprinkle on the basil and coconut flakes.

BETTER ENERGY BALLS WITH WALNUTS, APRICOTS, AND DATES

Makes about 35 balls

A quick whiz in the food processor turns dried fruit and nuts into a crunchy-creamy concoction that you roll into perfect, portable two-bite balls. High in protein and good fats, but tasty enough to count as treats, they kick a busy morning into gear or provide a super-powered midday boost.

1 cup raw cashews

1 cup unsweetened coconut flakes

1 cup unsulphured dried Turkish apricots

⅔ cup raw walnuts

20 Medjool dates, pitted (15 if large)

2 tablespoons virgin coconut oil

2 teaspoons flaky sea salt

MAKE THE BALLS

Working in batches if necessary, pulse all the ingredients in a food processor until a chunky, sticky mass forms. The nuts and coconut will be in small pieces and the dates will become a paste. This is important, because the date paste is the glue that holds the balls together.

Transfer the mixture to a medium bowl. Use your hands to roll tablespoon-size portions into balls. They keep in an airtight container at room temperature for up to 2 weeks.

WARM COCONUT CHIA PUDDING WITH DRIED MANGOES AND CHERRIES

Serves 4 to 6

This warm, creamy treat is full of great-for-you seeds and dried fruit. The star of the show is chia, an unassuming seed native to Mexico and Guatemala that tops every healthiest-foods chart—it's high in fiber, protein, and antioxidants and low in carbs. Better still, soaking chia (in the fridge, like overnight oats) gives it this incredible texture, gelatinous outside with a soft crunch inside, which adds to the pudding's creaminess.

For the Chia Mix
½ cup chia seeds
½ cup flax seeds
½ cup chopped (about ¼ inch) unsulphured dried mango
½ cup unsulphured dried cherries (tart or sweet)

¼ cup raw hulled sunflower seeds
¼ cup raw pepitas (hulled pumpkin seeds)
2 cups well-shaken coconut milk

For the Pudding
3 cups alternative milk, such as pecan, coconut, or hazelnut, homemade (page 321) or store-bought
¼ cup maple syrup
½ teaspoon kosher salt

MAKE AND SOAK THE CHIA MIX

In a medium bowl, combine all the chia mix ingredients along with 2 cups of water, and stir well. Cover and let soak in the fridge for at least 8 hours or up to 3 days, so the chia has time to absorb the liquid and take on its cool texture.

MAKE THE PUDDING

Once the chia mix has soaked, combine it in a medium pot along with the alternative milk, maple syrup, and salt. Stir well, then bring to a simmer over medium-high heat and cook, stirring occasionally, just until the pudding is hot, creamy, and slightly thickened and the chia seeds are tender but with some chew, about 10 minutes. Keep a close eye on the chia, which can get mushy quickly.

Serve hot or warm.

5

Dips

CREAMY CASHEW DIP WITH JALAPEÑO AND SEEDY SEAWEED CRACKERS

Serves 6 to 8

After a short soak, cashews blend to make a luscious, savory dip with a little vinegar for tang and jalapeño oil for heat and flavor. Your favorite cracker makes it a party, though I highly recommend baking these seedy seaweed ones. Inspired by a recipe from Angela Liddon of Oh She Glows, one of my favorite health food blogs, they offer an irresistibly salty, crispy nutrient-dense accompaniment.

For the Crackers
3 nori sheets

¼ cup chia seeds

¼ cup flax seeds

¼ cup raw hulled sunflower seeds

3 scallions, trimmed and thinly sliced

1 small garlic clove, very finely chopped

½ teaspoon red chile flakes

2 teaspoons flaky sea salt

For the Dip
3 cups raw cashews

1 medium shallot, roughly chopped

1½ teaspoons kosher salt

2 tablespoons white wine vinegar

3 tablespoons Jalapeño Oil (page 305)

Small handful mixed fresh herbs, like small dill and parsley sprigs and oregano leaves

MAKE THE CRACKERS

Preheat the oven to 300°F. Stack the nori sheets shiny-side down. Use kitchen scissors to cut along the indentations into long strips. Stack those strips and snip them crosswise into ½-inch-wide strips.

Combine the nori, chia seeds, flax seeds, sunflower seeds, scallions, garlic, chile flakes, and ¾ cup water in a medium mixing bowl. Stir well so the ingredients are evenly distributed and until a mixture forms as the chia absorbs the water and gets jelly-like. Let the mixture sit for about 3 minutes so the chia has time to fully bloom.

Cut two 17 x 12-inch sheets of parchment paper. Lay one of the sheets on a work surface. Scoop the chia mixture onto the sheet and use a flexible spatula to spread it into a thin (about ⅛-inch), even layer that covers more or less the whole sheet. Place the other sheet of parchment paper on top and use a rolling pin or round bottle to make sure the chia mixture is nice and even. Carefully transfer the two layers of parchment paper to a large sheet pan, then gradually and slowly peel off the top layer.

Evenly sprinkle on the flaky salt and bake in the oven until the mixture is completely dry to the touch and crispy even in the center, about 45 minutes. If the center is not completely crispy after 45 minutes, remove the sheet pan from the oven, flip the entire cracker, and cook for 10 minutes more.

Let the cracker cool on the sheet pan, then break it into any size crackers you'd like. They keep in an airtight container in the pantry for up to 1 week.

MAKE THE DIP AND SERVE

Combine the cashews and 1½ cups of water in a narrow jar (it's fine if the cashews float) and let the nuts soak for 1 hour.

Meanwhile, combine the shallot and kosher salt in a small bowl, toss well, and let sit for 10 minutes to soften a bit. Add the vinegar, stir well, and let the mixture hang out until the cashews are done soaking.

Transfer the cashews and the soaking water to a blender, add the shallot mixture and 2 tablespoons of the jalapeño oil, and blend on high speed until as smooth as possible. This might take up to 2 minutes in a standard-speed blender and require you to occasionally stop the blender and stir and scrape the sides to encourage blending. The dip keeps in an airtight container in the fridge for up to 1 week.

When ready to serve, transfer the cashew dip to a bowl and drizzle with the remaining jalapeño oil. Serve with the crackers and the herbs.

CASHEW "HUMMUS" WITH CHILE AND HERBS

Serves 8 to 10

One of the dishes my legume-free friends miss most is hummus. I know I do. But I promise you, when you give cashews the full hummus treatment, you may never go back to chickpeas. Instead of dried beans that require long-cooking or overnight soaking, cashews take just half an hour to get tender and blend to a super-silky puree. (The secret is in the addition of baking soda to the cooking water, which true hummus maestros like my friend Michael Solomonov, chef/owner of Zahav, use for the traditional version.) An aromatic chile paste provides a little thrill to the dip. Serve this with cold, crunchy raw vegetables to contrast the richness and heat.

For the "Hummus"
2 cups raw cashews

½ teaspoon baking soda

1 tablespoon plus 2 teaspoons kosher salt

¾ cup fresh lemon juice (from 5 or 6 juicy lemons)

8 medium garlic cloves, peeled

½ teaspoon cumin seeds, ground to a powder in a spice grinder

2 cups well-stirred tahini

For Serving
6 tablespoons Aromatic Chile Paste (page 298) or harissa, homemade (page 300) or store-bought

Smoked paprika

¼ cup plus 2 tablespoons extra-virgin olive oil

Handful small parsley sprigs

3 scallions, trimmed and thinly sliced

MAKE THE "HUMMUS"

In a medium pot, combine the cashews, baking soda, and 3 cups of water and bring to a boil over high heat. Reduce the heat and simmer, stirring occasionally and skimming off any foam, until the cashews are fully tender and creamy inside, like cooked beans, about 30 minutes.

Use a slotted spoon to scoop out ⅓ cup of the cashews and transfer them to a small bowl to cool. Continue to cook the remaining cashews until they're very soft and start falling apart and most of the liquid has been absorbed, 5 to 10 minutes more. You should be able to smoosh them between two fingers with almost no pressure. Drain the cashews, reserving 1 cup of the cooking liquid. Put the smooshable cashews and reserved cooking liquid into a blender, add 2 teaspoons of the salt, and puree on high speed until super smooth and silky, stopping and scraping the sides as needed, 3 to 5 minutes. Transfer the puree to a small mixing bowl.

Combine the lemon juice, garlic, cumin, and the remaining 1 tablespoon of salt in the blender and puree until very smooth. Pour the mixture into a medium mixing bowl and let it sit for 10 minutes so the garlic mellows and the flavors come together. Add the tahini and whisk to make a smooth, stiff mixture.

Add the cashew puree and whisk to combine well. It keeps in an airtight container in the fridge for up to 4 days.

SERVE THE "HUMMUS"

Scoop the hummus into a serving bowl and create a big well in the center. To the well, add the chile paste, whole cooked cashews, and smoked paprika. Drizzle on the olive oil, sprinkle on the parsley and scallions, and serve.

GUACAMOLE WITH ROASTED CHILES, POMEGRANATE, AND TORTILLA CRISPS

Serves 4

I love guacamole—the way a few key ingredients balance and enliven lush, mellow avocado. My version builds on the classic, swapping charred chiles for raw for another dimension of heat and flavor and augmenting the typical lime with pomegranate seeds for another sort of acidity and a little texture. Make sure you let those avocados get good and ripe—they should be soft but not mushy, giving slightly to a gentle squeeze—to enjoy their full, creamy potential.

Nowadays, stores are filled with grain-free chip options, but I recommend buying cashew, almond, or cassava tortillas and crisping them in a little hot oil so they're warm when you serve them.

For the Guacamole
½ small white onion, cut into ⅛-inch dice

2 tablespoons lime juice (from 1 juicy lime)

2 tablespoons flaky sea salt

2 medium jalapeño or large serrano chiles

2 moderately spicy fresh red chiles, like Fresnos or ripe jalapeños

3 large ripe Hass avocados

2 tablespoons extra-virgin olive oil

½ cup pomegranate seeds

1 tablespoon Jalapeño Oil (page 305; optional)

Handful mixed fresh herbs, like small cilantro and dill sprigs and oregano leaves

For the Crisps
¼ cup extra-virgin olive oil

6 grain-free tortillas (such as cashew, almond, or cassava), halved

Kosher salt

MAKE THE GUACAMOLE

Combine the onion, lime juice, and flaky salt in a large bowl, stir well, and set aside for 15 minutes to soften the onion and mellow its sharpness.

Lay the green and red chiles on the stove rack of a gas burner, turn on the burner, and char them over the flames, using tongs to flip them occasionally, just until their skins are blistered and black all over but the flesh is still bright and firm, about 3 minutes. (No gas burner? Broil them in the oven close to the heat, turning occasionally, for 3 to 4 minutes.) Let the chiles cool briefly, then scrape off the skins with a small knife. Remove the stems, halve the chiles lengthwise, and scrape out the seeds. Discard the skins, stems, and seeds, then finely chop the chiles and scrape them into the bowl with the onion.

Halve the avocados and remove the pits. Score the flesh in a crisscross pattern, stopping at the skin, and use a spoon to scoop the flesh into the bowl with the onion and chiles. Use a fork to mash about half of the avocado to a creamy texture, leaving the rest chunky. Drizzle in the olive oil and use a spoon to stir gently but well until there's no more visible oil.

Scoop the guacamole into a shallow serving bowl, sprinkle on the pomegranate seeds, drizzle with the jalapeño oil (if using), and scatter on the herbs.

MAKE THE CRISPS AND SERVE

Line a sheet pan with paper towels. Heat the olive oil in a large, heavy skillet over medium heat until hot but not quite shimmery. To test whether it's ready, dip a corner of a tortilla into the oil—when it's hot enough, the oil will bubble right away.

Fry the tortillas, two pieces at a time and flipping once, just until crispy and golden, about 30 seconds on each side. Transfer them to the paper towels to drain and sprinkle with kosher salt. Repeat with the remaining tortilla pieces.

Serve the guacamole with the warm crisps.

CHARRED EGGPLANT DIP WITH GARLIC CONFIT AND HERBS

Serves 6 to 8

The key to this dip is the way you cook the eggplant. Poking it here and there provides an escape hatch for the moisture inside so it can evaporate as the eggplant cooks, intensifying the flavor. Charring the eggplant—not just a little but so much that some of skin burns off entirely—under the broiler or directly on the hot coals of a grill gives the flesh an irresistible smokiness. From there, it's simply pureed with nutty tahini, scattered with herbs, and topped with whole cloves of garlic that you've slow-cooked in good-for-you fat. It's essentially confit, but don't let the French term put you off this virtually effortless technique that leaves you with sweet, lusciously tender garlic and aromatic oil.

Serve it with crunchy vegetables or crackers.

For the Garlic Confit
⅔ cup peeled garlic cloves (about 45)
½ cup extra-virgin olive oil
½ teaspoon kosher salt

For the Dip
2 pounds whole globe eggplants (about 3 large)
2 tablespoons well-stirred tahini
1½ teaspoons kosher salt

3 small dried red chiles, crumbled
Handful mixed herbs, such as parsley, rosemary, and thyme

MAKE THE GARLIC CONFIT

Combine the garlic, oil, and salt in a small saucepan (the garlic won't be completely submerged yet, but it will be as it cooks and shrinks), set it over medium-low heat, and bring it to a gentle gurgle. Cook, stirring every 5 minutes or so, until the garlic is golden on the outside and creamy-tender all the way through (but still holds its shape), about 15 minutes.

Let the garlic cool in the oil. It keeps, submerged in the oil, in an airtight container in the fridge for up to 3 weeks.

MAKE THE DIP

Preheat a broiler and position an oven rack in the top position. Use the tip of a small, sharp knife to make eight tiny slits all over each eggplant, so the moisture escapes and the flavor concentrates as it cooks. Put the eggplants on a sheet pan with some space between them.

Broil on the top rack, turning the eggplants every 6 to 8 minutes to expose all the skin to the broiler's heat, until they have collapsed, the flesh is super creamy, and the skin is completely charred, 18 to 20 minutes.

Let the eggplants cool on the sheet pan until you can handle them. Halve them, then scoop out the flesh, discarding the skin and any dark juices that have accumulated on the sheet pan, and put it in a blender or food processor. Add the tahini and the salt and puree until it's as smooth as possible.

Scoop the eggplant mix into a serving bowl and create a big well in the center. To the well, add the garlic cloves and 2 tablespoons of the garlicky oil. Sprinkle on the chiles and herbs and serve.

SOUR COCONUT CREAM RANCH DIP WITH RAW VEGETABLES

Serves 8 to 10

Once you've turned coconut cream into coconut crème fraîche—via one of the world's easiest fermentations—the tangy rich product makes a perfect stand-in for the traditional buttermilk and sour cream in ranch dressing. Dosed with garlic, chives, and dill, the dip has all the creamy pleasures of the original but with a lightness that doesn't dominate the vegetables or undo the radiant feeling they give you.

The vegetables, of course, are up to you, though the list I give is a particularly nice assortment, especially when they're arranged in rainbow order for that ombré effect. Whatever you do, make sure to give them a soak in ice water so they're cold and super crisp. I like to go even further, serving them over a bowl of ice to preserve the texture and temperature.

For the Dip
1 medium shallot, finely chopped

2 garlic cloves, finely chopped

2 teaspoons flaky sea salt

2 cups Coconut Crème Fraîche (page 270), chilled

2 tablespoons thinly sliced chives

1 tablespoon lemon juice (from 1 juicy lemon)

1 teaspoon ground black pepper

For Serving
4 Persian cucumbers, halved lengthwise

2 heads baby bok choy, bottoms trimmed and leaves separated

1 head fennel, trimmed of thick stems and blemishes, cut lengthwise into ¼-inch-thick slices

1 small jicama, peeled and julienned (3 x ¼ inch)

1 small golden beet, peeled and thinly sliced on a mandoline

1 small orange bell pepper, cut into ½-inch strips

8 sweet mini peppers, halved

1 bunch small radishes, tops trimmed, halved

8 small young carrots, peeled and quartered lengthwise

3 cups cauliflower florets

Extra-virgin olive oil

Small handful small dill sprigs

MAKE THE DIP
Combine the shallot, garlic, and salt in a medium mixing bowl, mix well, and let sit for 15 minutes to soften the bite of the shallot and garlic. Add the coconut crème fraîche, chives, lemon juice, and pepper and stir well. Chill the dip in the fridge until you're ready to serve (the coconut crème fraîche melts at room temperature), up to 12 hours.

Ten minutes or so before you plan to serve, fill a large mixing bowl with ice water, add the vegetables, and let them hang out for 10 to 15 minutes. Right before serving, drain the vegetables well and pat them completely dry with clean kitchen towels.

SERVE THE DIP
Arrange the vegetables on a platter. Serve the dip, drizzled with the olive oil and sprinkled with the dill, alongside the vegetables.

6

Soups

CHILLED TOMATO, WATERMELON, AND STRAWBERRY SOUP WITH CRAB

Serves 6

When summer turns muggy, I practically wade through thick air into the farmers market, grabbing heavy tomatoes, late-season strawberries, and a baby watermelon or two to make this bracing cold soup. A little garlic, chile, and quick-pickled onions keep all that lovely sweetness in check, and taking the time to freeze half the soup and scrape it into fluffy, flaky ice creates a really cool textural contrast—and keeps things extra refreshing.

Finish it with crab for a bit of luxury, swap in simply cooked shrimp, or skip the seafood altogether.

2½ pounds peeled watermelon

2½ pounds large, very ripe tomatoes, cored and roughly chopped

2 pints strawberries, hulled

1 moderately spicy fresh red chile, such as Fresno, stemmed and roughly chopped

1 medium garlic clove, peeled

2½ tablespoons red wine vinegar

2 tablespoons kosher salt

¼ cup lime juice (from 2 juicy limes)

½ cup drained Quick-Pickled Red Onions (page 286)

½ pound lump crabmeat

Small handful basil leaves

MAKE THE SOUP

Cut enough of the watermelon into 1-inch cubes to give you 2 cups, put them in a medium bowl, and refrigerate to chill. Roughly chop the rest of the watermelon and put it in a big mixing bowl along with the tomatoes, strawberries, chile, garlic, vinegar, salt, and lime juice. Toss well.

In a blender and working in batches, blend the tomato mixture on high until very smooth, pour into a large container, and stir well. Pour about half the soup into a glass or ceramic container that will hold the amount in a depth of about 1½ inches (a 9 x 12-inch baking dish works well). Freeze uncovered until frozen through, about 3 hours, then cover and freeze for up to 2 days. Chill the rest of the soup in the fridge for up to 2 days.

Half an hour before you're ready to serve, take the soup from the freezer and use the tines of a fork to scrape the mixture into fairly fine, flaky shaved ice. Return the ice to the freezer for about 30 minutes more, so it's nice and firm. Freeze six serving bowls as well.

To serve, divide the chilled watermelon cubes among the chilled serving bowls. Pour in the remaining soup from the refrigerator and top with the pickled onions and crab, then spoon on the shaved ice.

Garnish with the basil and serve immediately.

TOMATO–HAZELNUT MILK SOUP WITH GARAM MASALA

Serves 4

When summer bleeds into fall and hot days are followed by chilly nights, I start dreaming of this creamy soup made with tomatoes so ripe they're nearly bursting. Nutty and rich, hazelnut milk carries all that late-summer flavor, and the warm spices in garam masala—fragrant from cardamom, coriander, and clove—brings depth and complexity. Top-notch fresh tomatoes and homemade hazelnut milk (active time: 5 minutes) will give you something truly special. Good canned tomatoes and the store-bought stuff is pretty damn good, too.

For the Garam Masala Hazelnuts

½ cup avocado oil

1½ teaspoons garam masala, preferably homemade (page 324)

¼ teaspoon kosher salt

½ cup unsalted roasted hazelnuts, very roughly chopped

For the Soup

¼ cup extra-virgin olive oil

1 small red onion, thinly sliced

4 garlic cloves, roughly chopped

½ small moderately spicy fresh red chile, such as Fresno, stemmed

1 tablespoon kosher salt

2½ pounds very ripe tomatoes, cored and quartered

2 cups hazelnut milk, store-bought or homemade (page 321)

Small handful cilantro sprigs

MAKE THE GARAM MASALA HAZELNUTS

Combine the avocado oil, garam masala, and salt in a small skillet, give it a stir, and warm gently over low heat just until the oil takes on a golden-brown color and the spices smell especially fragrant and have infused the oil, about 4 minutes. Add the hazelnuts, stir well, heat for 30 seconds, then set aside.

MAKE THE SOUP

Heat the olive oil in a medium pot over medium heat until shimmery. Add the onion, garlic, chile, and salt, and cook, stirring occasionally, until the onion softens, about 3 minutes.

In the meantime, put the tomatoes in a large mixing bowl and crush them with your hands. When the onion mixture is ready, add the crushed tomatoes to the pot and cook over medium-high heat for 5 minutes, so the tomatoes cook quickly while retaining their fresh flavor.

Stir in the hazelnut milk, let it come to a strong simmer, and cook until the liquid reduces by half and thickens to the texture of heavy cream, about 10 minutes. The mixture may separate a bit as it cooks, but don't worry, it will come together again in the blender. Turn off the heat and let it cool slightly. Transfer the mixture to a blender and blend on high speed until very smooth, 1 to 2 minutes.

Divide the soup among four bowls, spoon in the garam masala hazelnuts (oil and all), and garnish with the cilantro. Serve hot.

BUTTERNUT SQUASH SOUP WITH CASHEW CREAM AND SMOKY PEPPERS

Serves 8

I love those moments when the seasons overlap. Take this soup, for example. Sure, you can find butternut squash and peppers from January to January, but the combination conjures that special late-September moment when pepper season peaks as squash season begins. Those peppers provide seductive sweetness when they're slow-cooked in olive oil and spiked with smoked paprika, setting off a savory soup of butternut squash made velvety and rich from cashews.

For the Cashew Cream
¾ cup raw cashews
1 teaspoon kosher salt

For the Soup
1 large butternut squash (about 4 pounds), peeled, seeded, and cut into 2-inch chunks
5 garlic cloves, peeled
1 large yellow onion, chopped

1 small jalapeño chile, stemmed and halved
4 cups chicken or vegetable stock, salted homemade or store-bought
1 cup cashews
1½ tablespoons kosher salt

For the Smoky Peppers
¼ cup extra-virgin olive oil

3 medium red bell peppers, stemmed, seeded, and deveined, cut into long ¼-inch-wide strips
10 garlic cloves, cut into ⅛-inch slices
1½ teaspoons kosher salt
1 small dried red chile, crushed, or ½ teaspoon red chile flakes
1½ teaspoons smoked paprika
1 tablespoon sherry vinegar

MAKE THE CASHEW CREAM
Combine the cashews, salt, and ¾ cup of water in a small mixing bowl and let the nuts soak at room temperature for 1 hour. Transfer the mixture to a blender and blend on high speed until very smooth, about 2 minutes. It keeps in an airtight container in the fridge for up to 4 days.

MAKE THE SOUP
In a large pot, combine the squash, garlic, onion, jalapeño, stock, cashews, and salt and bring to a simmer over medium heat. Cook, adjusting the heat to maintain the simmer, until the squash is so tender it starts to fall apart, about 30 minutes. Let it cool slightly, then transfer to the blender in batches and blend on high speed until smooth, about 1 minute per batch. Cover to keep warm.

MAKE THE SMOKY PEPPERS AND SERVE
While the soup simmers, heat the oil in a medium pot over medium heat until shimmery. Stir in the peppers, garlic, salt, and chile and cook until the peppers sweat and leach out liquid, about 3 minutes, then reduce the heat to low and continue to cook, stirring, until the peppers are very tender, about 5 minutes. Add the paprika, stir well, and cook for 1 minute more so the flavors can meld. Stir in the vinegar, turn off the heat, and set aside.

Ladle the soup into eight bowls. Divide the peppers among the bowls and drizzle each with about 2 tablespoons of the cashew cream. Serve right away.

GUYANESE-STYLE VEGETABLE SOUP WITH COCONUT MILK AND CHILES

Serves 6

This is inspired by metemgee, the very comforting Guyanese stew of hearty vegetables simmered in coconut milk. What began as an African dish, whose name essentially means "plantains make it good" in the Twi dialect spoken in Ghana, has evolved in the generations since it was cooked to feed the enslaved. Plantains, along with yucca and sweet potatoes, do indeed make this version good, and so do ginger, bay leaves, and fruity chiles, which are left large so they contribute their flavor and just enough of their heat—though expect a wallop if you chomp on one. All those aromatics mean that the chicken stock can be swapped out for vegetable stock or water for a vegan version that's equally excellent.

3 tablespoons extra-virgin olive oil

20 garlic cloves, halved

3 large shallots, quartered

2 tablespoons kosher salt

4 cups well-shaken coconut milk

4 cups chicken or vegetable stock, salted homemade or store-bought

6 bay leaves, preferably fresh

2 Scotch bonnet or habanero chiles, stemmed and halved

2-inch knob ginger, peeled, halved, and very thinly sliced

1 tablespoon fresh thyme leaves

2 ripe plantains (see page 17), cut into ½-inch-thick half-moons

1½ cups peeled and diced (about ¾ inch) yucca

1½ cups peeled and diced (about ¾ inch) sweet potato

½ pound very small potatoes (1 to 2 inches), halved or quartered if large

MAKE THE SOUP

Heat the oil in a big soup pot or Dutch oven over medium heat until shimmery. Add the garlic, shallots, and salt, and cook, stirring every minute or so, until the shallots start to soften and turn translucent, about 3 minutes.

Add the coconut milk, stock, bay leaves, chiles, ginger, and thyme and raise the heat to high to bring it to a boil. Adjust the heat and cook at a moderate simmer until the liquid takes on some of the ginger and chile flavors and reduces by about a quarter, about 15 minutes. Add the plantains, yucca, sweet potato, and potatoes, bring to a gentle simmer, and cook until the vegetables are fully tender (the yucca and plantains will lose their starchy interiors and become creamy), about 15 minutes more.

Serve hot.

THAI-STYLE HOT AND SOUR SOUP WITH SHRIMP, LEMONGRASS, AND LIME

Serves 6

Like just about every American, I'd eaten plenty of tom yum in Thai restaurants, but it wasn't until I went to Thailand that I felt like I'd truly encountered the iconic soup. My first bite shocked me—how could this light broth with few garnishes explode with flavor? I found out a few years later, during a stint at Nahm, the acclaimed Bangkok restaurant run at the time by the legendary David Thompson.

The first step is infusing the stock with the all-important aromatics—lemongrass and galangal, Thai chiles and makrut lime leaves. Then you season it with a carefully calibrated balance of fish sauce and lime juice, electrifying the broth so it exceeds the sum of its ingredients. My rendition of this salty, sour, spicy dish features shrimp gently cooked in the stock and a drizzle of toasted chile oil at the end for another layer of fragrance and heat.

Remind friends to eat around the pieces of lemongrass, galangal, and makrut lime leaves that bob in the bowls and to bite into those chiles at their own risk.

8 cups chicken stock, salted homemade or store-bought

12 medium fresh or frozen makrut lime leaves, center ribs removed

8 fresh Thai chiles, stemmed and halved lengthwise

6 stalks lemongrass, trimmed (see page 15), bruised, then cut into 2-inch pieces

6 medium shallots, halved

4 medium tomatoes (about 1 pound total), cored and cut into 1-inch pieces

4-inch knob fresh galangal, scrubbed and cut into ¼-inch-thick rounds

2 tablespoons kosher salt

¼ cup plus 2 tablespoons fish sauce

1½ pounds jumbo shrimp, peeled and deveined

½ cup plus 2 tablespoons lime juice (from 5 or 6 juicy limes)

Large handful small cilantro sprigs

2 tablespoons Toasted Chile Oil (page 306)

MAKE THE SOUP

Combine the stock, makrut lime leaves, chiles, lemongrass, shallots, tomatoes, galangal, salt, and 1 cup of water in a large pot, set it over high heat, and bring to a boil. Reduce the heat to cook at a lively simmer for 20 minutes to extract all those wonderful aromatic flavors and umami.

Stir in the fish sauce, then add the shrimp and reduce the heat to low and cook at a bare simmer just until the shrimp are just cooked through (pink on the outside and opaque in the center), about 2 minutes. Turn off the heat, add the lime juice, and stir well.

Divide the cilantro among six bowls, add about 1 teaspoon of the toasted chile oil to each, and ladle in the soup. Serve right away.

CLAM-COD CHOWDER WITH BACON, JALAPEÑO, AND CREAMY DASHI

Serves 8

They really did it to us. The producers of *Top Chef*: Boston made me and my fellow contestants cook chowder for Jasper White, the guy who wrote the book on chowder—literally. My strategy was to make something that ate like the creamy New England classic but had an element of surprise. So I made dashi, the quick and incredible Japanese stock, the base of the chowder, fortifying it with chicken stock for extra body. Bacon echoes the smoky quality of the dashi, jalapeño brings a tingle, and coconut milk contributes its creaminess and mild sweetness. It goes so well with the clams, though its coconut flavor recedes into the background, letting the plump, briny bivalves and tender cod shine. For *Top Chef* fans playing catch up, spoiler alert: My chowder won.

For the Dashi

5 x 10 inches kombu (dried kelp), broken into several pieces if necessary

5 cups chicken stock, salted homemade or store-bought

2 cups lightly packed katsuobushi (bonito flakes)

For the Chowder

2 tablespoons extra-virgin olive oil

½ pound nitrate-free slab bacon, cut into ¼-inch cubes

2 medium onions, cut into ¼-inch dice

12 garlic cloves, roughly chopped

2-inch knob ginger, peeled, halved lengthwise, and thinly sliced

1 large jalapeño chile, very thinly sliced

2 tablespoons fresh thyme leaves

6 cups well-shaken coconut milk

½ teaspoon kosher salt

2 pounds small clams, such as Manila or Littlenecks, scrubbed under cold water

1 pound cod fillets (or rockfish, halibut, or hake), preferably center cut, cut into 1-inch pieces

3 scallions, trimmed and thinly sliced

MAKE THE DASHI

Combine the kombu and stock in a medium pot, bring to a simmer over high heat, then reduce the heat to low and gently simmer for 20 minutes. Remove the kombu and reserve for another use (see page 24). Add the katsuobushi, stir well, then turn off the heat. Cover the pot and steep for 20 minutes. Strain the liquid into a container, discarding the solids. It keeps in an airtight container in the fridge for up to 3 days.

MAKE THE CHOWDER

In a large, wide, heavy pot, like a Dutch oven, heat the olive oil over medium heat until shimmery. Add the bacon and cook, stirring every couple of minutes, until it's golden brown, about 5 minutes. Add the onions, garlic, and ginger and cook, stirring occasionally, until the onions are translucent and the garlic has begun to soften, about 4 minutes. Add the jalapeño and thyme and cook about 30 seconds longer.

Add the dashi, coconut milk, and salt, increase the heat to high, and stir well. Let it come to a boil, then lower the heat to maintain a lively simmer. Cook until the liquid has reduced by about one third (it'll thicken to the texture of heavy cream), about 35 minutes.

Add the clams and cod to the chowder, stirring gently so everything is submerged, then reduce the heat to low. Cover the pot, adjusting the heat to maintain a very gentle simmer, and cook until all the clams have popped open and the cod is cooked through, about 5 minutes. Turn off the heat and stir in the scallions, then serve right away.

THAI-STYLE CHICKEN SOUP WITH COCONUT MILK, LEMONGRASS, AND GALANGAL

Serves 4 to 8

Like my take on tom yum (page 160), this recipe channels my favorite versions of another familiar Thai soup called tom kha gai. In both soups, the same aromatics come into play—lemongrass and galangal, Thai chiles and makrut lime leaves—but here coconut milk adds its richness and subtle sweetness, turning the soup into something else altogether. Dodge the aromatics as you eat, but don't neglect the slick oyster mushrooms and gently simmered chicken, which I packed in to make this into a one-pot meal.

2 pounds boneless, skinless chicken thighs, cut into bite-size pieces

2 tablespoons kosher salt

8 cups well-shaken coconut milk

2 cups chicken stock, salted homemade or store-bought

10 fresh Thai chiles, cut in half lengthwise

5 large shallots, peeled and halved

3-inch knob fresh galangal, scrubbed and thinly sliced

5 stalks lemongrass, trimmed (see page 15)

½ pound oyster mushrooms, pulled into bite-size pieces

½ cup fish sauce

15 fresh or frozen makrut lime leaves, center ribs removed

3 tablespoons lime juice (from about 2 juicy limes) or more to taste

Toasted Chile Oil (page 306)

Small handful cilantro sprigs

MAKE THE SOUP

Season the chicken all over with the salt and set aside.

In a large pot or Dutch oven, combine the coconut milk, stock, chiles, shallots, and galangal and set over medium heat. Whack the lemongrass with the back of a heavy knife or rolling pin to bruise it, cut it into 2-inch pieces, and add it to the pot as well.

Let the liquid come to a simmer, reduce the heat to maintain a gentle simmer, and cook until the shallots are tender and the liquid is infused with the flavor of the aromatics, about 25 minutes. Add the mushrooms, fish sauce, and makrut lime leaves, let it return to a simmer, and cook until the mushrooms are tender, about 5 minutes. Add the chicken and simmer until it's fully cooked, 5 to 10 minutes. Stir in the lime juice or more to taste.

Divide among eight bowls, drizzle with toasted chile oil to taste, and sprinkle with the cilantro.

WHOLE CHICKEN ZOODLE SOUP WITH SHIITAKE AND WHITE PEPPER

Serves 8

A whole chicken simmered gently in stock gives you a doubly flavorful broth and especially tender meat. This trick alone raises the bar on your typical chicken noodle soup, while shiitake, ginger, and lots of garlic transform the mild-mannered dish into something that's rousing and comforting at once. If you're gluten free, you're probably already familiar with the zoodle. If not, embrace these noodle-shaped strips of zucchini, added at the last minute so they stay bright and crisp.

1 whole chicken (4 to 4½ pounds)

6 cups chicken stock, salted homemade or store-bought

20 large garlic cloves, peeled

1 large yellow onion, halved and thinly sliced

1 medium jalapeño chile, stemmed and thinly sliced

4-inch knob ginger, peeled and cut into ⅛-inch-thick coins

2½ tablespoons kosher salt

1 pound fresh shiitake mushrooms, stemmed and cut into ¼-inch-thick slices

1 teaspoon ground white pepper

4 medium zucchini, cut into spaghetti-like strips on a mandoline or spiralizer

Jalapeño Oil (page 305)

MAKE THE SOUP

Rinse the chicken inside and out with cold water and put it in a large soup pot. Add 3 cups of water as well as the stock, garlic, onion, jalapeño, ginger, and salt. (It's okay if the liquid doesn't completely cover the chicken.) Set the pot over medium heat to gently bring the liquid to a bare simmer (with tiny bubbles barely breaking the surface). Partially cover with a lid, adjust the heat to maintain the simmer, and cook just until the chicken breast feels plump but still gives slightly when you poke it and you can use tongs to easily wiggle the drumsticks, 30 to 35 minutes.

Turn off the heat and carefully use the tongs (one side inserted into the cavity and one gripping the exterior) to pull the chicken from the pot, tipping any liquid inside the chicken back into the pot and transferring the chicken to a sheet pan.

When it's cool enough to handle, remove the wings and break them into wingettes and drumettes. Then remove the skin from the breasts, thighs, and drumsticks and pull the meat into large bite-size pieces, discarding the skin and bones. Scour the carcass for any hidden bits of meat, like the oysters underneath. Set the meat and wings aside.

Add the mushrooms to the pot, return the heat to medium, let the soup come to a gentle simmer, and cook for 5 minutes. Stir in the chicken and white pepper and simmer very gently, lowering the heat if need be, for 2 minutes. Stir in the zucchini and cook just until it turns bright green, about 1 minute. Turn off the heat.

Divide the soup among eight bowls, drizzle with jalapeño oil, and serve right away.

7

Seafood

ALBACORE TATAKI WITH AVOCADO AND GRILLED CUCUMBER VINAIGRETTE

Serves 4

In the Pacific Northwest, the return of albacore tuna is one of the first signs of summer. And every year, I can barely wait. Best known as fodder for canned tuna, albacore is exceptional when it's fresh, and indulging is way better for the ocean than eating bluefin. It needs nothing more than a kiss in a searing hot pan, so the flesh is luscious, tender, and mostly raw—in the style of Japanese tataki. Creamy avocado and vinaigrette made from crunchy cucumbers, grilled to give them a little smoky char, adds texture and brightness.

For the Vinaigrette
3 Persian cucumbers, tops and bottoms trimmed
½ teaspoon avocado oil
½ teaspoon kosher salt
½ cup unseasoned rice vinegar
¼ cup honey
2 large garlic cloves, thinly sliced

1 large shallot, cut into thin half-moons
½ small jalapeño chile, thinly sliced

For the Dish
1 tablespoon avocado oil
1¼ pounds albacore or yellowfin tuna loin

1 teaspoon kosher salt
1 large ripe Hass avocado
2½ tablespoons extra-virgin olive oil
½ tablespoon lime juice (from 1 juicy lime)
½ teaspoon flaky sea salt, plus extra for finishing
Handful dill sprigs

MAKE THE VINAIGRETTE

Fire up a grill to cook with high heat. Rub the cucumbers with the avocado oil and ¼ teaspoon of the kosher salt. Grill the cucumbers, turning occasionally, just until they have dark grill marks all over, about 10 minutes. Let the cucumbers cool briefly. Cut them into thin half-moons and put them in a medium mixing bowl.

Combine the vinegar, honey, garlic, shallot, jalapeño, and the remaining ¼ teaspoon of kosher salt in a small pot and set it over medium-high heat. When it comes to a simmer, turn off the heat. Let cool for a couple of minutes, then pour it over the cucumbers. Let the cucumbers pickle at room temperature for at least 1 hour.

MAKE THE DISH

Heat the avocado oil in a large, heavy skillet over high heat. Pat the tuna dry with paper towels and evenly season it all over with the kosher salt. Right before the oil starts to smoke, add the tuna and cook for 20 seconds on each side, just until it turns creamy white. (To grill, get the grill good and hot, rub the tuna with a very thin layer of oil, season with the kosher salt, and cook for 20 seconds on each side.)

Transfer the tuna to a cutting board and let it rest for 2 minutes. While it rests, halve and pit the avocado. Scoop the flesh into a small bowl, add ½ tablespoon of the olive oil, the lime juice, and the flaky salt, then mash until creamy but still a little chunky.

Slice the tuna into ½-inch-thick slices. I like to plate the avocado first, set the tuna on top, then spoon the cucumbers, aromatics, and 3 tablespoons of the pickling liquid onto the plate around the tuna. Sprinkle some flaky salt on the tuna, drizzle everything with the remaining 2 tablespoons of olive oil, sprinkle on the dill, and serve.

QUICK-SEARED TUNA WITH BLISTERED TOMATOES AND TARRAGON-MUSTARD VINAIGRETTE

Serves 4 to 6

I can't help it. Every time I go to a French brasserie, I order salade Niçoise. I love the down-home versions made with nice canned tuna. I especially love luxe versions that flaunt barely cooked fresh tuna, which is so good with sharp mustardy vinaigrette. This version is an entire ocean away from what you'd find in Nice—teaming up tuna and avocado feels so right and also so very American to me—but the dressing conjures the French Riviera and burst high-summer cherry tomatoes stay true to the market-driven spirit of the original.

For the Vinaigrette
¼ cup plus 2 tablespoons red wine vinegar

2 tablespoons grainy Dijon mustard

2 tablespoons drained capers, roughly chopped

2 tablespoons roughly chopped fresh tarragon leaves

1 large shallot, very finely chopped

¼ cup plus 2 tablespoons extra-virgin olive oil

For the Dish
2 tablespoons avocado oil

One 1½-pound yellowfin tuna steak (about 1 inch thick)

1½ teaspoons kosher salt

½ teaspoon ground black pepper

2 pints cherry tomatoes

10 medium garlic cloves, thinly sliced

2 medium ripe Hass avocados, pitted, peeled, and cut into 1-inch pieces

Small handful mixed herbs, such as torn basil and tarragon leaves and small parsley sprigs

1 teaspoon flaky sea salt

MAKE THE VINAIGRETTE
In a small mixing bowl, combine the vinegar, mustard, capers, tarragon, and shallot. Stir well, then slowly drizzle in the olive oil, whisking while you do, until the dressing looks creamy. Set aside.

MAKE THE DISH
Heat 1 tablespoon of the avocado oil in a large, heavy skillet over high heat. Pat the tuna dry with paper towels and evenly season both sides with 1 teaspoon of the kosher salt and the pepper. Right before oil starts to smoke, add the tuna and cook for 20 seconds on each side, just until it turns creamy white. Transfer the tuna to a cutting board and let it rest while you finish the dish.

Add the remaining 1 tablespoon of avocado oil, reduce the heat to medium-high, wait a couple of seconds, then add the tomatoes and toss well. Shaking the skillet occasionally so they roll around, let the tomatoes char, puff, burst, and release their juices, about 5 minutes. Add the garlic and the remaining ½ teaspoon of salt and give the garlic a toast so it gets golden while the tomatoes finish cooking, carefully poking any stubborn, unburst tomatoes with the tip of a sharp knife. When all the tomatoes have collapsed and their juices have thickened to a saucy consistency, a couple of minutes, take the skillet off the heat.

Scatter the avocado pieces on a serving plate. Slice the tuna against the grain into 1-inch-thick slices, arrange them on top of the avocado, then spoon on the saucy tomatoes and drizzle on all of the vinaigrette. Finish with the herbs and flaky salt and serve.

SEARED SCALLOPS WITH ASPARAGUS, YUZU KOSHO, AND DILL

Serves 4

This bright, thrilling treatment for scallops is perfect for spring, when the markets are filled with bunches of asparagus. A flash in a hot pan keeps the asparagus crisp and juicy, dill steps in for a fresh, unexpected element, and yuzu kosho, a bold paste of salty fermented green chile and fragrant Japanese citrus, ignites a simple vinaigrette. When it's time to cook the scallops, you take them *almost* all the way on one side in a hot pan, so they develop an enticing brown crust but the other sides stay sweet, silky, and just warmed.

For the Yuzu Kosho Dressing
¼ cup unseasoned rice vinegar
1 teaspoon green yuzu kosho
½ teaspoon kosher salt
¼ cup extra-virgin olive oil

For the Pickled Jalapeño
1 small jalapeño chile, thinly sliced

1 large shallot, cut into thin
   half-moons
¼ teaspoon kosher salt
¼ cup unseasoned rice vinegar
1 teaspoon honey

For the Asparagus
1 bunch asparagus

1 tablespoon extra-virgin olive oil
½ teaspoon kosher salt

For the Scallops
1½ pounds medium scallops
   (about 20)
2 tablespoons avocado oil
1 teaspoon kosher salt
Large handful small dill sprigs

MAKE THE YUZU KOSHO DRESSING
Combine the vinegar, yuzu kosho, and salt in a small bowl. Whisk well, then slowly pour in the olive oil, whisking while you do, until the dressing looks creamy.

PICKLE THE JALAPEÑO
Combine the jalapeño, shallot, and salt in a small bowl and mix well. Let sit for 10 minutes to draw out some liquid. Transfer the jalapeño mixture to a small saucepan, add the vinegar and honey, and set over medium heat. Once it comes to a simmer, immediately turn off the heat. Let cool to room temperature while you complete the next steps.

COOK THE ASPARAGUS
One by one, bend each asparagus spear to break off the tough bottoms and discard them. Cut the asparagus into 2-inch pieces. Heat the olive oil in a wide, heavy skillet over high heat until shimmery and cook the asparagus, stirring occasionally, until bright green, just slightly charred, and tender but with a snap, 2 to 3 minutes. Season with the salt and transfer to a plate in a single layer. Keep in a warm place while you cook the scallops. Give the pan a quick wipe to make sure it's dry.

COOK THE SCALLOPS AND SERVE
Pat the scallops very dry with paper towels. Heat the avocado oil in the same wide, heavy skillet over medium-high heat until very shimmery.

If the scallops won't fit in the pan with at least half an inch of space between them, work in two batches to season and cook so they can brown nicely. Evenly season the scallops with the salt, top and bottom. Add the scallops to the skillet and cook, without messing with them, until the bottom layer is a rich golden brown and the top turns opaque at the edges but is still translucent at the center, about 2 minutes. Flip the scallops and cook for 15 seconds more. Transfer the scallops, pretty-side up, to a platter. Keep in a warm place while you cook the remaining scallops.

To serve, spoon the dressing on and around the scallops, scatter on the asparagus, drain and scatter on the pickled jalapeño and shallot. Sprinkle on the dill and serve right away.

SEARED SCALLOPS WITH BUTTERNUT SQUASH AND CHILE HAZELNUTS

Serves 4

Two time-tested partners for scallops come together on one plate. And they bring surprises. The easy butternut squash puree has the fragrant sweetness of coconut milk and the toasty, crunchy hazelnuts get tossed in chile paste, so they deliver warm, welcome heat.

For the Squash Puree

3 cups peeled, seeded, chopped (about 1-inch pieces) butternut squash (from a 3-pound squash)

1 cup well-shaken coconut milk

3 large garlic cloves, peeled

1-inch knob ginger, peeled and roughly sliced against the grain

1 teaspoon kosher salt

For the Chile Hazelnuts

½ cup unsalted roasted hazelnuts, roughly chopped

¼ cup plus 2 tablespoons extra-virgin olive oil

2 tablespoons sherry vinegar

2 tablespoons Aromatic Chile Paste (page 298)

2 teaspoons kosher salt

For the Scallops

1½ pounds medium scallops (about 24)

2 tablespoons avocado oil

1 teaspoon kosher salt

Small handful basil leaves

MAKE THE SQUASH PUREE

Combine all of the puree ingredients in a medium pot and bring to a simmer over medium-high heat. Reduce the heat to maintain a fairly lively simmer and cook until the squash is so tender it starts to fall apart and the liquid has almost completely evaporated, 15 to 17 minutes. Let cool slightly, then transfer to a blender and blend the mixture on high until silky smooth, about 1 minute. Keep warm until ready to serve.

MAKE THE CHILE HAZELNUTS

Combine all of the chile hazelnuts ingredients in a small saucepan, stir well, and heat gently over low heat just until warmed through, about 5 minutes. Set aside in a warm place.

COOK THE SCALLOPS AND SERVE

Pat the scallops very dry with paper towels. Heat the avocado oil in a wide, heavy skillet over medium-high heat until very shimmery.

If the scallops won't fit in the pan with at least half an inch of space between them, work in two batches to both season and cook, so they can brown nicely. Evenly season the scallops with the salt, top and bottom. Add the scallops to the skillet, and cook, without messing with them, until the bottom layer is a rich golden brown and the top turns opaque at the edges but is still translucent at the center, about 2 minutes. Flip the scallops and cook for 15 seconds more.

Transfer the scallops, pretty-side up, to a plate. Keep in a warm place while you cook the remaining scallops.

To serve, spoon the warm butternut squash puree onto a platter, top with the scallops, and spoon on the chile-hazelnut mixture. Sprinkle on the basil and serve right away.

SPICY SAUTÉED SHRIMP WITH SCALLIONS, CASHEWS, AND PINEAPPLE

Serves 4 to 6

With my aromatic chile paste in your kitchen arsenal, dinner comes together in minutes. It's as easy as quickly sautéing shrimp, ginger, garlic, and scallions, then tossing in that chile paste and a few friends for a sauce that's bold, hot, sweet, and savory. Juicy roasted pineapple and crunchy cashews add still more texture and fun.

Once the stove is on, this dish comes together especially quickly. To avoid accidentally overcooking the shrimp, make sure you're all prepped and ready to go, so you're not fiddling with measuring spoons as they cook.

For the Pineapple
3 cups cubed (1 inch) pineapple
1 tablespoon avocado oil

For the Dish
1½ tablespoons Aromatic Chile Paste (page 298)
1 tablespoon honey

½ tablespoon toasted sesame oil
1½ teaspoons Toasted Chile Oil (page 306)
7 scallions, greens cut into 2-inch pieces, whites halved lengthwise, separated
2 tablespoons avocado oil
5 garlic cloves, thinly sliced

4-inch knob ginger, peeled and cut into thin matchsticks
2 teaspoons kosher salt
1½ pounds medium shrimp, peeled, deveined, and patted dry
3 tablespoons coconut aminos
1 cup unsalted roasted cashews
Handful small cilantro sprigs

ROAST THE PINEAPPLE
Preheat the oven to 450°F. In a medium mixing bowl, toss the pineapple with the avocado oil. Spread the pineapple on a sheet pan in a single layer and roast until it turns bright yellow and starts to concentrate a bit, about 10 minutes. Give it a stir, then cook it for 5 minutes more, so it's nice and dry on the outside but still juicy inside. If any edges turn light golden brown, that's lovely.

MAKE THE DISH
In a small bowl, combine the chile paste, honey, sesame oil, toasted chile oil, and scallion greens. Set aside.

Heat the avocado oil in a large, wide, heavy pot (a Dutch oven works great) over medium heat until shimmery. Add the garlic, ginger, and scallion whites, season with ½ teaspoon of the salt, and cook, stirring frequently, just until the edges of the garlic and scallions turn golden, about 2 minutes.

In the meantime, season the shrimp on both sides with the remaining 1½ teaspoons of salt. Add the coconut aminos to the pot, give it a quick stir, then immediately add the shrimp to the pot. Stir well to coat the shrimp in the aromatics and oil, then cook, tossing occasionally, until the shrimp just start to turn light pink, about 1 minute.

Add the chile paste mixture and roasted pineapple and stir well. Cook, stirring occasionally, until the shrimp are just cooked through, about 2 minutes. Add the cashews, toss well, and transfer to a platter. Sprinkle with the cilantro and serve right away.

SHRIMP WITH CURRIED WATERMELON AND QUICK-PICKLED RIND

Serves 4

I had the same thought you're probably having now: Which oh-so-creative chef came up with cooked water-melon? Yet what sounds like a fanciful modern creation has time and tradition behind it. Just ask cooks from the Indian state of Rajasthan, where the fruit is simmered and masterfully spiced to make curry. I take my version in a Thai direction, applying a lemongrass-and-galangal-powered red curry paste (which will become a staple of your pantry) that teams up with the juice released by the melon as it cooks to create a beguiling sweet-savory sauce for luscious chunks of fruit, shrimp, and tangy pickled watermelon rind.

For the Quick Pickle
One seedless watermelon (about 5½ to 6 pounds)
½ cup unseasoned rice vinegar
¼ cup maple syrup
¼ teaspoon kosher salt

For the Curry
2 tablespoons extra-virgin olive oil

8 large garlic cloves, finely chopped
3-inch knob ginger, peeled and very finely chopped
1 tablespoon kosher salt
3 tablespoon red curry paste, homemade (page 297) or store-bought
1 tablespoon lime juice (from 1 juicy lime)

For the Dish
1 tablespoon extra-virgin olive oil, plus more for drizzling
1½ pounds medium shrimp, peeled and deveined
1 tablespoon kosher salt
Small handful cilantro sprigs

QUICK-PICKLE THE WATERMELON RIND

Trim just enough off the top and bottom of the watermelon to reveal the flesh, then stand it up and carve off the peel, reserving it. Cut enough flesh into 1-inch cubes to give you 8 cups, reserving it for the curry and any remainder for another time. Next, trim the green skin from some of the reserved peel. Cut the pale rind into long, 1-inch-wide pieces, then cut them crosswise into ¼-inch slices. Reserve 1 cup of these slices for the pickle.

Combine the 1 cup of rind slices with the vinegar, maple syrup, and salt in a small saucepan and bring to a simmer over medium heat. Reduce the heat to low and gently simmer until the rind turns translucent and gets soft with a tender bite, about 10 to 12 minutes. Let cool to room temperature.

It keeps in an airtight container in the fridge for up to 3 months.

MAKE THE CURRY

Heat the oil in a large Dutch oven or heavy pot over medium heat until shimmery. Add the garlic, ginger, and salt, and cook, stirring frequently, until lightly golden brown, about 2 minutes.

Stir in the curry paste and cook, stirring often, until the mixture is fragrant and a shade or two darker, about 1 minute. Add the 8 cups of reserved watermelon flesh and give everything a good stir. Taste it—it'll help you note the progress later.

Increase the heat to medium-high and wait for the watermelon to start to release its juice, 3 to 4 minutes. Cook at a lively simmer until the mixture has reduced from 8 cups to about 4 cups (the sauce will lightly coat the back of a spoon) and the watermelon cubes turn deep red and are tender with the slightest bite, 10 to 12 minutes more. Taste it again—it will have gone from a sort of spiced watermelon juice to a richer, more deeply flavored stew with a bit of heat and complexity from the curry paste. Turn off the heat, stir in the lime juice, and cover to keep warm while you cook the shrimp.

MAKE AND SERVE THE DISH

In a wide skillet, heat the 1 tablespoon of oil over high heat until shimmery. Season the shrimp on both sides with the salt. Working in batches if necessary to avoid crowding, cook the shrimp in a single layer, flipping once, until light pink on both sides and just opaque in the center, 1 to 2 minutes per side.

Divide the curry among four serving bowls and top each with shrimp, pickled watermelon rind (and a tiny drizzle of the pickling liquid), a drizzle of olive oil, and a sprinkle of cilantro. Serve warm.

STEAMED CLAMS WITH GINGER, SCALLIONS, AND XO SAUCE

Serves 2 to 4

Clams take so well to briny, spicy XO sauce, a Hong Kong invention that'll quickly become your new favorite pantry item. Executing this dish requires only a little attention, so those clams don't overcook and lose their plump juicy meat. As they bubble away, take frequent peeks into the pot, with a bowl and tongs at the ready, to pluck out any that have popped open. Add them back just before you serve.

Before you cook, make sure the clams you bought have tightly closed shells or shells that close with a gentle tap against the counter. Discard any that remain open or any with cracked shells. I've found that wild clams need a little more cleaning than farmed clams. Soak them in cold water for about 20 minutes so they eject any sand from inside. Farmed or wild, clams should be scrubbed and rinsed to dislodge any grit on the shells.

2 tablespoons extra-virgin olive oil

4-inch knob ginger, peeled and cut into thin matchsticks

6 garlic cloves, thinly sliced

4 scallions, trimmed and cut into ¼-inch-thick slices

2 pounds small clams, such as Manila or Littleneck, scrubbed

2 tablespoons coconut aminos

¼ cup XO Sauce (page 299)

2 tablespoons sherry vinegar

Handful small cilantro sprigs

MAKE THE DISH

Find a pot (or deep skillet with a lid) wide enough so the clams fit in two layers at most. This will help them cook more evenly.

Set a medium mixing bowl next to the stove. Heat the oil in the pot over high heat until shimmery. Add the ginger, garlic, and scallions and cook, stirring constantly, until the garlic is light golden and everything smells great, 1 to 2 minutes. Add the clams, quickly followed by the coconut aminos, then immediately stir to coat the clams with the aromatics and oil.

Cover the pot and keep cooking over high heat for about 5 minutes, peeking under the lid every couple of minutes or so and using tongs to transfer any clams that pop open to the mixing bowl.

After 5 minutes, turn off the heat. Discard any clams that haven't opened. Add the clams in the bowl back to the pot. Add the XO sauce and vinegar and stir gently to combine. Sprinkle on the cilantro and serve right away.

STEAMED MUSSELS WITH TAMARIND, CHILE, AND BASIL

Serves 2 to 4

I learned to make French-style steamed mussels back in culinary school, but now my favorite way to make them is to give them the Thai treatment. Here there's garlic, scallions, and chiles instead of garlic and onions, a dose of tangy tamarind instead of white wine, and some sweet, anise-y Thai basil instead of parsley. Don't let the "tamarind water" dissuade you—it's just the tangy fruit pulp soaked in hot water, then strained of any fibrous solids.

Note: Just as you would with clams, inspect your mussels before you cook them to make sure they have tightly closed shells or shells that close with a gentle tap against the counter. Discard any that remain open or any with cracked shells. They need a little more cleaning than clams, so scrub them especially well under cold running water to dislodge any grit and barnacles that may be clinging to their shells. If your mussels still have so-called "beards," the small stringy clusters poking out from their sides, get a firm grip on them, with the help of a paring knife for leverage, and yank them out.

2 tablespoons extra-virgin olive oil

6 garlic cloves, thinly sliced

5 scallions, trimmed and cut into 2-inch pieces, whites halved lengthwise

3-inch knob ginger, peeled and cut into long, thin matchsticks

2 moderately spicy fresh red chiles, like Fresnos, thinly sliced

½ teaspoon kosher salt

½ cup Tamarind Water (page 327)

1 tablespoon fish sauce

2 pounds mussels, scrubbed and debearded

Large handful basil leaves, preferably Thai

1 juicy lime, cut into wedges

MAKE THE DISH

Heat the oil in a medium pot or high-sided skillet with a lid over medium-high heat until shimmery. Add the garlic, scallions, ginger, chiles, and salt and stir well. Cook, stirring occasionally, until the garlic turns golden at the edges, about 2 minutes. Stir in the tamarind water and fish sauce.

Once the tamarind mixture comes to a simmer, add the mussels and stir well to coat them with the tamarind and aromatics. Add most of the basil and quickly stir again. Cover the pot and cook just until the mussels pop open (even if it's just a little), 3 to 4 minutes. Discard any that don't open after this time.

Sprinkle on the remaining basil and serve with the lime wedges.

TURMERIC-MARINATED COD WITH GINGER AND LOTS OF DILL

Serves 6

Like so many eager eaters before me, I, too, ascended the stairs at Cha Ca La Vong, a restaurant in Hanoi, to sample the dish that is its namesake, and the only one on the menu. The turmeric-marinated fish, served with dill and scallions, noodles, and peanuts, has spawned many copycats—the restaurant is located on what has become Cha Ca Street, with competitors galore. And now, there is one more, me. Okay, mine is more riff than imitation. Cod stands in for snakehead fish, and there are no peanuts or rice noodles to be found on my legume- and grain-free table. But the earthy turmeric and funky fish sauce and heaps of herbs bring me right back to the table in Vietnam.

For Marinating the Fish
3 large garlic cloves, roughly chopped

1 medium shallot, roughly chopped

3-inch knob fresh turmeric, peeled and roughly chopped

2-inch knob ginger, peeled and roughly sliced against the grain

3 tablespoons fish sauce

2 pounds cod, hake, or halibut fillets, preferably center cut, cut into 6 similar-size pieces

For the Dish
3 tablespoons avocado oil

2 large baby bok choy bulbs, gently pulled apart into individual leaves

1 bunch scallions, trimmed and cut into 2-inch pieces, whites halved lengthwise

1 large serrano or medium jalapeño chile, thinly sliced

½ teaspoon kosher salt

Large handful dill sprigs

Large handful small cilantro sprigs

3 juicy limes, cut into wedges

MARINATE THE FISH
Combine the garlic, shallot, turmeric, ginger, and fish sauce in a blender and puree until smooth, stopping and stirring if necessary. Transfer the mixture to a medium mixing bowl. Add the fish and toss to coat the pieces well in the marinade. Marinate in the fridge for at least 4 hours or up to 24 hours.

MAKE THE DISH
Preheat the broiler and position a rack 6 inches from the heat. Remove the fish from the marinade, but don't wipe any marinade off. Rub 1 tablespoon of the oil onto a sheet pan, arrange the fish in a single layer, and broil until the fish is a vivid yellow color and just cooked though (the center will be milky white and flake easily with the poke of a finger), 8 to 10 minutes.

In the meantime, cook the vegetables. Heat the remaining 2 tablespoons of oil in a large skillet over high heat until shimmery. Add the boy choy, scallions, and chile and cook, stirring occasionally, until the bok choy is bright green and slightly wilted but with a tender crunch to the stems, 1 to 2 minutes. Season with the salt and turn off the heat.

When the fish is done, transfer it to a platter, scatter on the bok choy mixture, and shower everything with the dill and cilantro. Serve right away with the lime wedges.

HALIBUT WITH SUMMER SQUASH AND SPICED TOMATOES

Serves 4

Summer is halibut season, so I look to hot-weather produce like zucchini and tomatoes. But don't mistake this preparation for Provençal. I stew the tomatoes with coriander, cardamom, fresh turmeric, and ginger and brighten them with lime juice. This adds surprise and complexity to an otherwise straightforward dish. Cod and rockfish would also work well here, if you follow my lead and roast them at a relatively low temperature so the lean fish stay tender and lush.

For the Tomatoes
20 green cardamom pods
2 tablespoons coriander seeds
¼ cup extra-virgin olive oil
10 large garlic cloves, cut into ¼-inch-thick slices
2-inch knob ginger, peeled and cut into long, thin matchsticks

3-inch knob fresh or frozen turmeric, peeled and thinly sliced
3 pounds ripe tomatoes, cored, halved, and deseeded
1 tablespoon plus 1 teaspoon kosher salt

For the Dish
Four 5-ounce halibut or cod fillets, preferably center cut

1½ teaspoons kosher salt
2 tablespoons extra-virgin olive oil, plus more for finishing
¾ pound summer squash or zucchini, cut into ⅛-inch half-moons
1 juicy lime, halved
Small handful basil leaves, torn

MAKE THE TOMATOES

Combine the cardamom and coriander in a medium skillet, set over high heat, and toast, shaking and tossing occasionally, until the pods and seeds are very fragrant and toasty, about 2 minutes. Let them cool slightly, then grind in a spice grinder to a fine powder. Set aside.

Heat the oil in a medium, heavy pot or Dutch oven over medium heat until shimmery. Add the garlic and ginger and cook, stirring frequently, until the garlic is golden, about 3 minutes. Add the turmeric and all but ½ teaspoon of the cardamom mixture, reserving the remainder for later. Cook, stirring, for 2 minutes to bring the flavors together.

Use your hands to crush the tomatoes as you add them to the pot, then add the salt, stir well, and increase the heat to high. The tomatoes will begin to release their liquid. Let the sauce come to a simmer, reduce the heat to medium and cook at a moderate simmer, stirring often and occasionally scraping the bottom, until the tomatoes break down and the sauce thickens to the texture of marinara, 20 to 25 minutes. (If it splatters a lot, reduce the heat slightly and/or partially cover the pot.) Turn off the heat and cover to keep warm.

MAKE THE DISH

Preheat the oven to 350°F. Pat the fillets dry with paper towels and season them all over with the salt. Drizzle on 1 tablespoon of the oil and gently rub to coat the fillets. Drizzle the remaining 1 tablespoon olive oil on a sheet pan, add the fillets in a single layer with some space between each one, and sprinkle the remaining ½ teaspoon of the cardamom mixture on top of them.

Bake until the fillets are milky white (bright white means they're overcooked) and flake with gentle pressure (125°F on a thermometer), about 10 to 12 minutes. About 5 minutes before the fish is ready, bring the tomatoes to a gentle simmer, stir in the summer squash, and cook just until tender with a slight crunch, about 3 minutes. Squeeze in half a lime or more to taste.

Spoon the tomato mixture into a serving dish, add the fillets, drizzle with more olive oil, and add the basil.

CRISPY SKIN SNAPPER WITH CHILE-LIME SAUCE AND LOTS OF HERBS

Serves 4

Ever have fish at a nice restaurant and wonder how in the world someone got the skin so crisp it shatters beneath your fork? Well, good news: It takes no magic, just a bit of technique. In this recipe, I walk you through it. Sneak preview: Dry the skin well, use a nonstick skillet, and cook the fish virtually all the way on the skin side. Besides contributing delightful texture, crispy skin also means everyone can enjoy those heart-protecting omega-3s.

From there, a squeeze of lemon will do. But Vietnamese flavors—sweet-tart pickles, bright garlic-and-chile-laced fish sauce dressing, and a heap of herbs—make it extra special and cut through the richness of the fish.

1¼ pounds skin-on snapper or sea bass fillets, cut crosswise into ten 2-ounce pieces

1 teaspoon kosher salt

1 tablespoon avocado oil

1½ cups drained Vietnamese-Style Pickles (page 291)

½ cup Vietnamese-Style Chile-Lime Sauce (page 302)

Extra-virgin olive oil

A giant handful mixed herbs, such as basil leaves, mint leaves, and cilantro sprigs

MAKE THE DISH

Pat the fish pieces dry with paper towels, then lay the pieces, skin-side down, on fresh paper towels to dry them really well as you heat the skillet.

Heat a large nonstick skillet (or two skillets if necessary to avoid crowding) over medium-high heat for a minute or so until it gets nice and hot. Just before you cook the fish, remove the pieces from the paper towels and season on both sides with the salt.

Once the pan is hot, add the avocado oil and swirl the pan. Add the pieces, skin-side down, to the skillet and reduce the heat to medium. Use a spatula to gently press each piece for a few seconds so it lays flat in the pan (fillets like to curl up). Cook until the skin is completely crispy and golden brown (beware of small lingering soggy spots), about 5 minutes. The fish should release easily from the pan; if it doesn't, keep cooking until it does.

Reduce the heat to low, flip the pieces, and cook just until the fish is milky white and just cooked through, about 1 minute more.

Scatter the pickles on a large platter and spoon on the dressing. Top with the fish, skin-side up, drizzle on some olive oil, and top with the herbs. Serve immediately.

ROASTED SEA BASS WITH HARISSA, OLIVES, AND PRESERVED LEMON

Serves 4

Once you've got the crispy-skin technique down pat, you'll find yourself taking it in many directions, from the Vietnamese-ish preparation on page 191 to this one-pan North African one. Complexly spiced harissa, bright preserved lemon, and briny olives make a high-flavor combination that you can pull from the fridge anytime.

Four 5-ounce skin-on sea bass or red snapper fillets

3 tablespoons extra-virgin olive oil

1½ teaspoons kosher salt

¼ cup harissa, homemade (page 300) or store-bought

1 cup mixed pitted olives

2 large garlic cloves, thinly sliced

2 tablespoons thinly slivered preserved lemon peel, homemade (page 188) or store-bought

Handful small parsley sprigs

MAKE THE DISH

Preheat the oven to 400°F. Pat the fish dry, then rest it, skin-side down, on fresh paper towels to absorb any liquid left on the skin. Heat 2 tablespoons of the oil in a large, ovenproof, nonstick skillet (wide enough to hold the fillets without crowding) over medium-high heat until shimmery. While the oil is heating up, evenly season the fish with the salt on both sides.

Put the fish, skin-side down, in the skillet, reduce the heat to medium and use a spatula to gently press each fillet for a few seconds so it lays flat in the pan (fillets like to curl up). Cook until the skin is completely crispy (beware of small lingering soggy spots) and golden brown, about 5 minutes. The fillets should release easily from the pan; if they don't, keep cooking until they do.

Put the skillet in the oven to finish cooking. Cook until the visible flesh goes from translucent to creamy white at the sides with just a sliver of translucence in the middle, about 3 minutes.

While the fish is in the oven, spread the harissa on a serving platter. When the fish is ready, use a thin spatula to transfer the fillets, skin-side up, to the platter.

Add the olives, garlic, and remaining 1 tablespoon of olive oil to the skillet and set over medium heat. Let the garlic turn golden and the olives warm up, about 2 minutes. Turn off the heat, stir in the preserved lemon peel, then spoon it all over the fish. Sprinkle on the parsley and serve.

FISH IN GREEN CURRY WITH ASPARAGUS AND SPINACH

Serves 6

This style of Thai green curry is one of many dishes that bowled me over when I had the joy to spend time in chef David Thompson's restaurant kitchen in Bangkok. The curry is so vibrant because of aromatics like lemongrass and makrut lime leaves, and because of the chiles that give the cream-colored curry its name. Speaking of "green," I like to add leafy vegetables for a nutritional boost, though I have a feeling Chef Thompson wouldn't approve of this breach of tradition. Note that I take the time to brown the skin of the fish that I later plunk into the curry, not because it stays crisp but because I love the depth of flavor it adds.

For the Curry Paste

1½ teaspoons coriander seeds

½ teaspoon cumin seeds

½ teaspoon white peppercorns

1 cup packed roughly chopped cilantro stems

2 large shallots, roughly chopped

5 large garlic cloves, peeled

6 fresh green Thai chiles, stemmed

3-inch knob fresh turmeric, peeled and roughly sliced against the grain

2-inch knob fresh galangal, peeled and roughly sliced against the grain

2-inch knob ginger, peeled and sliced against the grain

6 fresh or frozen medium makrut lime leaves, center ribs removed

2 large stalks lemongrass, trimmed (see page 15), bruised, then thinly sliced

For the Dish

Six 4-ounce sea bass or red snapper fillets

1½ teaspoons kosher salt

2 tablespoons avocado oil

2 tablespoons virgin coconut oil

6 cups well-shaken coconut milk

16 fresh or frozen makrut lime leaves, center ribs removed

¼ cup plus 2 tablespoons fish sauce

2 fairly spicy fresh red chiles, such as Fresnos or ripe red jalapeños, stemmed, seeded and quartered lengthwise

4 fresh red or green Thai chiles, split lengthwise to just below the stem

1 small bunch asparagus, tough bottoms snapped off and discarded, cut into 2-inch pieces

1 small bunch kale, center stems removed, roughly chopped

1 small bunch mature spinach, stem bottoms trimmed

Large handful basil leaves, preferably Thai

MAKE THE CURRY PASTE

Combine the coriander, cumin, and peppercorns in a small skillet, set it over high heat, and toast, shaking and tossing the pan every 30 seconds or so, until the spices are very fragrant and toasty, about 1 minute. Let cool briefly, transfer the spices to a spice grinder and grind to a slightly coarse powder, and transfer to a medium bowl.

Combine the cilantro, shallots, garlic, and chiles in a blender and alternate between blending and stopping to scrape down the sides and stir until you have a slightly chunky paste (think pesto), adding a couple of tablespoons of water if necessary. Then add the remaining curry paste ingredients and blend, stopping and stirring, to a chunky paste. Be patient—you'll get there! Transfer the mixture to the bowl with the spice powder and stir really well.

MAKE THE DISH

Pat the fillets dry with paper towels, then lay the fillets, skin-side down, on fresh paper towels to dry them really well as you heat the skillet.

Heat a large Dutch oven over medium-high heat for a minute or so, until it gets nice and hot. Just before you cook the fillets, remove them from the paper towels and season on both sides with the salt.

Once the pot is hot, add the avocado oil and swirl the pan. Add the fillets, skin-side down, to the pot. Reduce the heat to medium and use a spatula to gently press each fillet for a few seconds so it lays flat in the pot (fillets like to curl up). Cook until the skin is completely crispy and golden brown, about 5 minutes. The fillets should release easily from the pan; if they don't, keep cooking until they do. Transfer them to a large plate (the flesh will still be mostly raw) and set aside while you make the curry.

With the heat still on medium, add the coconut oil and curry paste to the pot. Stir and cook until it's especially fragrant, about 2 minutes. Add the coconut milk and makrut lime leaves, bring to a simmer, then adjust the heat to cook at a moderate simmer, stirring if it threatens to bubble over, until the liquid thickens to the consistency of a slightly creamy soup, 20 to 25 minutes.

Add the fish sauce and both kinds of chiles, stir well, and cook for 1 minute more. Stir in the asparagus, kale, and spinach, and cook, stirring again as the greens wilt, for 1 minute or so. Finally, return the fish fillets, skin-side up, to the pot, reduce the heat, and gently simmer just until the fish finishes cooking (it'll flake at the thickest part), about 3 minutes.

Divide among six serving bowls, scatter with basil, and serve right away.

GRILLED TROUT WITH SAUTÉED SPINACH AND VEGETABLE-PACKED PONZU

Serves 4

In this ponzu—a bright, umami-rich Japanese sauce—coconut aminos take the place of soy sauce and asparagus and jicama add some crunch. With quick-wilted spinach and that sauce waiting on the table, you can focus on grilling the fish. Practically any fish would be a pleasure, but I love grilled trout because of its high ratio of crispy charred skin to flaky flesh.

Note that you'll have plenty of the versatile ponzu left over, which is good news for that week's lunches and dinners since it lasts in the fridge for a week.

For the Vegetable Ponzu
1 cup coconut aminos

½ cup unseasoned rice vinegar

3-inch square kombu (dried kelp), broken into several pieces

2 tablespoons katsuobushi (bonito flakes)

1 small shallot, finely chopped

½ teaspoon kosher salt

4 stalks asparagus, tough ends snapped off and discarded, cut into ¼-inch slices

½ cup diced (about ¼ inch) jicama

2 tablespoons finely chopped ginger

½ small jalapeño or serrano chile, seeded and cut into ¼-inch dice

2 tablespoons lemon juice

For the Spinach
2 tablespoons extra-virgin olive oil

2 pounds mature spinach (about 3 bunches), stem bottoms trimmed

1 teaspoon kosher salt

For the Dish
4 whole butterflied trout (about ¾ pound each)

1 tablespoon plus 1 teaspoon avocado oil

1½ teaspoons kosher salt

Handful mixed basil leaves and small dill sprigs

MAKE THE VEGETABLE PONZU

Combine the coconut aminos, vinegar, and kombu in a small saucepan, set it over medium heat, and bring to a lively simmer. Cook until the liquid has reduced by about half, about 12 minutes. Turn off the heat and stir in the katsuobushi. Let cool to room temperature.

In the meantime, combine the shallot and salt in a medium mixing bowl, toss well, and let sit for 10 minutes. Once the vinegar mixture has cooled, set a mesh strainer over the bowl with the shallot and strain in the vinegar mixture, gently pressing then discarding the solids. Add the remaining ponzu ingredients and stir well. Let sit at least 20 minutes.

COOK THE SPINACH

Heat the olive oil in a wide, heavy skillet over high heat until shimmery. Add the spinach and cook, tossing every 30 seconds or so, until the spinach is just wilted and bright green, about 2 minutes. Season with the salt, transfer to a plate, and keep warm while you cook the trout.

MAKE THE DISH

Fire up a grill to cook with medium-high heat. Pat the trout dry with paper towels, then lay them, skin-side down, on fresh paper towels to dry them really well as you heat the grill.

Just before you cook the fillets, drizzle on the avocado oil and rub to coat both sides in a thin layer. Evenly season both sides with the salt. Grill the trout, skin-side down, uncovered and without messing with it, until the skin is crispy and golden with charred spots and the visible flesh is just opaque with a tinge of translucence at the thickest part, about 4 minutes.

Drain off any liquid that has accumulated on the plate of spinach and transfer the spinach to a platter. Top with the trout, drizzle on ½ cup of the vegetable ponzu, add the herbs, and serve.

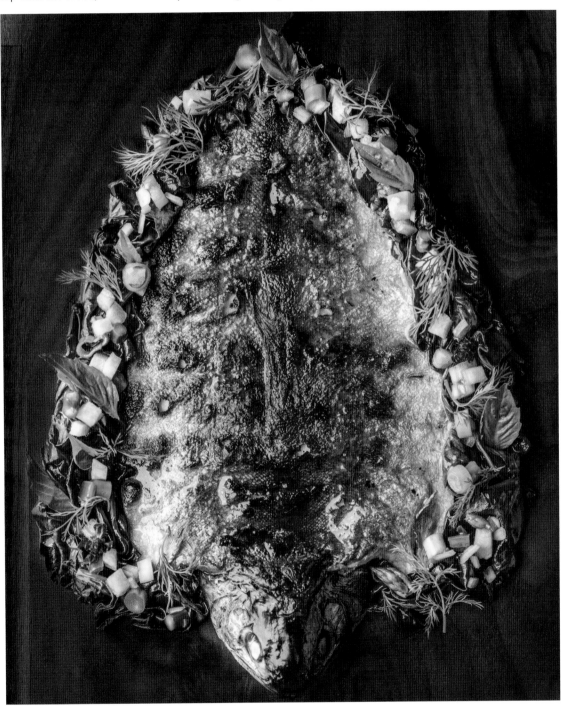

SWEET AND SALTY BLACK COD WITH BACON AND SUNCHOKES

Serves 4

There's no fish quite like black cod. Also known as sablefish, black cod cooks to an unbelievable silky, melty texture, and the super-fatty flesh solves the standard fish-at-home dilemma, because it makes overcooking highly unlikely. In this dish, the sweet-salty marinade becomes a sticky drizzle that balances the fish's richness and sunchokes and bacon add earth and smoke. Just be sure to broil the fish until its thick skin is crispy all the way through—otherwise, it won't be as much fun to eat.

Note that black cod fillets have pesky bones that are difficult to remove yourself. Ask your fishmonger for help.

For Brining the Fish
¾ cup coconut aminos

3 tablespoons honey

3-inch knob ginger, peeled and cut into thin half-moons

3 large garlic cloves, thinly sliced

1 moderately spicy fresh red chile, such as Fresno, thinly sliced

2 scallions, trimmed and cut into 2-inch pieces, whites halved lengthwise

1 teaspoon toasted sesame oil

1¼ pounds skin-on black cod fillets, cut into about 3-inch pieces

For the Dish
1 tablespoon avocado oil

12 ounces nitrate-free fatty slab bacon, cut into 1-inch cubes

1 pound sunchokes, scrubbed and cut crosswise into ¼-inch-thick slices

½ teaspoon kosher salt

2 scallions, trimmed and cut into 2-inch pieces then lengthwise into thin strips

BRINE THE FISH
Combine the coconut aminos and honey in a medium mixing bowl and stir until the honey dissolves. Add the ginger, garlic, chile, scallions, and sesame oil, and stir to combine. Add the fish and mix gently but well, so the ingredients are well distributed and the fish is more or less submerged in the brine. Cover and brine in the fridge for at least 6 hours or up to 24 hours.

MAKE THE DISH
Rub the avocado oil onto a heavy ovenproof skillet that's wide enough to hold the fish in a single layer with a little space between the pieces. Remove the fish from the brine and put the pieces, skin-side up, in the skillet and set aside for the moment. Transfer the brine, including the aromatics, to a small saucepan, set it over medium heat, and bring it to a lively simmer. Cook, stirring once or twice, until the aromatics are tender and the liquid has reduced to about ½ cup (it'll be a little thicker and saucy), about 8 minutes. Set it aside.

Set a mesh strainer over a small heatproof container and put it near the stove. Heat another large, heavy skillet over low heat for a minute or so, then add the bacon, spreading the pieces to form a single layer. Let the bacon slowly render its fat, stirring occasionally, until the bacon has shrunk and the fat-to-meat ratio on the pieces looks about even, about 10 minutes. Turn up the heat to medium and cook, stirring to get relatively even color, until crisp and golden brown, about 5 minutes more.

Scrape the bacon and fat into the mesh strainer, reserving 3 tablespoons of the fat for the next step and the rest for another use. Transfer the bacon to towels to drain and keep it in a warm place.

Reheat the skillet, this time over medium heat, and add the reserved 3 tablespoons of bacon fat. Add the sunchoke slices, sprinkle on the salt, and cook, flipping the sunchokes once, until both sides are golden and the sunchokes are creamy with a slight bite, 10 to 12 minutes.

In the meantime, preheat the broiler and move an oven rack to the top position. Transfer the skillet with the black cod to the top rack and broil until the skin is completely crispy and charred and the fish is firm and opaque in the center, about 10 minutes.

Scoop the sunchokes onto a serving platter, top with the bacon, then use a sturdy spatula to add the black cod, trying your best to keep the tender pieces intact. Drizzle with the reduced marinade, sprinkle on the scallions, and serve.

GRAVLAX WITH LEMON, PEPPER, AND DILL

Serves 8 to 10

This one will definitely impress your brunch guests—just don't mention how easy it was to make. Barely any effort, and a robust cure of lemon zest, black pepper, and fragrant dill transforms the salmon into a true showstopper to be carved into velvety slices. Have fun with the rest and compile a mix of crunchy raw vegetables; rich and creamy things (alternative yogurts and boiled eggs, perhaps); and tart, tangy, pickle-y things, from this book or from the jar.

3 tablespoons black peppercorns

4 small dried red chiles, crumbled, or 1 teaspoon red chile flakes

⅓ cup plus 1 tablespoon kosher salt

⅓ cup plus 1 tablespoon coconut sugar

1 large bunch dill, finely chopped, a few whole sprigs spared for garnish

2 large lemons, for zesting

One 2-pound skin-on salmon fillet

MAKE THE DISH

In a spice grinder, grind the black peppercorns and chiles to a fine powder. Transfer it to a small mixing bowl, then add the salt, sugar, and dill. Use a Microplane to grate in the lemon zest, reserving the lemons for another time. Stir well, making sure there are no clumps.

Take a sheet of parchment paper that's at least 3 times longer than the salmon is wide and lay it on a work surface, with one of the long sides facing you. You're going to position the salmon so it runs top to bottom. But first, sprinkle about a quarter of the cure onto the center of the paper and spread it to approximate the shape of the salmon. Lay the salmon, skin-side down, on the cure. Sprinkle and spread the remaining cure on the flesh in an even layer (though use a bit less on the thin, tapered tail side), making sure the flesh is completely covered.

Wrap the salmon in the parchment to create a nice, tight package. Put the package in a baking dish, skin-side down, then put a small cutting board on the package and set a weight on top (for example, a couple of big cans of tomatoes). You don't want to smoosh the fish—you want to just give it a little hug as it cures. Cure the salmon in the fridge, untouched, for 48 hours or up to 60 hours.

When the salmon is ready, remove it from the parchment paper and rinse it gently under cold water, wiping off any loose cure from both sides. Some will have become embedded in the fish and that's quite okay. Pat the salmon very dry with paper towels. To serve, use a very sharp knife to cut thin, even slices. I shoot for slices that are about as thick as a nickel. If the salmon fillet is especially wide, it helps to halve it lengthwise first, then slice from the narrow pieces.

Wrapped well in parchment paper and stored in a container with a tight lid, the cured salmon keeps in the fridge for up to 5 days.

SLOW-COOKED SALMON WITH TI MALICE SAUCE

Serves 6

Slow-cooked salmon was my initiation to the perfection-through-simplicity ethos at the famed Jean-Georges, where I had my first job in a professional kitchen. Today, I still cook salmon this way, and you won't believe how easy it is to turn the ubiquitous, frequently overcooked fish into a tender treat.

Something this rich needs acidity to shine, so I look to sos ti malice, named for a mischievous character from Haitian folklore. The story goes: Ti-Malice was tired of his friend Bouki coming over for lunch, overstaying his welcome, and eating all his food, so the trickster made a sauce so fiery that it would surely make Bouki run screaming from his house. And Bouki did indeed run into the street—shouting about how much he loved Ti-Malice's sauce.

One part of the story is definitely true. The Haitian condiment, a pickle that doubles as a sauce, is that good. Mine has plenty of fruity heat from Scotch bonnet or habanero chiles, the zip of citrus and vinegar, and a little crunch from red pearl onions. Peeling and separating the onions into tiny petals takes time, but the result is gorgeous. But sure, shallots cut into ¼-inch half-moons work great, too.

For the Ti Malice Sauce
3 cups red pearl onions
1½ tablespoons kosher salt
3 limes
1 large Scotch bonnet or habanero chile, very finely chopped

6 tablespoons white vinegar
6 tablespoons extra-virgin olive oil
1 tablespoon fresh thyme leaves

For the Salmon
One 2-pound salmon fillet
2 teaspoons kosher salt
3 tablespoon extra-virgin olive oil

MAKE THE TI MALICE SAUCE

Soak the pearl onions in a small bowl of warm water for 20 minutes to help loosen their skins. Take a few pearl onions at a time out of the water, then trim the tips and bottom nubs and use a small paring knife to peel off the skins. When you've peeled them all, halve them lengthwise.

In a medium mixing bowl, combine the onions and salt, toss well, and let them sit for 15 minutes to soften. Once they've softened, pull the pearl onion layers apart. Use a Microplane to grate the zest of the 3 limes into the bowl, then halve enough limes (1 or 2 juicy ones should do it) to squeeze in 3 tablespoons of juice. Reserve the remaining limes for another purpose. Stir in the chile and vinegar. Let everything sit for about 15 minutes more.

Transfer the mixture to a small pot, add the oil and thyme, and set it over medium heat. Let it heat up (you're not looking for a sizzle), stirring occasionally, until the onions are translucent and lose their harsh raw flavor but still have a slight crunch, 7 to 8 minutes.

The sauce keeps in an airtight container in the fridge for up to 2 weeks. Before serving, very gently reheat it (in a small pan or in a bowl set near a hot oven) until it's a little warmer than room temperature.

COOK THE SALMON AND SERVE

Preheat the oven to 300°F. Evenly season the salmon all over with the salt. Pour 1 tablespoon of the oil in a shallow baking dish and rub to coat the surface. Put the salmon in the dish (skin-side down, if your salmon has skin) and drizzle on the remaining 2 tablespoons of oil so it completely covers the top and sides of the salmon. Bake just until the salmon goes from bright pink to light orange and you see the tiniest white beads on the surface of the fish at the thickest part (the center will register 120°F on a thermometer), 20 to 25 minutes.

Transfer to a platter, spoon the sauce over the salmon, and serve.

CRISPY-SKIN SALMON WITH PLANTAINS AND AFRICAN PEPPER SAUCE

Serves 4

Salmon gets the crispy-skin treatment, the crackling texture a fine foil to the fish's rich, tender flesh. Plantains contribute their complex sweetness, mushrooms deliver umami, and just-wilted spinach provides silky greenery. A tangy, tongue-tingling sauce, hailing from West Africa, ties it all together.

For the Vegetables
3½ tablespoons extra-virgin olive oil
2 ripe plantains (see page 17), peeled and cut into ½-inch-thick slices
1½ teaspoons kosher salt

1 pound mixed mushrooms, such as button, oyster, and shiitake, stemmed and cut into bite-size pieces
5 large garlic cloves, thinly sliced
1 large bunch spinach, stem bottoms trimmed

For the Salmon
Four 5-ounce skin-on center-cut salmon fillets
1½ teaspoons kosher salt
1 tablespoon avocado oil
¾ cup African Pepper Sauce (page 308)

MAKE THE VEGETABLES

In a large, heavy skillet, heat 1½ tablespoons of the olive oil over medium heat until shimmery. Cook the plantains in a single layer, flipping halfway through, until golden brown and slightly crispy on both sides and creamy in the middle, about 2 minutes per side. Sprinkle on ½ teaspoon of the salt and give them a stir. Transfer the plantains to a serving platter.

Heat the remaining 2 tablespoons of olive oil over medium-high heat until shimmery. Add the mushrooms and cook, tossing every few minutes, until golden brown, 8 to 10 minutes. Reduce the heat to medium, add the garlic and the remaining 1 teaspoon of salt, and stir well. Cook until the garlic is golden at the edges, about 2 minutes more. Finally, crank the heat up to high, add the spinach, cook until it's just wilted and still bright green, about 1 minute.

Transfer the mixture to the platter with the plantains, give it a toss, and keep it in a warm place while you cook the salmon.

COOK THE SALMON AND SERVE

Preheat the oven to 400°F. Pat the salmon dry with paper towels, then lay the fillets, skin-side down, on fresh paper towels to dry them really well as you heat the skillet.

Heat a large, heavy nonstick or well-seasoned skillet (wide enough to hold the fillets without crowding) over medium-high heat for a minute or so, until it gets nice and hot. Just before you cook the fillets, remove them from the paper towels and season on both sides with the salt.

Once the pan is hot, add the avocado oil and swirl the pan, then add the fillets, skin-side down. Reduce the heat to medium and use a spatula to gently press each fillet for a few seconds so it lays flat in the pan (fillets like to curl up). Cook until the skin is completely crispy and golden brown, about 5 minutes. The salmon should release easily from the pan; if it doesn't, keep cooking until it does.

Transfer the skillet to the oven and cook, skin-side still down, until most of the visible flesh goes from pink to light orange with a patch of slightly translucent pink in the middle, 4 to 6 minutes, depending on the thickness of the fillets.

Serve the salmon with the vegetables and the pepper sauce.

GRILLED SALMON WITH PEACH CURRY AND COCONUT CREAM

Serves 6

Juicy ripe peaches and beautiful pink salmon scream summer. A little curry paste and herbs keep this sweet-spicy curry squarely in the savory realm, and a drizzle of reduced coconut cream cools things off. I like grilling to char the skin, the whisper of bitterness complementing the sweetness of the stone fruit. I prefer the flavor of the curry when it's served warm or at room temperature, perfect for relaxed summer dining.

To cook the salmon without grilling, follow the method on page 205 to get the same lovely crisp skin.

For the Curry
3 tablespoons virgin coconut oil
2 garlic cloves, thinly sliced
1 tablespoon finely chopped ginger
1½ teaspoons kosher salt
1 tablespoon red curry paste, homemade (page 297) or store-bought

2½ pounds ripe peaches, halved, pitted, and cut into 1-inch pieces
3 tablespoons finely chopped palm sugar or coconut sugar
2 cups freshly squeezed orange juice

For the Dish
1¾ cups well-shaken coconut cream

Six 5-ounce skin-on salmon fillets
1½ tablespoons avocado oil
2 teaspoons kosher salt
Jalapeño Oil (page 305; optional)
Handful Thai basil leaves

MAKE THE CURRY

In a large skillet or sauté pan, heat the coconut oil over medium heat until shimmery. Add the garlic, ginger, and salt and cook, stirring frequently, until the garlic begins to turn golden, about 3 minutes. Add the curry paste and cook, stirring often, until very fragrant and a shade darker in color, about 4 minutes more. Add the peaches, stir well, and cook for a minute or so to allow the curry flavors to begin to season the peaches.

Add the palm sugar and orange juice, increase the heat to medium-high, and let it all come to a strong simmer. Cook, adjusting the heat to maintain the simmer, until the peaches are cooked through but not mushy and the sauce has thickened enough to coat the back of a spoon, 10 to 15 minutes. Keep warm.

MAKE THE DISH

In a small pot, bring the coconut cream to a simmer over medium heat and cook, stirring frequently, until it has reduced by about half (it'll have the texture of barely whipped cream), 18 to 20 minutes. Keep warm.

Fire up a grill to cook with an area of medium heat and an area of low heat.

Pat the salmon dry, spending a little extra time on the skin side. Rub just enough of the avocado oil onto the fillets to coat them with a very thin layer (excess oil will lead to flare-ups). Once the grill is ready, evenly season the salmon all over with the salt. Grill the salmon, skin-side down, on the area of medium heat until the skin is golden, a bit charred, and crispy, about 3 minutes.

Carefully run a metal spatula between the grates and the skin (if the skin hasn't released from the grates just yet, wait another minute), then flip the fillets onto the area of low heat and cook until the salmon is cooked to your preference. For me, that's medium-rare to medium, when the center is light pink with a bit of translucence, about 3 minutes.

Transfer the peach curry to a serving bowl or platter and top with the salmon, skin-side up. Drizzle on the coconut cream, then the jalapeño oil, and sprinkle on the Thai basil. Serve right away.

WHOLE GRILLED LOBSTER WITH PIKLIZ AND JALAPEÑO OIL

Serves 2 to 4

This one takes me right back to the beach in Haiti, where men hawk lobsters—split, seasoned with a splash of sea-water, and grilled to order over blazing wood. The succulent, briny sweetness of the lobster is treated to nothing more than a bit of pikliz (crunchy, tart, fiery pickled cabbage and onion) and a drizzle of grassy, spicy jalapeño oil. Have a lobster cracker? That's great news if you do, but you can also access the claw meat by whacking them with the back of a sturdy knife's blade.

Two 1½- to 2-pound live lobsters
1 teaspoon kosher salt

1 tablespoon avocado oil
½ cup Jalapeño Oil (page 305)

Pikliz (page 285)

MAKE THE DISH

Fire up a grill to medium-high heat.

Now, you're going to humanely kill the lobsters one by one. Lay a clean kitchen towel on a cutting board. This will help keep the lobsters docile and absorb any liquids released in the next steps. Put one of the lobsters on the towel, top-side up and with the head facing you. If the lobster is lively, you might have to move its claws so you have a clear go at its head.

Steady the lobster by putting one hand firmly on the body, right below its head. With the other hand, plunge the tip of a large, sharp knife into the very back of its head, right in the middle, then quickly and firmly bring the knife down between its eyes to cut the head completely in half. The lobster is now dead, even though it may still move a bit.

Flip the lobster onto its back with its tail facing you. Hold the lobster in place with one hand and with the other, insert the knife tip where the first cut started, then halve the lobster completely through the tail, trying your best to make the two halves even. You might need to manually spread out the tail fins. Repeat with the other lobster. Working with one half at a time, use a spoon to scrape out and discard the soft, light-green tomalley and dark-green roe.

Season the tail meat with the salt. Drizzle and rub a little of the oil on the cut side of each lobster, then flip them over and rub the remaining oil on the shells.

Lobster overcooks very easily, so you just want to give the meat a bit of char. If you cook it until the lobster meat turns white, it'll be overcooked and tough. Because the claws typically take longer than the tail, we're going to perform a little acrobatics here to ensure they cook at the same time. Put the lobsters, cut-side up, on the grill, so that the tails are close to the edges of the grill, where the heat tends to be slightly lower, and the claws are in the center, where the heat is higher.

Cook, uncovered, until the tail meat goes from translucent to mostly opaque and the claw shells look dusty white, about 6 to 8 minutes. Flip the lobsters and continue cooking, with the tails at the edges and claws in the center still, keeping a close eye on the tail meat and removing the lobsters when just a sliver of translucence remains, about 3 minutes more.

Transfer the lobsters to a platter, drizzle the tail meat with the jalapeño oil, and serve with plenty of pikliz.

CURRY-RUBBED WHOLE FISH WITH CHILE-LIME SAUCE AND HERBS

Serves 4 to 6

Dramatic to serve and wildly delicious, this whole fish takes its cues from Southeast Asia, and it's way easier to make than its conversation-stopping presentation might suggest. I rub it with salt and curry paste and leave it to cure, uncovered, seasoning the flesh and drying the skin, so it roasts crisp and abounding with flavor. A bright, sour, and spicy dressing along with herbs gives contrast to the rich, savory fish. If you have Jalapeño Oil (page 305) on hand, now's a great time to drizzle it on before serving.

Take a look at this neat technique for cooking the fish in the oven. A rack in the sheet pan elevates the fish, so it's better exposed to the welcome dry heat of the oven. Getting that rack hot before adding the fish helps prevent sticking.

For Marinating the Fish

Two whole 1½- to 2-pound mild, white-fleshed fish (such as bass, snapper, or branzino), scaled, gutted, and fins snipped

2 tablespoons kosher salt

¼ cup Red Curry Paste (page 297)

3 tablespoons avocado oil

For the Dish

2 tablespoons avocado oil

Big handful mixed herbs, such as basil and mint leaves and cilantro sprigs

¾ cup Vietnamese-Style Chile-Lime Sauce (page 302)

MARINATE THE FISH

Rinse the fish under cold running water, inside and out, rubbing with your fingers to loosen any stray scales. Pat dry with paper towels. Using a sharp knife, make a cut, deep enough to reach the bone, from the start of the head to the start of the tail on both sides of the two fish. Then, also on both sides, make three cuts—from back to belly, about 2 inches apart, and deep enough to reach the bone. Put the fish on a large tray. Season each fish generously, inside and out, with 1 tablespoon of the salt per fish.

In a small bowl, mix the curry paste with the oil, then use your hands to rub it all over the fish—inside and out—so they're well coated. Put the fish on a wire rack set over a large sheet pan and marinate the fish, uncovered, in the fridge, for at least 12 hours or up to 48 hours.

MAKE THE DISH

About 20 minutes before you're ready to cook, remove the fish from the fridge to take the chill off. It'll cook more evenly that way.

Preheat the oven to 450°F. Take the fish off the rack, wrap the rack in foil, and put it back in the sheet pan. Rub 1 tablespoon of the oil on the foil and put the whole sheet pan in the oven to get it hot. When it's hot but before it smokes, carefully remove the sheet pan from the oven and add the fish, with some space between them, and drizzle on the remaining 1 tablespoon of oil. Roast, basting once or twice with the liquid collecting on the foil, until the fish are just cooked to the bone (the flesh visible from the cuts should be milky white), about 15 minutes.

Transfer the fish to a large platter, drizzle on any remaining liquid, and top with the herbs. Serve with a bowl of the sauce.

PWASON BOUKANNEN

Serves 4 to 6

Along the rocky beaches of Haiti, men roam the shores fishing for hungry customers. They're on their hustle, waving prize crustaceans at beachgoers and beckoning to nets full of fish, and I'm always happy to take the bait.

Once you select your meal, maybe a yellowtail snapper or grouper, from their stash, they disappear to gather a handful of parched driftwood, make a pile, and set it aflame. Out of sight of the customer, they grill fish between two warped metal racks over the fire until the skin chars and the flesh sizzles. Then they return with the feast in hand, passing you a Styrofoam plate dwarfed by the fish. On top, they add pikliz, the ubiquitous tangy, crunchy, Scotch bonnet chile–spiked pickle of cabbage and onion, here cut into rustic chunks and spooned from a repurposed soda bottle.

Devouring grilled fish by the sea, my fingers searching the bones for every last morsel—the cheeks, the flesh clinging to the bones, the crispy skin on the face—is one of my earliest memories of Haiti. And only during a recent trip did I discover why the dish made such an impression, aside from the obvious magic of eating just-caught seafood feet from the water in the land where my parents were born. As I watched my aunt's cook, Ginette, slather the whole fish inside and out with scallions, thyme, chile, and lime, I discovered the secret behind the Haitian classic—a marinade that permeates the flesh with flavor and helps keep it moist during cooking.

The marinade is a blessing for home cooks who are intimidated by the prospect of making whole fish. Along with the skin and bones, it safeguards against overcooking. A poke with a thermometer or peek at the flesh near the bones is all it takes to tell if it's ready. Serve with plenty of pikliz (page 285), repurposed soda bottle optional.

NOTE: Two grilling baskets deep enough to contain the whole fish (or one basket, if you cook one fish at a time) make your task easy. You can grill without a basket so long as you wipe off the marinade, dry the fish very well (moisture equals sticking), and rub it with a little oil. Alternatively, you can cook the fish in the oven using the technique on page 211.

For Marinating the Fish
8 scallions, trimmed and roughly chopped

1 cup packed roughly chopped parsley (leaves and tender stems)

3 small shallots, peeled and roughly chopped

3 garlic cloves, peeled

1 small Scotch bonnet or habanero chile

2 tablespoons distilled white vinegar

1 tablespoon fresh thyme leaves

2 teaspoons kosher salt

1 teaspoon black peppercorns

4 juicy limes, halved

Two whole 1½- to 2-pound mild, white-fleshed fish (such as bass, snapper, or branzino), scaled, gutted, and fins snipped

1 tablespoon flaky sea salt

For the Dish
Avocado oil

2 tablespoons extra-virgin olive oil

Handful of roughly chopped parsley

Big pinch of fresh thyme leaves

MARINATE THE FISH

Combine the scallions, parsley, shallots, garlic, chile, vinegar, thyme, kosher salt, peppercorns, and the juice of two of the limes in a blender and blend on high speed until smooth, about 1 minute.

Rinse the fish under cold running water, inside and out, rubbing with your fingers to loosen any stray scales. Pat dry with paper towels. Using a sharp knife, make three cuts—from back to belly, about 2 inches apart, and deep enough to reach bone—on both sides of the two fish.

Put the fish in a large, nonreactive dish or baking pan. Squeeze the juice of the remaining two limes over the fish, rubbing each one against the fish, inside and out, as you squeeze. Season the fish, inside and out, with the flaky salt. Divide the marinade between the two fish and use your hands to rub it all over them—inside, including the head cavity, and out—so they're well coated.

Cover and marinate the fish in the fridge for at least 12 hours or up to 48 hours.

MAKE THE DISH

Fire up a grill to cook with an area of medium heat and another of low heat. Use a rag dipped in a little avocado oil to rub the grill grates to prevent sticking.

Use your hands to wipe the marinade from the fish, reserving the marinade, and transfer the fish to a large clean dish. Pat the fish dry with paper towels and rub a very thin layer of the avocado oil on each side of the fish, then enclose them in two fish grilling baskets.

Scrape the reserved marinade into a small saucepan, stir in ¼ cup water and the olive oil, and bring it to a simmer over high heat, stirring occasionally, and cook until the marinade and oil come together, about 1 minute. Turn off the heat, cover to keep warm, and set aside.

Set the baskets with the fish on the hotter area of the grill and cook until the skin on both sides is crispy, golden, and slightly charred, about 2 minutes per side. Move the basket to the other side of the grill, close the grill lid, and cook until the fish is just cooked to the bone, 6 to 8 minutes more. To tell that it's ready, use the tip of a small knife to peek at the flesh at the thickest part of the fish. When the flesh near the bone is left with just the slightest bit of translucence, then it's done. Alternatively, a thermometer should register 130°F to 135°F when inserted in the fish. I like to check the thick part right behind the head, sliding the thermometer into the flesh parallel to the bones.

Serve the grilled fish right away on a platter, spoon on the warm marinade sauce, and sprinkle with the parsley and thyme leaves.

8

Birds

VIETNAMESE-STYLE DUCK CURRY

Serves 4 to 6

On my first trip to Vietnam, I had lunch at a restaurant in Ho Chi Minh that served only duck—duck salad, duck soup, and most memorable to me, duck curry, which I almost immediately set about reimagining when I got home. This rich curry, just the thing for a special night in, shines with lemongrass and black pepper; contains hearty taro chunks; and comes crowned with tender, rosy slices of duck, each one capped with crackling skin. If you've got them, serve sweet, crunchy Vietnamese-Style Pickles (page 291) alongside for nibbling.

For the Curry
2 medium yellow onions, roughly chopped
3-inch knob ginger, peeled and thinly sliced against the grain
4 large stalks lemongrass, trimmed (see page 15), bruised, then thinly sliced
5 medium garlic cloves, peeled
1 moderately spicy fresh red chile, such as Fresno, stemmed and roughly chopped

3 tablespoons Red Curry Paste (page 297)
1½ tablespoons kosher salt
1½ teaspoons black peppercorns
½ cup avocado oil
2½ cups well-shaken coconut milk
2½ cups chicken stock, salted homemade or store-bought
3 tablespoons fish sauce
2 tablespoons finely chopped palm sugar or coconut sugar

1 pound piece taro root or sweet potato, peeled and cut into ½-inch pieces

For the Dish
4 duck breasts (about 2 pounds total), preferably Pekin
Kosher salt
Large handful Thai basil leaves
3 scallions, trimmed and thinly sliced

MAKE THE CURRY

Put the onions and ginger in a blender first (this will help the mixture blend more easily), then add the lemongrass, garlic, chile, curry paste, salt, and peppercorns and blend on high speed, occasionally stopping to scrape down the sides and stir, until very smooth, about 3 minutes.

Heat the oil in a medium, heavy pot over medium heat until shimmery. Add the onion mixture and cook, stirring frequently, until it turns golden brown and the garlic-and-onion flavor goes from raw and sharp to cooked and sweet, about 15 minutes. Some of the mixture will stick to the pot and turn deep brown. This is good!

Add the coconut milk and stock, increase the heat to medium-high, and bring to a simmer. Adjust the heat to medium to maintain a moderate simmer and start scraping the flavorful brown bits from the bottom of the pan into the sauce. Continue to cook until the liquid reduces by about one third, about 15 minutes. Stir in the fish sauce and sugar. Add the taro and continue to cook at a gentle simmer until the taro is tender, about 15 minutes more. It should have a rich gravy-like consistency. Turn off the heat and keep it covered while you cook the duck.

(cont.)

MAKE THE DISH

Use a sharp knife to score the skin of the duck breasts in a crisscross pattern (fifteen or so cuts one way, then fifteen or so the other), cutting almost all the way through the skin but not quite. Generously season them all over with salt. (Because your breasts might range in size, a good rule of thumb is 1 teaspoon of salt per pound of duck.)

Set aside for 5 minutes so the salt has a chance to penetrate the skin and season the meat.

Working in two batches or in two large, wide, heavy skillets at the same time, add the duck breasts, skin-side down, with a little space between each one, and set over medium-low heat (don't rush the process with higher heat). After a few minutes, the skin will gently sizzle and the fat will start to render into the pan. Keep cooking until the skin is golden brown and completely crispy, about 15 minutes, draining the fat as you cook before it submerges the duck skin. (Hold the breasts in place and tip the skillet to pour the flavorful fat into a heatproof container, reserving it to use another day.)

Once the skin is crispy, reduce the heat to low, and flip the breasts. Cook, using tongs to make sure the sides and entire bottoms spend some time against the hot skillet, until the breasts are medium-rare to medium (springy when poked with your finger or 130°F to 135°F on a thermometer), 2 to 3 minutes more.

Transfer the breasts to a wire rack and let them rest for about 20 minutes. Duck breast needs a really long time to rest or else all its delicious juices will spill out when it's cut.

Bring the curry back to a simmer and turn off the heat. Stir most of the Thai basil into the curry and spoon the curry into shallow bowls. Slice the duck breasts against the grain into ½-inch-thick slices, divide them among the bowls, and garnish with the scallions and remaining Thai basil.

PRUNE CHAR SIU DUCK LEGS

Serves 4 to 6

The flavors of char siu, Chinese barbecued pork, merge with duck confit, a French preparation designed to preserve. In the fall, birds were salted and cooked slowly in their own fat, which when cooled served as a low-tech force field that safeguarded the meat through the winter months. Like many other means of preservation (I'm thinking of you, fermentation!), the process incidentally created something delicious.

At home, while the duck meat turns falling-apart tender in its fat bath, whip up the savory, sweet sauce you'll use to glaze the legs, which get lovably charred and sticky under the broiler. If you've made Ginger-Scallion Sauce (page 303), bust some out for serving.

Note: Don't you dare toss all that tasty duck fat! Strain it, keep it in the fridge for months, and pull it out for roasting hearty vegetables, frying eggs, making a warm vinaigrette for bitter greens, or preparing your next batch of duck confit.

For Curing the Duck
4 duck legs (about 1¾ pounds total), preferably Pekin

1 tablespoon plus 1 teaspoon kosher salt

5 garlic cloves, crushed

3 scallions, trimmed and cut into thirds

4-inch knob ginger (no need to peel), halved and chopped into ½-inch pieces

5 small dried red chiles, crumbled

For Confiting and Serving the Duck
3 cups rendered duck fat

1 cup Prune Char Siu Sauce (page 311), at room temperature

CURE THE DUCK

Season the duck legs all over with the salt. Find a baking pan, casserole dish, or Dutch oven (it should fit the legs snugly, with a little overlap) and add the duck legs one by one, tucking in some of the garlic, scallions, ginger, and chiles between each leg as best you can. Cover tightly (with a lid or foil) and cure in the fridge overnight or up to 24 hours.

CONFIT AND SERVE THE DUCK

When the duck has cured, preheat the oven to 250°F. Melt the duck fat in a small pot over low heat until warm. Pour the fat over the duck legs, cover the pot with a lid, and cook in the oven until the flesh is fall-apart tender, about 2½ hours. To test whether they're ready, use tongs to pull at one of the duck legs and wiggle the drumstick—if it moves easily, you're good.

Take the pot out of the oven. To finish the dish the same day, let the legs cool in the fat for 1 hour. Otherwise, let them cool to room temperature, then refrigerate for up to 2 weeks (they get even better as time passes). When you're ready to proceed, heat over very low heat just until the cold fat becomes liquid again.

Preheat the broiler and position an oven rack in the middle position. Set a wire rack in a sheet pan. Use tongs and a spatula for support (the legs are so tender they could fall apart without its help) to transfer the legs to the wire rack, leaving the fat and aromatics behind. Strain the fat through a fine-mesh strainer into a container, pressing on the aromatics to extract their flavor. Discard the aromatics and reserve the fat for another use.

Broil the duck legs on the middle rack until the skin gets crispy and golden brown with a few black spots, about 4 minutes. Remove the sheet pan and evenly brush or spoon on about ¼ cup of the char siu sauce over the top of each leg. Return them to the oven and broil until the sauce is shiny, sticky, and slightly charred, about 5 minutes more.

Serve the duck legs on plates with the remaining char siu sauce for dunking.

SPICED YOGURT-MARINATED CORNISH HENS WITH SWEET ONION-ROASTED POTATOES

Serves 4

A savory alternative-yogurt marinade spiced with black pepper, ginger, and turmeric simultaneously seasons and tenderizes these pint-size birds. While they roast, they spill deliciousness onto potatoes that you've tossed with caramelized onions.

For Marinating the Hens
½ cup plain alternative yogurt, such as almond, cashew, or coconut

¼ cup coconut aminos

9 large garlic cloves, peeled

1½ tablespoons kosher salt

1 tablespoon black peppercorns

3-inch knob yellow turmeric root, peeled and roughly chopped

3-inch knob ginger, peeled and thinly sliced against the grain

2 juicy lemons

3 Cornish hens (about 1¼ pounds each)

For the Dish
¼ cup extra-virgin olive oil

2 large yellow onions, thinly sliced

3 teaspoons kosher salt

1 pound tiny potatoes (1 to 2 inches in diameter), halved if bigger than 1 inch

MARINATE THE HENS

Combine the yogurt, coconut aminos, garlic, salt, peppercorns, turmeric, and ginger in a blender. Use a Microplane to grate in the zest of both lemons, then halve one and squeeze in the juice. Reserve the remaining lemon for another purpose. Blend on high speed until smooth, about 1 minute.

Rinse the hens under cool water, inside and out, and pat dry very well. Put them in a large bowl or pan and spoon about one third of the yogurt marinade into the cavities of the birds, spreading it around as best you can. Pour the rest of the marinade over the hens, using the spoon to make sure they're completely coated, tops and bottoms, including the wings and crevices between the legs and breasts.

Cover and marinate in the fridge for at least 16 hours or up to 2 days.

MAKE THE DISH

About half an hour before you're ready to cook the hens, remove them from the fridge to take the chill off. Heat the oil in a wide, heavy skillet over medium heat until shimmery. Add the onions and 1½ teaspoons of the salt, stir well, and cook, stirring occasionally, until the onions start to soften and release liquid, about 3 minutes. Reduce the heat to a gentle simmer, stirring occasionally, until all the liquid has evaporated and the onions have a creamy texture, turn a deep golden color, and taste very sweet, about 20 minutes.

Preheat the oven to 450°F. Spread the potatoes on a large sheet pan, sprinkle with the remaining 1½ teaspoons of salt, and toss well. Add the cooked onion mixture, stir well, and spread them to make a bed for the hens—a snug single layer in the center of the pan.

Take the hens out of the marinade (don't scrape any off, but do leave behind anything left in the bowl) and put them on the potato-onion mixture, with a few inches of space between each one. Roast until the hens are golden brown with some dark patches and poking the thighs reveals juices with no trace of pink (a thermometer inserted into the thickest part of the breast should register 150°F), 40 to 45 minutes.

Let the hens rest in the pan for 15 minutes, then transfer to a platter to serve.

STICKY CHICKEN WINGS WITH SPICY HONEY AND FISH SAUCE

Serves 4 to 6

The same marinade that infused these wings with flavor becomes a glaze that caramelizes as they cook, bringing all the sweet, savory, funky, salty qualities I crave with wings.

For Marinating the Chicken

1 cup honey

¼ cup Aromatic Chile Paste (page 298)

3 tablespoons fish sauce

2 tablespoons coconut aminos

1½ tablespoons kosher salt

1 tablespoon ground black pepper

9 large garlic cloves, finely chopped

3 pounds chicken wings, attached or separated

1 teaspoon avocado oil

MARINATE THE WINGS

In a large mixing bowl, combine the honey, chile paste, fish sauce, coconut aminos, salt, pepper, and garlic and stir well. Add the wings and toss to coat them well. Cover and refrigerate for at least 12 hours or up to 24 hours, tossing halfway through for even marination.

COOK THE WINGS

When you're ready to cook, preheat the oven to 425°F. Line a large plate or tray with paper towels. Transfer the wings to the paper towels, reserving the marinade, and let them hang out for a few minutes, so the towels absorb the excess marinade.

Line a large sheet pan with aluminum foil and put a roasting rack in it. Use a piece of paper towel to rub the avocado oil onto the top of the rack. Put the wings on the rack in a single layer and roast until they're lightly browned and nearly cooked through, about 15 minutes.

In the meantime, pour the reserved marinade into a medium skillet, set it over medium-high heat, and cook at a simmer until it's thickened to the consistency of barbecue sauce, stirring occasionally, about 8 minutes.

When the wings have cooked for about 15 minutes, generously brush or drizzle all over with a little more than half of the cooked marinade, then return the wings to the oven and keep cooking until the glaze is shiny, sticky, and nicely charred, about 8 minutes more.

Transfer to a platter and serve with the remaining marinade for dipping.

CRISPY FRIED CHICKEN WITH SMOKY CHILE SALT

Serves 8

Tapioca flour gives this fried chicken a super crispy crust, and the overnight marinade, which includes habanero, ginger, and lime, is inspired by the seasonings in my favorite versions of West African fried chicken, ensuring that the result is incredibly flavorful and juicy. Avocado oil makes it a bit better for you, too, so you can feel (a bit) better when you inevitably go back for that fourth piece.

Note: This dish does require a lot of avocado oil, which is not cheap, so be sure to save and strain it to use for your next few deep-frying projects.

For Marinating the Chicken
2 large shallots, roughly chopped
3 large garlic cloves, peeled
1 habanero or Scotch bonnet chile, stemmed
1½-inch knob ginger, peeled and roughly sliced against the grain
1½ tablespoons black peppercorns

1½ tablespoons coconut aminos
1½ tablespoons kosher salt
1 tablespoon apple cider vinegar
2 teaspoons paprika
2 juicy limes
4 pounds skin-on chicken pieces (boneless breasts, bone-in thighs, drums, and wings)

For Frying and Serving
Avocado oil, for deep frying (about 6 cups)
2 cups tapioca flour
1 teaspoon baking powder
¼ cup Smoky Chile Salt (page 325)
Lemon and lime wedges, for serving

MARINATE THE CHICKEN
Combine the shallots, garlic, chile, ginger, peppercorns, coconut aminos, salt, vinegar, and paprika in a blender. Use a Microplane to grate the limes' zest into the blender, then halve the limes and squeeze in the juice. Blend on high speed to a thick smooth paste, about 1 minute.

Rinse the chicken under cold water and pat it dry. Cut the breasts crosswise into thirds. Halve the thighs lengthwise, so one half is boneless and the other isn't. Combine the chicken and blended marinade in a large mixing bowl and toss to coat the chicken really well with the marinade. Cover and marinate in the fridge for at least 12 or up to 24 hours.

FRY AND SERVE
About an hour before you cook, remove the chicken from the fridge to take the chill off so it doesn't crater the temperature of the frying oil. Preheat the oven to 300°F.

Set a wire rack over a sheet pan. Pour enough avocado oil into a 3-quart pot to give you a depth of 4 inches and heat it over medium heat until the oil registers 350°F on a deep-fry thermometer (check in a few places to make sure it's evenly hot). In the meantime, combine the tapioca flour and baking powder in a large mixing bowl, mix very well, and put it next to the stove.

When the oil reaches 350°F, add 4 pieces of the chicken to the bowl with the flour and toss to coat well, making sure that the flour coats the entire surface of each piece, including any nooks and crannies. Take a moment to pull the skin on each piece taut, so it isn't bunched up and covers as much of the flesh as possible.

One by one, give the pieces a shake so any excess flour falls back into the bowl and carefully add them to the oil. Fry until the chicken's craggy crust is golden brown and crispy (when done, the breast pieces will register 150°F and the thighs and drums 160°F on a meat thermometer), 8 to 10 minutes. Transfer the chicken to the wire rack.

Between each batch, use a small strainer to scoop out any crispy bits floating in the oil and let the oil return to 350°F before cooking the next batch of 4 pieces. Repeat until you've fried all the chicken.

When it's all been fried, transfer the sheet pan to the oven to reheat the chicken, 5 to 10 minutes. Sprinkle on the smoky chile salt and serve with lemon and lime wedges.

GLAZED CHICKEN THIGHS WITH GARLIC, GINGER, AND SCALLIONS

Serves 4 to 6

The magic of these chicken thighs all happens in the oven. By the time the sweet, tangy cooking liquid has made the meat perfectly tender, it has reduced to a bold, teriyaki-like glaze and the ginger, scallions, and chiles that simmer along with it have turned roasty and inviting.

For the Sauce
½ cup coconut aminos
1 teaspoon arrowroot starch
¼ cup honey
¼ cup apple cider vinegar

For the Dish
3½ pounds bone-in, skin-on chicken thighs
1 tablespoon avocado oil
1½ tablespoons plus ½ teaspoon kosher salt
10 medium scallions, trimmed and cut into 2-inch pieces, whites halved lengthwise

10 large garlic cloves, thinly sliced
1 moderately spicy fresh red chile, such as Fresno, thinly sliced
3-inch knob ginger, peeled and cut into very thin matchsticks
1 cup chicken stock, salted homemade or store-bought
Handful small cilantro sprigs

MAKE THE SAUCE
Combine the coconut aminos and arrowroot starch in a small mixing bowl and whisk until the starch dissolves, including any clumps. Pour the mixture into a small saucepan, add the honey and vinegar, and bring to a boil over medium heat. Reduce the heat to cook at a lively simmer until it's glossy and thick enough to lightly coat a spoon, about 1 minute. Set aside. The sauce keeps in an airtight container in the fridge for up to 3 weeks.

MAKE THE DISH
Preheat the oven to 350°F.

Pat the chicken thighs dry, then lay them, skin-side down, on fresh paper towels to dry the skin especially well to prevent splattering. In a wide, heavy, ovenproof skillet that's at least 2 inches deep, heat the oil over high heat until shimmery. Working in two batches if need be, evenly season the chicken all over with 1½ tablespoons of the salt and add the chicken, skin-side down, to the skillet. Reduce the heat to medium and cook until the skin is deep golden brown and crisp, 8 to 10 minutes. Flip the chicken and cook to give the bottoms a little color, about 3 minutes more, transferring the thighs to a plate as they're done.

When all the thighs are ready, return them, skin-side up, to the skillet. Evenly scatter on the scallions, garlic, chile, ginger, and the remaining ½ teaspoon of salt, then evenly pour in the stock and the reserved sauce, giving the skillet a gentle shake so they come together.

Transfer the pan to the oven and cook, basting after about 15 and 25 minutes, until the sauce is slightly sticky but still plenty saucy and the meat pulls easily away from the bone, about 30 minutes. Sprinkle on the cilantro and serve.

CHICKEN ROASTED OVER ROOT VEGETABLES WITH GINGER AND ROSEMARY

Serves 4 to 6

It's tough for me to imagine cooking a whole chicken any other way. I remember the first time I tried it. Me and the other young cooks at Jean-Georges would ogle the fabled recipe printouts that circulated through the kitchen as chefs de parties prepped the next day's menus. These printouts were our windows into the genius we were chasing, wisdom distilled from Chef himself.

One night, I got my hands on a piece of paper scribbled with a simple picture of a whole chicken sitting over potato rounds. The title at the top read The Potatoes Taste Better Than the Chicken. I was intrigued, because how could the modest potato taste better than a juicy, bronze-skinned bird?

I found out the next afternoon when my prep shift began and, as per tradition, the dinner cooks would devour anything left over from lunch service. The chicken was indeed exquisitely golden and tender, salty and juicy, but the potatoes underneath were the thing, bathed in the chicken's fat and juices and slightly crushed under its weight. It was essentially a sheet-pan dinner at a four-star restaurant. Nowadays, I often use an assortment of tasty roots and tubers, plus some jalapeño for a little zip, and rub the chicken with a mixture of rosemary and ginger, the pairing another first I had at the restaurant that shaped me.

Note on Spatchcocking

Put the chicken, breast-side down, on a cutting board. Use kitchen shears or a sharp knife to remove the backbone, cutting along one side of the tail all the way to the neck and then along the other side, removing the backbone. Give the chicken and backbone a quick rub and rinse to remove any dark and squishy matter and pat dry. Toss the backbone in with the vegetables. It's quite good.

  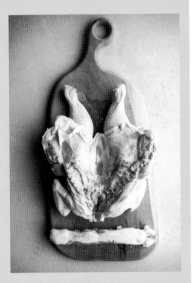

For the Aromatic Oil

3 tablespoons extra-virgin olive oil

2 tablespoons kosher salt

2 tablespoons finely chopped ginger

2 tablespoons chopped fresh or 1 tablespoon dried rosemary

1 tablespoon ground black pepper

2 tablespoons coconut aminos

For the Dish

One 4- to 4½-pound chicken, spatchcocked (see Note)

3 medium carrots, trimmed, peeled, and cut into 1-inch pieces

1 medium yellow onion, cut into ½-inch half-moon slices

1 medium sweet potato, cut into ¼-inch half-moon slices

8 trimmed baby turnips, halved

10 garlic cloves, peeled

1 medium jalapeño chile, stemmed and cut into ¼-inch-wide slices

1 teaspoon kosher salt

2 tablespoons extra-virgin olive oil

Flaky sea salt, for finishing

MAKE THE AROMATIC OIL

In a small bowl, combine all the aromatic oil ingredients and stir well.

MAKE THE DISH

Preheat the oven to 450°F. Pat the chicken dry with towels. Scatter the vegetables on a sheet pan in a single layer. Evenly sprinkle on the kosher salt, then evenly drizzle on the olive oil. Give it all a quick toss.

Set the chicken, breast side up, on top of the vegetables in the center of the sheet pan with the legs facing one of the short sides. Tuck the wing tips behind the breast. Because folds in the skin won't get crispy, stretch the bird a bit so it lays as flat as possible, especially where the legs connect to the breasts. Rub the aromatic oil mixture all over the chicken, including any nooks, so it's completely and evenly coated. Drizzle any of the remaining mixture over the vegetables.

Put the sheet pan in the oven (chicken legs first, if you can). Roast until the skin turns golden, about 20 minutes. Reduce the oven heat to 350°F and keep roasting until the juices that come out of the thigh when you poke it have no trace of pink, about 40 minutes more. (If you're using a thermometer, the thick part of the thigh should register 160°F when it's ready.)

Let the chicken rest in the pan for at least 15 minutes. Carve the chicken, then return it to the pan, sprinkle on some flaky salt, and serve.

POULE NAN SOS

Serves 4

When I was a kid, we often left Queens on Sunday mornings to visit Mémère, my paternal grandmother, in New Jersey. Along with warm kisses and a few words of broken English, this chicken stew would greet us. Its official name (poule nan sos in Haitian Creole, or "chicken in sauce") is quite an understatement. The meat is marinated overnight with onions, garlic, thyme, and chiles along with citrus, the fruits juiced and then rubbed forcefully onto the chicken to access the fragrant oils as well. After the meat takes on all that flavor, it's stewed with the marinade and loads of bell peppers for a satisfying, thrilling stew. This dish *is* Haiti, something we make time and time again. I suspect you will, too.

For Marinating the Chicken

3 pounds mixed bone-in chicken thighs and drumsticks, rinsed and patted dry

3 tablespoons kosher salt

1 juicy orange, halved

1 juicy lime, halved

1 juicy lemon, halved

2 medium yellow onions, cut into ⅛-inch half-moon slices

8 garlic cloves, roughly sliced

2 Scotch bonnet or habanero chiles, cut in half and sliced thin

¼ cup fresh thyme leaves

For the Dish

⅓ cup extra-virgin olive oil

½ cup tomato paste

1 tablespoon kosher salt

2 red bell peppers, seeded and deveined, cut into long, thin slices

2 yellow bell peppers, seeded and deveined, cut into long, thin slices

2 cups chicken stock, salted homemade or store-bought

Small handful roughly chopped parsley sprigs

MARINATE THE CHICKEN

Put the chicken pieces in a large bowl and season with the salt. Squeeze the citrus halves over the chicken, then spend a minute or so rubbing the cut sides of the citrus against the chicken. Add the onions, garlic, chile, and thyme and toss well, rubbing the chicken as you do.

Cover and marinate in the fridge for at least 12 hours or up to 48 hours.

MAKE THE DISH

Preheat the oven to 375°F.

Remove the chicken from the marinade, guiding any stuck-on aromatics back into the bowl. Set a strainer over a small mixing bowl. Pour the marinade through the strainer, reserving the solids and liquid. Pat the chicken very dry with paper towels.

Heat the oil in a wide heavy, ovenproof pot (I use a 3½-quart braiser) over medium-high heat just until shimmery. Cook the chicken, skin-side down, occasionally turning the drumsticks but not the thighs, until the skin is deep brown about 8 minutes. Transfer the chicken pieces to a plate.

Reduce the heat to medium-low, add the tomato paste and salt, and cook, stirring often, until it turns several shades darker, about 3 minutes. Add the bell peppers and the reserved solids from the marinade, and cook, stirring occasionally, until the peppers soften slightly and take on a little color, about 8 to 10 minutes.

Return the chicken to the pan, skin side up and in a single layer, then take a minute to pile the peppers, onions, and other aromatics on top of the chicken. Then evenly pour in the reserved liquid from the marinade along with the stock. Cook in the oven, basting every 15 minutes to coat the chicken with the peppers and sauce, until the sauce has thickened slightly and the meat pulls off the bone with a gentle tug from a fork, about 1 hour. Garnish with the parsley and serve.

MY FAVORITE GRILLED CHICKEN

Serves 4 to 6

If the words "grilled chicken" conjure dry, mild-mannered breasts, this dish should fix that. Bone-in meat, a blend-and-go marinade made with lemongrass, cilantro, and fish sauce, and rather slow grilling gives you the kind of juicy, boldly seasoned chicken you'd find in Thailand.

Serving tamarind chile sauce (page 122) alongside takes the chicken to the next level.

¾ cup avocado oil

½ cup fish sauce

1 tablespoon plus 2 teaspoons kosher salt

4 lemongrass stalks, trimmed (see page 15), bruised, then thinly sliced

1 small bunch cilantro, stems roughly chopped, upper leaves reserved for garnish

¼ cup finely chopped palm sugar or coconut sugar

¼ cup black peppercorns

3 tablespoons coconut aminos

2 tablespoons coriander seeds

8 garlic cloves, peeled

6 fresh Thai chiles, stemmed

4 to 4½ pounds bone-in, skin-on chicken parts

MARINATE THE CHICKEN

In a blender, combine the avocado oil, fish sauce, 1 tablespoon of the kosher salt, the lemongrass, cilantro stems and lower leaves, palm sugar, black peppercorns, coconut aminos, coriander, garlic, and chiles. Blend to a coarse puree, about 2 minutes.

Season the chicken all over with the remaining 2 teaspoons of salt, put it in a large container along with the marinade, and toss to coat well, making sure the marinade gets into the nooks and crannies. Cover and refrigerate for at least 12 hours and up to 3 days.

MAKE THE DISH

When it's time to cook the chicken, fire up a grill so there's a high-heat area and a medium-heat area. Remove the chicken from the marinade, giving each piece a brief shake and reserving the marinade, and transfer it to a large plate or tray. Pour the reserved marinade into a small pot, bring it to a boil over high heat, and turn off the heat. You'll use it in a bit to glaze the chicken.

Grill the chicken, skin-side down and uncovered, on the hot area until it's charred and the skin is crispy, about 4 minutes. Flip the chicken as you move it to the area of medium heat, baste with some of the reserved marinade, then cover the grill. Cook until the breasts are just cooked through (I prefer 150°F to the standard 165°F), 20 to 25 minutes, and the drum and thigh meat pulls easily from the bone, 25 to 30 minutes. When the chicken is ready, flip it back to skin-side down and cook for about 30 seconds more, rubbing the remaining marinade on the meat side as the skin side crisps up.

Let the chicken rest for 5 minutes. Serve, garnishing with the remaining cilantro.

MOM'S (HAITIAN) MEATLOAF

Serves 6

Few foods say comfort like meatloaf. That's true even for a Queens boy who grew up eating poule nan sos and griyo. To hers, Mom added classic Haitian seasonings—thyme, parsley, and fruity, fiery chile—as well as pimento-stuffed olives. I do things only a little differently, using ground turkey, the kind with some fat, as a lighter alternative to the traditional beef and glazing the top with ketchup, which I'm just a sucker for. Eat the meatloaf hot for dinner, then try it cold the next day.

3 tablespoons extra-virgin olive oil

1 large yellow onion, cut into ¼-inch dice

7 medium garlic cloves, roughly chopped

2 medium bell peppers (preferably red and yellow), stemmed, seeded, and cut into ¼-inch dice

1½ tablespoons kosher salt

2 pounds ground dark meat turkey

1 large egg, lightly beaten

½ Scotch bonnet or habanero chile, finely chopped

½ cup all-natural ketchup

3 tablespoons extra-fine almond flour

3 tablespoons Epis (page 296)

1 tablespoon umami mushroom powder, homemade (page 326) or the Nom Nom Paleo brand

1 teaspoon smoked paprika

1 cup drained pimento-stuffed olives, roughly chopped

Large handful small parsley sprigs, roughly chopped

MAKE THE DISH

Preheat the oven to 350°F. Line a 9 x 5–inch loaf pan with parchment paper so that it overhangs on both long sides of the pan by at least an inch.

Heat the oil in a medium skillet over medium heat until shimmery, add the onion and garlic, and cook, stirring occasionally, until they start to soften, about 3 minutes. Add the bell peppers and ½ tablespoon of the salt, and cook, stirring occasionally, until the onions are translucent and soft and the peppers are bright and tender, about 12 minutes. Turn off the heat and let cool.

In a large mixing bowl, combine the turkey, egg, chile, ¼ cup of the ketchup, the almond flour, epis, mushroom powder, paprika, and the remaining 1 tablespoon of salt. Stir well, then use your hands (gloved ones, if you're worried about the chile) to mix and knead well for a minute or so to make a smooth mixture that's all one color.

Stir in the onion mixture, olives, and parsley and mix really well. Transfer the meatloaf to the prepared loaf pan, smooth and even out the top, and cover with the remaining ¼ cup of ketchup, spreading it into an even layer.

Bake until a thermometer inserted into the center of the meat registers 160°F (it's the best way to gauge doneness for this meatloaf), 50 minutes to 1 hour. Let the meatloaf rest for at least 15 minutes. Use the parchment paper overhang to carefully pull the meatloaf out of the pan and transfer to a cutting board. Slice and serve.

TURKEY IN RED MOLE

Serves 6

My red mole, like the incredible genre of sauces on which it's based, is so complex and satisfying that it needs little embellishment, just meat (or sweet potato, see page 99) and perhaps some tortillas (grain-free for me, such as those made by the Siete brand). The meat could be chicken, but I especially love serving the mole with turkey. In small part, it's because turkey is said to be what the nuns who first created mole in Puebla in the seventeenth century served with the sauce, but mostly I look to the underused bird—at least, not counting Thanksgiving Day—because its meat is flavorful enough to stand up to the bold sauce without overpowering its subtleties.

3 tablespoons avocado oil

2½ pounds mixed turkey parts, such as wings (separated and tips removed), boneless skin-on breasts (cut into about

5-ounce pieces), thighs (cut in half along the bone), or drumsticks

1 tablespoon kosher salt

My Red Mole (page 313)

½ cup roasted unsalted pecans, roughly chopped

MAKE THE DISH

Heat the oil in a large Dutch oven over medium-high heat until shimmery. Pat the turkey dry and season all over with the salt.

Cook any wings, thighs, or drumsticks until deep golden brown all over, about 15 minutes. Cook any breast meat, skin side only, until deep golden brown, 5 to 8 minutes. Transfer the turkey parts to a plate as they're done.

If necessary, reheat the mole, covered, in the large Dutch oven over low heat. Add any wings, thighs, or drumsticks to the pot so they're submerged in the mole, then cover the pot, adjusting the heat to maintain a very gentle simmer. Cook over very low heat until the meat is very tender (it'll pull easily from the bone), about 1 hour, ensuring that the simmer is very gentle and cracking the lid an inch or so if it's simmering too rapidly. If using breast meat, cook, covered, until just cooked through (it'll feel just bouncy when poked with a finger), about 15 minutes.

To serve, sprinkle the pecans over turkey and mole.

9

Meats

VIETNAMESE-STYLE GRILLED PORK WITH LEMONGRASS, HONEY, AND BLACK PEPPER

Serves 6

Succulent pork shoulder, cut into steaks, takes well to a marinade that does double duty as a sauce. It's a pleasure to taste what's at play: the sweet-salty push and pull of honey and fish sauce, the way floral lemongrass sets off the burn of black pepper. Do not be afraid of char here. The bitter edge is lovely with the honey. Pork shoulder doesn't see the grill as often as chops, but make this dish and you'll see it should.

For Marinating the Pork

2 pounds pork shoulder (Boston butt)

1 teaspoon kosher salt

1 cup Lemongrass–Black Pepper Dressing (page 304)

For the Dish

1½ tablespoons avocado oil

2 cups drained Vietnamese-Style Pickles (page 291)

Extra-virgin olive oil

Large handful mixed basil and mint leaves and cilantro sprigs

MARINATE THE PORK

If necessary, trim the fat layer on the pork to ½ inch. Cut the pork with the grain into long, narrow steaks that are about 2 inches wide and 2 inches thick. Season the pork all over with the salt. Put it in a medium mixing bowl, pour on ¾ cup of the lemongrass dressing, and toss to coat well. Cover and marinate in the fridge for at least 24 hours or up to 3 days.

MAKE THE DISH

Fire up a grill to cook with an area of high heat and an area of medium heat. Remove the pork from the marinade, letting the excess drip off and reserving the marinade, and transfer to a platter. Drizzle both sides with the avocado oil.

Grill the pork on the hot area of the grill and cook, flipping occasionally, until it's deep golden brown with a few black spots, 6 to 8 minutes. Use tongs to dunk the pork in the leftover marinade, then grill again briefly on the hot area, flipping it a few times to avoid crossing the line from charred to burned. Finish cooking the pork on the area of medium heat to medium doneness (just a trace of pink inside or 140°F on a thermometer), 10 to 12 minutes more.

Let the pork rest for 10 minutes or so before slicing it against the grain and plating it with the pickles. Pour on the remaining ¼ cup lemongrass dressing, drizzle with the olive oil, and scatter on the herbs.

SPICY LARB-STYLE LETTUCE WRAPS WITH MAKRUT LIME AND HERBS

Serves 4

I model this dish after the larb, the bright, spicy jumble of ground meat, shallots, and herbs that's made in the Northeast region of Thailand. It's often served with vegetation on the side for nibbling between bites, so I don't feel like I'm so far off when, at home, I serve it with crisp, cooling cucumbers and lettuce for making wraps in the Vietnamese manner.

Pork is a common and excellent fodder for larb, but try it with ground chicken, turkey, or even duck. Mushrooms are tasty here, too. If you can find them, fresh betel leaves add a hugely herbaceous, fragrant bonus.

2 tablespoons avocado oil

1½ pounds ground pork

3 medium shallots, halved and thinly sliced

5 small dried red chiles, crumbled

3 tablespoons fish sauce

1½ teaspoons finely chopped palm sugar or coconut sugar

3 tablespoons lime juice (from 2 juicy limes)

1½ cups mixed small cilantro sprigs, mint leaves, and basil leaves (preferably Thai), plus a handful for serving

12 fresh or frozen medium makrut lime leaves, center ribs removed, very thinly sliced

1 head butter lettuce, trimmed and leaves separated

2 Persian cucumbers, cut into spears

8 to 12 fresh betel leaves (optional)

MAKE THE DISH

Heat the oil in a large, heavy skillet over medium heat until shimmery. Add the pork and use a sturdy spoon or spatula to stir and break up the clumps as it cooks until it's no longer pink and liquid has accumulated in the skillet, 4 to 5 minutes.

Stir in the shallots, dried chiles, fish sauce, and sugar, then raise the heat to high and cook, stirring every 30 seconds or so, until the liquid has evaporated and the pork takes on a golden hue, about 6 minutes. Add the lime juice and cook until it has completely absorbed into the pork, 1 minute more. Turn off the heat.

Roughly chop the herbs. Stack, roll, then very thinly slice the makrut lime leaves. Add the herbs and makrut lime leaves to the pork and stir well. Set out a platter with the lettuce, cucumbers, remaining herbs, and betel leaves (if using), and serve the pork alongside.

STEWED PORK SHOULDER WITH CUMIN, CHIPOTLE, AND POBLANO CHILES

Serves 6 to 8

The so-very-stewable pork shoulder anchors this smoky, beguiling braise. Poblano chiles and carrots turn it into a hearty one-pot meal. Serve it with the garnishes for pozole, the pork and hominy of which it's reminiscent: radishes and onions for crunch and oregano to echo the herb's presence in the stew.

For the Stew

2 tablespoons cumin seeds

2 tablespoons coriander seeds

3 pounds boneless pork shoulder (Boston butt), cut into 2-inch pieces

1 tablespoon plus 1 teaspoon kosher salt

1 tablespoon ground black pepper

⅓ cup avocado oil

3 medium cored green tomatoes or 3 ounces husked tomatillos, roughly chopped

3 tablespoons fresh oregano, or 1½ tablespoons dried

3 dried hoja santa leaves (optional)

2 dried or canned chipotle chiles

8 garlic cloves, roughly chopped

3 medium carrots, peeled and sliced into ¼-inch rounds

1 large yellow or white onion,

cut into ½-inch pieces

2 medium poblano chiles, stemmed, deseeded, and cut into long ¼-inch-wide strips

2 cups chicken stock, salted homemade or store-bought

For Serving

Thinly sliced white onions and radishes

Cilantro and fresh oregano leaves

MAKE THE STEW

Combine the cumin and coriander in a small skillet, set it over high heat, and toast, shaking the pan and tossing the spices every 30 seconds or so, until the spices are very fragrant and toasty, about 2 minutes. Set them aside in a small bowl.

Season the pork evenly all over with 1 tablespoon of the salt and the pepper. Heat the oil in a large pot or Dutch oven (7- to 9-quart works well) with a lid over medium-high heat until shimmery. Working in batches to avoid crowding, brown the pork on all sides, 6 to 8 minutes per batch, transferring each batch to a plate when it's done. In the meantime, combine the toasted cumin and coriander, the green tomatoes, oregano, *hoja santa* (if using), and chipotles in a blender and blend on high speed until smooth, about 1 minute.

When you've browned all the pork, add the garlic, carrots, and onion to the pot and cook, stirring occasionally and scraping any pork bits from the bottom of the pot, until they brown a bit at the edges, about 3 minutes. Add the poblanos and cook, stirring, for a couple of minutes more.

Return the pork to the pot, add the blended mixture, the stock, and the remaining 1 teaspoon of salt and stir well. Let it come to a simmer, then reduce the heat to maintain a very gentle simmer and cook, covered, until the pork is very tender (you should be able to easily cut it with a spoon) but not falling apart, about 2 hours. Cooled and refrigerated, the stew keeps for up to 5 days.

SERVE THE DISH

Soak the onions and radishes in a small bowl of ice water for 10 minutes or so, to wash away some sharpness and crisp them. Drain them really well. Serve the pork stew garnished with the onions, radishes, and herbs.

SPICE-CRUSTED PORK CHOPS WITH CHERRIES AND OREGANO

Serves 4

An effortless brine ensures these pork chops are incredibly juicy, and a crust of toasted coriander and cumin seeds delivers a welcome crackle as well as exciting pops of fragrance and flavor. On weeknights, you might stop there to revel in the love from your guests, while on weekends you might go the extra mile, whipping up this quick summery sauce of sweet-tart cherries and smoky, spicy chipotles. Oregano stands strong among all those bold flavors, contributing a hit of freshness along with a little peppery heat.

Note: Once you pit the cherries, the sauce comes together in a flash. I'm a cherry fiend, so I have a cherry pitter, which makes quick work of the task. If you don't, just cut the cherries in half around the pit (just as you would an avocado), gently twist to separate the halves, and use your tiniest spoon to scoop out the pit.

For Brining the Pork Chops
¼ cup honey

¼ cup kosher salt

4 bone-in pork loin chops (about 1½ inches thick and 10 ounces each)

For the Cherries
1 large dried chipotle chile

2 tablespoons extra-virgin olive oil

4 large garlic cloves, thinly sliced

3-inch knob ginger, peeled and finely chopped

1 teaspoon kosher salt

2 pounds ripe sweet cherries, stemmed, halved, and pitted (about 6 cups)

¼ cup honey

2 tablespoons lime juice (from 1 juicy lime)

For the Dish
½ cup coriander seeds

½ cup cumin seeds

¼ cup black peppercorns

2 tablespoons avocado oil

Extra-virgin olive oil

Small handful mixed small cilantro sprigs and thinly sliced trimmed scallions

2 tablespoons fresh oregano leaves

BRINE THE PORK CHOPS

Combine the honey and salt with 1½ cups of warm water in a medium mixing bowl and stir to dissolve. Stir in 1 cup of cold water. Put the pork chops in a baking dish just large enough to fit them in a single layer and pour on the brine to submerge them. Cover and refrigerate for at least 12 hours or (even better) up to 24 hours. When you're ready to make the pork, drain the chops and pat them dry with paper towels.

MAKE THE CHERRIES

Put the chipotle in a small bowl, cover with warm water, and soak until supple, about 20 minutes. Drain, stem, and finely chop the chipotle.

Heat the olive oil in a large, heavy skillet or saucepan over medium-low heat until shimmery. Add the garlic, ginger, and salt and cook, stirring frequently, until the garlic is fragrant but hasn't taken on color, about 1 minute. Add the cherries and chipotle, raise the heat to high, and cook, stirring frequently, until the cherries release their juices and those juices reduce to a thick syrupy glaze, about 8 minutes. Slide the pan off the heat, stir in the honey and lime juice, then return to the heat and simmer for 30 seconds to meld the flavors.

Cover and keep warm while you cook the pork chops.

MAKE THE DISH

Combine the coriander, cumin, and peppercorns in a medium skillet, set over high heat, and cook, shaking the skillet frequently once it gets hot, until the spices are very fragrant, about 3 minutes. Working in batches if necessary, coarsely grind the spices in a spice grinder, stir well, and spread them on a large plate to cool.

Preheat the oven to 350°F. One at a time, dredge the pork chops in the spice mixture, turning to coat them on all over (top, bottom, and sides) in a thin, even layer and pat gently to help the mixture stick. As they're coated, transfer them to a plate in a single layer.

Heat a large, heavy ovenproof skillet over medium heat until it's good and hot. Work in two batches to brown the pork chops. Add half the avocado oil, swirl to coat the skillet, then cook two of the pork chops, flipping once and using tongs to stand the chops on their fatty edge for a minute, until the visible pork is golden brown on all sides and the spices turn a few shades darker, about 6 minutes total. Transfer the chops to a sheet pan lined with a wire rack, wipe the skillet clean, and repeat with the remaining avocado oil and chops.

Put the sheet pan in the oven and roast until the chops are cooked to your liking. I recommend medium doneness (slightly pink in the middle) or until a thermometer inserted into the center of each chop registers 130°F to 135°F, about 12 minutes.

Let the chops rest for at least 10 minutes. Divide the chops among four plates, spoon on the cherry sauce, and drizzle with a little olive oil. Sprinkle on the cilantro, scallions, and oregano, and serve.

TAMARIND BBQ SPARE RIBS WITH SMOKY LONG-COOKED GREENS

Serves 4 to 6

Ribs are great on the grill, but they're just as tasty baked slowly in the oven. These really glow bright thanks to an overnight spice cure and a quick BBQ sauce made with ketchup, chipotle, and tamarind that gets sticky and charred under the broiler. The ribs go for a while in the oven, so why not throw on a pot of greens as they cook? Serve it all alongside Bread-and-Butter Squash Pickles (page 290).

For Curing and Cooking the Ribs

3 dried chipotle chiles, stemmed

2 small dried red chiles or ½ teaspoon red chile flakes

2 tablespoons coriander seeds

3 tablespoons kosher salt

3 tablespoons coconut sugar

1 tablespoon hot smoked paprika

5 pounds St. Louis–cut spareribs (about 2 racks), membranes removed

For the Collards and Serving

2 tablespoon extra-virgin olive oil

1 medium yellow onion, cut into ¼-inch-thick slices

6 large garlic cloves, smashed and peeled

1 teaspoon kosher salt

8 cups tightly packed stemmed, very roughly chopped collard greens (about 2 large bunches)

3 cups chicken stock, salted homemade or store-bought

1 dried chipotle chile

2 tablespoons coconut aminos

2 tablespoons apple cider vinegar

1 cup Tamarind BBQ Sauce (page 310)

CURE AND COOK THE RIBS

Combine the chipotles, dried red chiles, and coriander in a spice grinder and grind to a fine powder. Put the powder in a small mixing bowl, add the salt, sugar, and paprika, then stir well.

Put the ribs in a large, deep pan (it's fine if they overlap or stack) and sprinkle on the cure, using your hands to pack it all over them—some on the bottom and sides and the majority on the top, where most of the meat is. Cover and cure in the fridge, top-side up, for at least 12 hours or up to 24 hours.

After curing, preheat the oven to 250°F. Wrap each slab of ribs tightly in two layers of aluminum foil. Set a wire rack in a large sheet pan, add the rib packets, and cook until they're very tender (carefully un-wrap them and poke the thickest part between the ribs with the tip of a knife—it should go through easily), about 2½ hours. Remove the ribs from foil and let them rest for 20 minutes or let them cool completely and refrigerate them for up to 1 day.

MAKE THE COLLARDS AND FINISH THE RIBS

While the ribs cook, heat the oil in a large pot over medium heat until shimmery. Add the onion, garlic, and salt and cook, stirring frequently, for 1 minute. Add the collards, stock, and chipotle, stir well, and let it come to a gentle simmer.

Cook, stirring occasionally, until the collards are very tender (they go from shiny to dull when they're done) and the liquid has reduced to about 2 cups, about 1 hour. If the collards are done before the liquid reduces, turn up the heat to speed up the process. Stir in the coconut aminos and apple cider vinegar, simmer for 3 minutes more, then turn off the heat. Keep the collards warm.

When you're about ready to serve, preheat the broiler and set an oven rack to the top position. Slather about half of the BBQ sauce all over the tops and sides of the ribs. Broil the ribs on a sheet pan on the top rack until the sauce is glossy, sticky, and slightly charred, 10 to 12 minutes (or closer to 15 minutes if your ribs come straight from the fridge). Let them cool slightly, then cut into individual ribs, and serve with the remaining BBQ sauce and the collards.

BOUYON BEF

Serves 6 to 8

In Haiti, refrigeration still isn't ubiquitous, so cooks aggressively clean meat, washing it in vinegar, scouring it with sour oranges, and blanching it before cooking. It's one reason Haitian stews are so good: those sanitary measures morphing into marinades meant to replicate flavors born of need that turn out to be quite delicious. This savory, citrusy beef stew is just one great example, fragrant with chile and lime, clove and thyme. Plenty of vegetables (plantain, yucca, spinach) make it a meal.

For Marinating the Beef

2 pounds beef chuck roast or other stewing beef, cut into 2-inch cubes

2 juicy limes, halved

1 tablespoon kosher salt

1 tablespoon ground black pepper

1 cup Epis (page 296)

For the Dish

3 tablespoons extra-virgin olive oil

1 large yellow onion, cut into ¾-inch pieces

1 cup Epis (page 296)

1½ tablespoons kosher salt

1 Scotch bonnet or habanero chile, stemmed and finely chopped

7 cups beef or chicken stock, salted homemade or store-bought

6 fresh or dried bay leaves

2 cups ½-inch-thick half-moon slices peeled yucca

2 medium carrots, peeled and cut into ¼-inch-thick rounds

2 celery stalks, cut into ¼-inch pieces

1 large unripe plantain, peeled (see page 17) and cut into ½-inch-thick slices

1 large bunch spinach, stem bottoms trimmed

2 juicy limes, cut into wedges

MARINATE THE BEEF

Rinse the beef under cool running water, pat it dry, and put it in a bowl. Squeeze the juice of the limes over the beef, then rub the cut sides of the spent lime halves all over beef as well.

Evenly season the beef all over with the salt and pepper. Add the epis to the bowl and toss well to coat the beef. Cover and marinate in the fridge for at least 1 hour or up to 24 hours.

MAKE THE DISH

Remove the beef from the fridge, scraping off the marinade and reserving it in the bowl. Pat the beef dry with paper towels and transfer it to a plate. Heat 2 tablespoons of the oil in a large, heavy skillet over medium-high heat until shimmery. Working in batches to avoid crowding, brown the beef on each side, about 8 minutes per batch, transferring each batch to a plate when it's done. Take your time and make sure all six sides have a deep mahogany crust—the stew will be much better for it. Once you've browned the beef, add the onion to the skillet and cook, stirring frequently and scraping up brown bits, until it starts to color and soften, about 2 minutes. Turn off the heat.

In a large Dutch oven or wide pot, heat the remaining 1 tablespoon of oil over medium heat until shimmery. Add the epis, salt, and chile along with the reserved marinade. Stir well and cook, stirring constantly, until it smells great, about 1 minute.

Transfer the beef and its accumulated juices, along with the onion in the skillet, to the Dutch oven, add the stock and bay leaves, and stir. Reduce the heat to low, and cover the pot. Cook, checking every hour or so and adjusting the heat to maintain a very gentle simmer, until you can insert a knife tip through the beef with little resistance, 2 to 2½ hours.

Stir in the yucca, carrots, celery, and plantain. Increase the heat to bring the stew to a simmer, then reduce the heat again to gently simmer until the vegetables (especially the plantain, which takes the longest to cook) are tender, about 15 minutes. Finally, add the spinach and cook just until it wilts and turns bright green, about 2 minutes more. Serve with the lime wedges.

ROASTED BEEF TENDERLOIN WITH PARSNIP-ALMOND PUREE AND PICKLED SHIITAKES

Serves 4

Beef tenderloin is the focus of this dish, and I share a technique to maximize the enticing crust and ensure a tender interior. Lightning-quick pickled shiitakes update the classic duo of mushrooms and beef, while almonds add interest to a silky, rich parsnip puree.

For the Pickled Shiitake
3 tablespoons extra-virgin olive oil
½ pound stemmed shiitake mushrooms, halved or quartered if large
5 garlic cloves, thinly sliced
½ medium jalapeño chile, thinly sliced

1 teaspoon kosher salt
¼ cup unseasoned rice vinegar

For the Dish
Four 6-ounce center-cut tenderloin steaks (about 1½ inches thick)
1½ teaspoons kosher salt

½ teaspoon freshly ground black pepper
1½ tablespoons avocado oil
Parsnip-Almond Puree (page 294), warm
Small handful parsley leaves

MAKE THE PICKLED SHIITAKE

Heat the olive oil in a medium skillet over medium heat until nice and hot. Add the mushrooms and cook, flipping each piece once, until both sides are deep golden, about 4 minutes total.

Add the garlic, reduce the heat to medium-low, and cook, stirring occasionally, until the garlic is soft and fragrant, about 1 minute. Stir in the jalapeño and salt, and cook for a few seconds more, to season everything. Turn off the heat.

Add the vinegar and stir and scrape to dislodge any tasty bits that may have stuck to the pan. Keep them at room temperature until you're ready to serve.

MAKE THE DISH

Preheat the oven to 300°F. Pat the steaks dry, then season all over with the salt and pepper. Let them sit for 5 minutes so the salt has a chance to penetrate the meat.

Heat the avocado oil in a large, heavy ovenproof skillet over high heat until shimmery. Add the steaks and cook until both sides have a nice brown crust, about 1 minute per side. Next, use tongs to briefly sear the edges of the steaks, just to get a little color, about another minute. Transfer the skillet to the oven and cook until the steaks are done to your liking—I like mine medium-rare (aim for about 120°F on a thermometer), which takes about 3 minutes.

Transfer the steaks to a wire rack and let them rest for about 20 minutes. (Tenderloin needs plenty of time to rest.) Halve the steaks horizontally to expose the rosy center and serve them over the parsnip-almond puree. Spoon on the pickled shiitakes and the pickling liquid. Sprinkle on the parsley and serve.

SEARED RIB EYE STEAKS WITH KOREAN BARBECUE–STYLE SAUCE AND BANCHAN

Serves 4

I love to serve simply cooked rib eye in the mode of Korean ssäm, for which leafy greens wrap fish and meat. The beefy star of the show shares the stage with a riff on sweet-salty ssäm sauce and a few vegetable-forward supporting players made in the style of banchan, the assortment of little dishes that flesh out the Korean meal.

For the Cucumbers
2 Persian or small Japanese cucumbers, thinly sliced

¼ teaspoon kosher salt

2 tablespoons unseasoned rice vinegar

1 teaspoon toasted sesame oil

1 teaspoon raw sesame seeds, toasted (see page 26)

For the Mushrooms
1 tablespoon avocado oil

5 ounces stemmed shiitake mushrooms (about 2 cups), halved or quartered if large

½ teaspoon kosher salt

2 tablespoons coconut aminos

1 teaspoon finely chopped ginger

1 medium garlic clove, finely chopped

1 scallion, trimmed and thinly sliced

For the Steaks
2 rib eye steaks (about 1 inch thick and about 2 pounds total)

1 tablespoon plus 1 teaspoon kosher salt

1 tablespoon coarsely cracked black peppercorns

2 tablespoons avocado oil

For Serving
2 heads butter lettuce, trimmed and leaves separated

1 cup Korean Barbecue–Style Sauce (page 309)

Kimchi, homemade (page 279) or store-bought

MAKE THE CUCUMBERS
Combine the cucumbers and salt in a small bowl, toss well, and let sit for 10 minutes. Drain the cucumbers and gently squeeze them, discarding any liquid. Put them back in the bowl, add the remaining ingredients, and toss well. Let pickle at room temperature until you're ready to serve.

MAKE THE MUSHROOMS
Heat the oil in a medium skillet over high heat until shimmery. Add the mushrooms, reduce the heat to medium-high, and cook, stirring now and then, until golden and softened, 3 to 5 minutes. Stir in the salt and turn off the heat. Transfer the mushrooms to a bowl and let them cool to room temperature. Stir in the remaining ingredients and let marinate at room temperature until you're ready to serve.

COOK THE STEAKS
Preheat the oven to 350°F. Set a wire rack in a sheet pan. Evenly season the steaks with the salt and pepper on both sides and let them sit at room temperature for about 10 minutes so the salt can penetrate the beef.

Heat the oil in a very wide, heavy skillet (13 inches should do it) or two heavy skillets over high heat until very shimmery. Then wait 30 seconds or so, until the oil is especially hot but not smoking. Put the steaks in the pan, reduce the heat to medium-high, and cook, without messing with them, until the first side has developed a deep-brown crust, 2 to 3 minutes. Flip the steaks and cook the other side the same way,

2 to 3 minutes more. Use tongs to stand the steaks on their fat caps and cook for about 30 seconds, until they're crispy and deep golden brown as well.

Transfer the steaks to the rack in the sheet pan and finish cooking the steaks in the oven. I like mine medium-rare, so the flesh is deep pink with a hint of red and the fat has had the chance to melt a bit. After the steak has been in the oven for about 5 minutes, insert a meat thermometer into the center or prod the middle with a finger. When it registers 120°F or the flesh feels soft but with a little spring to it, the steak is ready. Let the steaks rest for 15 minutes (their internal temperature will rise to 125°F and the juices will redistribute through the meat, so they're nice and juicy throughout).

SERVE THE DISH

Slice the steak against the grain into ½-inch-thick slices, then into 2-inch pieces. Serve with the lettuce, sauce, mushrooms, cucumbers, and kimchi for making lettuce wraps and eating between bites.

THAI MUSLIM–STYLE BEEF CURRY

Serves 6

Green and red curries might hog the spotlight in the United States, but let me show you the beauty of brown. To me, this is the king of curries, the crown jewel of Thai-Muslim cooking, rich from coconut milk and beef and fragrant from dried spices like cinnamon, cardamom, cloves, and bay leaves—ingredients that reflect the influence of Persian and Indian cuisine on Thai food. Making it is a project, but one that's more than worth the effort. Use short ribs for an especially lavish version. Make it a meal with Cauliflower-Cashew Puree (page 295).

For the Curry Paste
1½ tablespoons green cardamom pods
1½ tablespoons fennel seeds
1½ tablespoons coriander seeds
2 teaspoons cloves
2 dried ancho chiles
2 dried New Mexico chiles
2 dried chipotle chiles
¼ cup Red Curry Paste (page 297)

For the Curry
3 pounds bone-in beef short ribs or cubed (about 2½ inches) boneless beef chuck or brisket
1½ tablespoons kosher salt
¼ cup avocado oil
4 large shallots, quartered
2-inch knob ginger, peeled and finely chopped
1 tablespoon finely chopped palm sugar or coconut sugar

3 cups well-shaken coconut milk
2½ cups chicken or beef stock, salted homemade or store-bought
⅓ cup raw cashews
1 tablespoon fish sauce
12 fresh or dried bay leaves
Seven 3-inch cinnamon sticks

MAKE THE CURRY PASTE
Preheat the oven to 350°F. Put the cardamom, fennel, coriander, cloves, and dried chiles on a small sheet pan and toast in the oven, stirring only if the spices at the edges look darker than those in the middle and keeping a close eye on the chiles so they don't get too dark, until fragrant and everything turns a shade darker, 5 to 7 minutes. Let cool briefly, stem the chipotle chile, then working in batches if necessary, grind it all in a spice grinder to a fine powder. Combine the powder and the red curry paste in a small bowl, stir well, and set aside.

MAKE THE CURRY
Put the beef in a large mixing bowl, season evenly with the salt, then add ¼ cup of the curry paste and mix well to coat the beef.

Heat 2 tablespoons of the oil over medium-high heat in a large Dutch oven until shimmery. Working in batches to avoid crowding, brown the short ribs, turning to sear the tops, bottoms, and sides until they're deep mahogany, about 3 minutes per side. Keep an eye on the spices and lower the heat slightly if they threaten to burn rather than turn deep brown. Transfer each batch to a plate when it's done.

Reduce the heat under the pot to medium, then add the remaining 2 tablespoons of oil and the remaining curry paste; stir well. Cook over medium heat, stirring every 20 seconds or so, until fragrant and slightly darker in color, about 1 minute. Add the shallots, ginger, and palm sugar and cook, stirring, for 2 minutes more to lightly brown the shallots. Return the beef to the pot, stir well to get the pieces coated in good stuff, then add the coconut milk, stock, cashews, fish sauce, bay leaves, and cinnamon sticks.

Stir as best you can, then raise the heat to medium-high and let it come to a simmer. Reduce the heat to maintain a very gentle simmer and cook, covered, checking occasionally to keep the simmer gentle, until the meat is fall-apart tender and the liquid has thickened significantly to the texture of rich gravy, about 3 hours. A layer of flavorful, auburn-colored oil will cover the curry, so be sure to scoop deep and stir a bit when you serve.

The curry keeps in the fridge for up to 4 days.

SHORT RIBS BRAISED WITH TAMARIND, LEMONGRASS, CHILES, AND LIME LEAVES

Serves 8 to 10

I treat short ribs to a long cook in a mixture of tamarind, coconut milk, galangal, chiles, and dark spices for my take on Indonesian rendang. By the time the beef is meltingly tender, the stewing liquid has transformed into a curry that's as thick as heavy cream and unforgettably flavorful—deep and floral, spicy and bright.

Admittedly one of the book's more demanding dishes, it makes a Sunday project to remember, your home filling with the warm aromas. During the long, hands-off cook, make carrot puree (page 295) and quick-pickle some cucumbers (page 291) for a meal to remember.

For the Curry Paste

6 green cardamom pods

6 whole cloves

Three 3-inch cinnamon sticks, roughly broken

3 star anise

15 small dried red chiles, stemmed and soaked in hot water until soft

10 large shallots, peeled and roughly chopped

4 large stalks lemongrass, trimmed (see page 15), bruised, then thinly sliced

3-inch knob ginger, peeled and thinly sliced against the grain

2-inch knob fresh galangal, peeled and thinly sliced against the grain

2-inch knob fresh turmeric, peeled and thinly sliced against the grain

1 bunch cilantro, bottoms trimmed, stems roughly chopped, leaves reserved for garnish

For the Dish

3 pounds beef short ribs, chuck, or brisket, cut into 2 x 1-inch pieces

¼ cup kosher salt

¼ cup avocado oil

½ cup virgin coconut oil

1 cup Tamarind Water (page 327)

½ cup coconut sugar or finely chopped palm sugar

5 cups well-shaken coconut milk

Three 3-inch cinnamon sticks

10 small dried red chiles, stemmed

15 fresh or frozen makrut lime leaves, center ribs removed

MAKE THE CURRY PASTE

In a small pan, combine the cardamom, cloves, cinnamon, and star anise, set it over medium heat, and toast, tossing frequently, until very fragrant, about 4 minutes. Let cool slightly, then transfer to a spice grinder and grind to a slightly coarse powder.

Drain the chiles, discarding the water. In a medium mixing bowl, combine the shallots, lemongrass, ginger, galangal, turmeric, cilantro stems, and the soaked chiles and mix well. In a blender and working in batches if need be, blend the mixture on high speed, stopping often to scrape down the sides and stir, until smooth, up to 4 minutes. Be patient—you'll get there! Transfer to a medium bowl and stir in the ground spices. The curry paste keeps in an airtight container in the fridge for up to 3 days and in the freezer for up to 4 weeks.

MAKE THE DISH

Preheat the oven to 350°F. Season the short ribs all over with 2 tablespoons of the salt.

In a large ovenproof pot or Dutch oven (wide enough for the beef to fit in about two layers later), heat the avocado oil over medium-high heat until it's very hot. Working in batches to avoid crowding, sear the short ribs until deep golden brown on all sides, about 10 minutes per batch. As they're done, transfer them to a plate. (If any bits in the pot start to blacken, wipe out the pot and add fresh oil.)

When all the short ribs are browned, reduce the heat to medium-low and add the coconut oil. When it's warm, add all of the curry paste and the remaining 2 tablespoons of salt and cook, occasionally stirring and scraping the pot to dislodge any bits, until the paste turns several shades darker and the dried spices smell especially fragrant, about 5 minutes.

Stir in the tamarind water and sugar and cook for 2 minutes or so, then add the coconut milk. Increase the heat to high, bring to a simmer, and cook, stirring, for 5 minutes to meld the flavors. Add the short ribs, along with any juices on the plate, arranging them so they're all nearly submerged by the liquid.

Add the cinnamon sticks, chiles, and makrut lime leaves, cover the pot, and cook in the oven (there's no need to stir) until the short ribs are tender enough to cut easily with a spoon, about 2 hours.

Divide the meat and sauce among serving bowls. Garnish with a small handful of cilantro leaves.

10

Ferments, Pickles,
and Preserves

A Note on Fermentation

Fermentation is an age-old technique that, now-adays, is all the rage. And for good reason. When good bacteria convert an ingredient's natural sugars to lactic acid—aka lacto-fermentation!—the result is a big bump in acidity and umami (two vital elements of deliciousness) and probiotics (which are great for you).

For anyone eager to delve deep into the craft, there are several excellent books—to name just two, Sandor Katz's *The Art of Fermentation* and René Redzepi and David Zilber's *The Noma Guide to Fermentation*—devoted to the subject. In this book, however, you'll find just a dozen or so recipes that demonstrate both the relative ease of the process—no crocks and weights necessary!—and the thrilling results.

Each one takes just a handful of ingredients and guides you through creating the right conditions for whatever you're fermenting—essentially creating an environment where good bacteria thrive and bad bacteria don't.

Besides glorious classics like kimchi and sauerkraut, which complete their transformation over a week or two, you'll also find wildly simple examples of fermentation's magic—cashews and coconut cream, pineapple and pine nuts—that morph quickly and with little effort into new ingredients entirely. Once they're fermented, they can hang in your fridge, often for many months, a new culinary tool at your disposal.

Each recipe will guide you to successful fermentation. Here, though, I've collected some general advice to keep in mind as you go.

- Make sure to clean fruits and vegetables destined for your fermentations especially well. And save anything verging on over-ripe for another purpose. It could kick off a proliferation of the wrong stuff.
- I typically ferment in glass jars. They're easy to clean (just a scrub with soapy water—no sterilization needed) and since they're clear, you have a front row seat to the process. For kimchi, which I like to make the old-school way with cabbage wedges, a Dutch oven works perfectly.
- For longer fermentations, it's essential that the ingredients ferment in an anaerobic environment. In other words, they shouldn't come in contact with air. To that end, the ingredients are submerged in a salty solution called a brine—submerged to lock out air and salty to kill off bad bacteria and flavor the ingredients. Note that you shouldn't use iodized salt to ferment, because iodine can inhibit the process.
- In many fermentations, you'll be asked to press down on the ingredients. This serves two purposes: First, it ensures that there are no pockets of air hiding out amidst the ingredients, and second, it forces the brine to the surface so it can cover the ingredients, creating a sort of natural seal. I often suggest adding a piece of parchment paper to the surface as an extra layer of protection in case any stray ingredients float.
- Even like vegetables vary in moisture content, so once in a while, you might find yourself without enough liquid to submerge the ingredients. Not to worry! Just make a quick brine (see the next page).

Quick Brine: Combine 1 cup of water and ½ tablespoon of Diamond kosher salt, stir until the salt completely dissolves, and use it to top off the liquid in the jar.

- You always want to wipe the inside top of your container clean so no little bits are hanging out and risk getting moldy.
- When I cover my jars, I add the lids loosely—not ajar, but not airtight either. As the good bacteria break down the sugars in the ingredients, you get lactic acid, which gives fermentations like these their characteristic tang, and carbon dioxide, which will bubble up through the liquid. A loose lid lets this carbon dioxide escape. Without an outlet, it'll still manage to escape along with some of your brine—all over your counter. An airtight lid is fine, too, as long as you unscrew the lid every few days (also known as "burping" the jar) to let the gas escape.
- The ideal place to ferment is anywhere out of direct sunlight where the temperature is 65°F to 70°F, give or take a few degrees. Within this range of temperatures, the good bacteria flourish at just the right speed. Too hot and some bacteria multiply too quickly and others don't thrive, leaving you with an off-flavor and sometimes with mushy ingredients or even mold. Too cold and the bacteria may not multiply at all. Of course, temperature, like life, isn't always predictable. In summer and in winter, you'll need to find a different spot. And while temperature is important, there's no need to run around your home with a laser thermometer—a spot that's a bit warmer than room temperature does the trick.

- If you follow these recipes carefully, you shouldn't have to worry about mold developing. Still, you should check your fermentations daily and make sure it's always covered in brine. If you spot a white film on the surface, don't worry—it's kahm yeast, a sign that fermenting conditions are just a little less than perfect. It's harmless, but skim it off the brine and remove any ingredients that have it, because it can multiply and give the fermentation an off-flavor. And don't mistake the bold, sour, funky (and even, in the case of cabbages and radishes, sulfurous) aromas of proper fermentation for the rankness of rot.
- Mold, however, is another matter. Anything fuzzy or colored (green, blue, gray, black) should have your attention. Every fermenter has their own response to its presence. For instance, if I spot a speck of mold, I'll carefully remove it and transfer the ferment to a clean jar. Anything more than a speck, I take a deep breath, toss the whole thing, and start over.
- Be sure to label your jars with a piece of tape scribbled with the date you began the fermentation and the day you intend to end it. It'd be a shame to do the work and then lose track. And don't be afraid to taste as you go. Not only is it cool to see how the flavor changes over time, but you might find you prefer your kimchi slightly less fermented or your sauerkraut a bit more fermented than I do mine.
- Be a nerd and take notes. They'll make you even more successful the next time around.

CREAMY FERMENTED PINE NUT DRESSING

Makes about 3 cups

When my former chef de cuisine, Jami Flatt, and I set out to make a dressing with all the pleasures of Caesar but without the dairy, we hit upon this concoction with a dead-simple ferment at its base. After just three days and with barely any effort (no salting, crocks, or weights!), pine nuts transform from mild and nutty to tangy, funky, and complex, like Parmesan, ready to be pulsed with basil for dairy-free pesto, sprinkled over salads to add tangy pop, and as they are here, whizzed with lemon, garlic, fish sauce, and olive oil for a bold, creamy dressing that goes great with classic romaine but tastes even better with hearty, healthy greens like kale, mustards, and chard.

1½ cups pine nuts

¾ cup lemon juice (from about 5 juicy lemons)

2½ tablespoons maple syrup

1 tablespoon fish sauce

4 medium garlic cloves, roughly chopped

½ small shallot, roughly chopped

1 fresh red Thai chile, roughly chopped

2½ teaspoons kosher salt

3 tablespoons extra-virgin olive oil

FERMENT THE PINE NUTS

Put the pine nuts in a clean 1-quart jar and pour in 1½ cups of cold tap water (they'll float, which is just fine). Cover the jar with a lid that fits loosely (nothing airtight and nothing ajar—you want just a little bit of airflow so carbon dioxide can escape during the fermentation). Let it sit at room temperature to ferment for 24 hours. The water will look slightly cloudy and tiny bubbles may appear around the pine nuts.

Drain the mixture, discarding the water, and rinse the pine nuts and the jar under cold running water. Return the pine nuts to the jar, cover with a fresh 1½ cups of cold tap water, cover loosely with the lid, and let it sit at room temperature for another 24 hours. Drain, rinse, and repeat the process once more for a total fermentation time of 72 hours.

MAKE THE DRESSING

After they've fermented for 72 hours, drain and rinse the pine nuts one last time. Put them in a blender along with the lemon juice, maple syrup, fish sauce, garlic, shallot, chile, and salt and puree on high speed until as smooth and creamy as possible, about 2 minutes. With the blender running on low speed, slowly drizzle in the oil.

The dressing keeps in an airtight container in the fridge for up to 5 days.

SOURED CASHEW CREAM

Makes about 3 cups

Just like the pine nuts in the previous recipe, these cashews ferment for three days, then get blended to a velvety, nutty, dairy-free sour cream. It's wonderful as the backbone of an herby dressing for crunchy greens (page 35), for a tangy drizzle for soups and tacos, and as a topping for baked potatoes.

1½ cups raw cashews   2 teaspoons kosher salt

FERMENT THE CASHEWS

Put the cashews in a clean 1-quart jar and add 1½ cups of cold tap water (they'll float, which is just fine). Cover the jar with a lid that fits loosely (nothing airtight and nothing ajar—you want just a little bit of air-flow so carbon dioxide can escape during the fermentation). Let it sit at room temperature to ferment for 24 hours. The water will look slightly cloudy and tiny bubbles may appear around the cashews.

Drain the mixture, discarding the water, and rinse the cashews and the jar under cold running water. Return the cashews to the jar, cover with a fresh 1½ cups of cold tap water, cover loosely with the lid, and let it sit at room temperature for another 24 hours. Drain, rinse, and repeat the process once more for a total fermentation time of 72 hours.

MAKE THE SOURED CASHEW CREAM

After they've fermented for 72 hours, drain and rinse the cashews one last time. Combine the cashews, salt, and 1½ cups of fresh water in a blender and blend on high speed until super smooth, about 2 minutes.

The sour cream keeps in an airtight container in the fridge for up to 5 days.

COCONUT CRÈME FRAÎCHE

Makes about 2½ cups

The fat from coconuts is extremely versatile. Here I treat coconut cream like, well, actual cream and turn it into a kind of crème fraîche. A little heat, some vinegar, and a low-key ferment for three days gives you a tangy, satiny product with the mild sweetness and nutty quality of coconut. I love it with cold, crunchy vegetables, ranch-style please (page 148).

I highly recommend boxed coconut cream for this recipe. Look for the Aroy-D brand in markets with a robust Southeast Asian section.

One 33.8-fluid ounce box
coconut cream, refrigerated for
at least 16 hours

1 tablespoon apple cider
vinegar

PREP THE COCONUT CREAM

Flip the chilled box of coconut cream upside down and open it from the bottom. All the rich fat, which had risen to the top of the container in the fridge, will now be on the bottom. Pour off the liquid and because it's tasty, reserve it for another purpose. Give your blender an extra good cleaning.

Gently melt the fat in a small saucepan over low heat. Once it's completely melted, transfer the liquid to the blender, add the apple cider vinegar, and blend it for 5 seconds to combine the vinegar and cream. This brief blending helps emulsify the fat and vinegar, ensuring the final texture is nice and smooth.

FERMENT THE COCONUT CREAM

Transfer the mixture to a clean glass jar (you want at least an inch of space between the cream and the rim) and let cool, uncovered, for 30 minutes. Cover the jar opening with cheesecloth and secure it with a rubber band. Put the jar in a warm area out of direct sunlight (see page 267 for tips) and let the mixture ferment for 3 days. It'll thicken slightly but still be liquid.

After 3 days of fermenting, remove the cheesecloth and chill it in the fridge, uncovered, until it's cold and set (it'll get thick and creamy), at least 2 hours. Covered with an airtight lid, it keeps in the fridge for up to 10 days. If the mixture separates, just use the thick cream on top, not the liquid on the bottom.

SRIRACHA

Makes about 1¾ cups

Sriracha isn't just the familiar garlicky hot sauce (green cap, rooster on the bottle) invented in California by a Vietnamese immigrant. In Thailand, there's a product, said to be named for the Gulf Coast town of Si Racha, that has a different flavor profile with more brightness and sweetness and less heat. Mine clocks in somewhere in the middle with a nontraditional twist—it's fermented for a week, the seven days of hands-off waiting heightening the acidity and developing the umami. Pureed, the chiles and garlic become an all-purpose hot sauce you'll burn through at rapid speed. Leave it chunky and you have a sambal-like garlic-chile sauce with the same great flavors.

1 pound moderately spicy fresh red chiles, such as Fresnos or ripe jalapeños, roughly chopped

3 tablespoons finely chopped palm sugar or coconut sugar

15 medium garlic cloves, peeled

2 tablespoons kosher salt

PUREE THE INGREDIENTS
Combine all the ingredients in a food processor and process to an evenly coarse puree (the chiles and garlic should be no bigger than chile seeds). Transfer the mixture to a clean 16-ounce glass jar and cover with a lid that fits loosely (you want just a little bit of airflow to let carbon dioxide escape, so nothing airtight and nothing ajar).

FERMENT THE SAUCE
Put the jar in a warm area out of direct sunlight (see page 267 for tips) and let the mixture ferment for 7 days. You might spot some bubbles or a little foam. That's just fine.

   After the 7 days of fermentation, it's ready to be used as is or pureed in a blender on high speed until super smooth, about 1 minute. It keeps in an airtight container in the fridge for up to 6 months.

ACHAR

Makes about 3½ cups

This South Asian pickle comes packed with warm, nutty spices and develops its tang during a brief fermentation. I like to give the achar treatment to firm fall fruits and vegetables, like apples, roots, and winter squash. Choose one, use them all, or expand the roster with cauliflower, parsnips, persimmons, or the more traditional green mango.

1½ pounds assorted root vegetables (such as carrots, beets, turnips, celeriac), apples, and winter squash

1½ teaspoons yellow mustard seeds

1½ teaspoons fennel seeds

1½ teaspoons black peppercorns

1½ teaspoons coriander seeds

1 teaspoon cumin seeds

5 small dried red chiles

1½ tablespoons paprika

1½ teaspoons ground turmeric

1 tablespoon kosher salt

1½ cups avocado oil

MAKE THE ACHAR

Peel, rinse, and dry the vegetables well. Roughly chop them into about 1-inch pieces. You want to use about 4 cups. Working in batches if necessary, pulse the vegetables in a food processor until they're coarsely ground, similar to the texture of ground meat.

Combine the mustard, fennel, peppercorns, coriander, cumin, and dried chiles in a medium skillet, set over high heat, and toast, shaking the pan and tossing the spices every 30 seconds or so, until the spices are very fragrant and toasty, about 2 minutes. Add the paprika and ground turmeric to the pan, turn off the heat, and stir and toss for 15 seconds or so to warm up the ground spices. Grind in a spice grinder to a very coarse powder (the whole spices should be no larger than halved).

Transfer the spice mixture to a medium bowl, add the salt, and stir well. Add the vegetables and toss well to coat in the spice mixture. Transfer to a clean container, cover tightly, and let it sit in a warm area out of direct sunlight (see page 267 for tips) for 12 hours to ferment.

After the 12 hours, combine the vegetable mixture with the oil in a medium bowl, stir well, and transfer to a 1-quart jar. Gently press on the solids so they're submerged by a thin layer of oil. Cover tightly and store in the fridge for 1 week before you eat it.

The achar keeps in the fridge for up to 3 months.

FERMENTED CABBAGE WITH TURMERIC AND GREEN CHILES

Makes about 6 cups

The alchemy of sauerkraut is at work in this cabbage ferment. The addition of garlic, hot green chiles, and fresh turmeric creates a very refreshing pickle with round acidity, mellow garlic flavor, and bright heat.

A 3-pound head napa cabbage, wilted outer leaves removed, rinsed

1 large yellow onion, cut into ⅛-inch-thick half-moons

2 tablespoons kosher salt

15 large garlic cloves, thinly sliced

10 fresh green Thai chiles or 4 small serrano chiles, thinly sliced

6 inches turmeric root, peeled and sliced into ⅛-inch-thick coins

PREP THE CABBAGE

Quarter the cabbage lengthwise, and cut the cabbage into 1½-inch pieces. Transfer the cabbage to a large mixing bowl, add the onion and salt, and spend a good minute massaging the cabbage and onion with your hands, rubbing the salt against them. Let the mixture sit at room temperature for 30 minutes so the salt starts to draw out the cabbage juices (which mix with the salt to create a brine). The cabbage will have turned brighter green and gone slightly limp.

Repeat the massaging process, this time rubbing any visible salt and the brine against the surface and between the leaves of the cabbage. Add the garlic, chiles, and turmeric, toss well, and let the cabbage mixture sit for 30 minutes more.

Transfer the cabbage and the accumulated juices to a clean 2-quart glass jar (or divide it evenly between two 1-quart jars). Firmly press the cabbage mixture so a thin layer of liquid rises to the surface to submerge the mixture by at least 1 inch. If there's insufficient liquid, top it off with this quick brine (see page 267).

FERMENT THE CABBAGE

Cover the jar loosely with a lid (nothing airtight and nothing ajar—you want just a little bit of airflow so carbon dioxide can escape during the fermentation).

Put the container in a warm area out of direct sunlight (see page 267 for tips) and let the mixture ferment for 14 days or up to 30 days for an especially tangy and deep flavor. Sometimes the gas produced during the fermentation pushes some of the cabbage out of the brine; if so, use a clean fork to push the cabbage back into the brine to make sure it's submerged.

After it has fermented to your liking, close the lid tightly and keep in the fridge for up to 1 year.

SAUERKRAUT

Makes about 6 cups

Some histories trace fermented cabbage back to China, where the cruciferous vegetable was fermented with rice wine. By the time it made its way to Europe, and Germany in particular, salt replaced the wine and modern sauerkraut was born. At its heart, it's just two ingredients—three, if you count time—and the complex, sour, mouth-fillingly delicious product that it becomes demonstrates the miracle of fermentation. I like the subtle peppery, citrusy quality caraway seeds add to the picture, but they're optional. Not optional, in my opinion, is a kitchen scale. Because the ingredients are so few, a precise ratio of cabbage to salt by weight is vital to the success of the ferment. Note that I use Diamond kosher salt for this recipe.

3¾ pounds green cabbage, wilted outer leaves removed, rinsed

2 tablespoons caraway seeds (optional)

2 tablespoons Diamond kosher salt

PREP THE SAUERKRAUT
Quarter the cabbage, then cut out and discard the core. Use a sharp knife or mandoline to slice the quarters crosswise into very thin slices, about ⅛ inch thick. Use a kitchen scale to weigh 3½ pounds of the prepped cabbage to use for this recipe.

   Combine the cabbage, caraway seeds (if using), and salt in a large bowl and toss well. Let the cabbage sit for 30 minutes so the salt draws out the cabbage juices (they'll mix with the salt to create a brine). Next, spend a good minute squeezing and massaging the cabbage with your hands, rubbing any visible salt and the brine against it. The cabbage will have turned brighter green and gone limp. Let it sit 20 minutes more.

   Transfer the cabbage and the accumulated juices to a clean 2-quart glass jar (or divide it evenly between two 1-quart jars). Firmly press the cabbage, forcing it as far down as possible—to rid the mixture of any pockets of air and to bring liquid to the surface that submerges the cabbage by at least 1 inch. If there's insufficient liquid, top it off with this quick brine (see page 267).

FERMENT THE SAUERKRAUT

Cover the jar loosely with a lid (nothing airtight and nothing ajar—you want just a little bit of airflow so carbon dioxide can escape during the fermentation). Put the jar in a warm area and out of direct sunlight (see page 267 for tips) and let the cabbage ferment for 14 days (for kraut with a nice balance of sour and crunch) or up to 28 days (for kraut that's extra sour and more tender). Sometimes the gas produced during the fermentation pushes some of the cabbage out of the brine; if so, use a clean fork to push the cabbage back into the brine to make sure it's submerged.

Once it's fermented, close the lid tightly and keep the sauerkraut in the fridge for up to 1 year.

CABBAGE KIMCHI

Makes about 12 cups

Kimchi, the Korean fermented pickle, comes in more than 200 varieties, spicy and not, made with everything from radishes and cucumber to mustard greens and, best known in the West, cabbage. The jarred product is easier to get than ever, but that doesn't mean you shouldn't make it yourself. The project is extremely gratifying and not difficult. You salt cabbage, massaging to help the vegetable expel its water. The water and salt mingle to make a brine, then you mix in gochugaru (the hot, slightly smoky Korean chile flakes) and aromatics like ginger and garlic. Fermentation melds and transforms these flavors, creating a tangy, funky, pungent, and vibrant condiment that enlivens anything you eat it with.

Once it's fermented, it's charged with flavor and also sufficiently preserved to keep for a long, long time in the fridge. (I don't think I can legally recommend this, but I have five-year-old kimchi in my fridge that's slightly fizzy and completely delicious.) I like to ferment the cabbage in large wedges, snipping off pieces with scissors when I want some, but you can absolutely use chopped cabbage (into, say, 2-inch pieces) to make kimchi that's ready to use straight out of the jar.

Note: As kimchi ferments, it has a pungent aroma that overtakes all others in your home. Embrace it—it means you're creating something delicious.

A 3-pound head napa cabbage, wilted outer leaves removed, rinsed

⅓ cup kosher salt

1 large yellow onion, cut into ⅛-inch-thick half-moons

1 large carrot, cut into ⅛-inch-thick matchsticks (a mandoline helps)

3 x 3-inch piece daikon radish, peeled and cut into ⅛-inch-thick matchsticks (a mandoline helps)

7 large garlic cloves, finely chopped

6 scallions, trimmed and cut into 2-inch pieces

2-inch knob ginger, peeled and finely chopped

¾ cup gochugaru (Korean chile flakes)

PREP THE KIMCHI

Cut the cabbage into eighths through the core, so the pieces remain intact. Transfer the cabbage to a large mixing bowl.

Sprinkle on the salt and spend a good minute massaging the cabbage with your hands, rubbing the salt against the surface and between the leaves of the cabbage. Let the cabbage sit at room temperature for 30 minutes so the salt starts to draw out the cabbage juices (which mix with the salt to create a brine). The cabbage will have turned brighter green and gone slightly limp. Repeat the massaging process, this time rubbing any visible salt and the brine against the surface and between the leaves of the cabbage. Let the cabbage sit for 30 minutes more.

In the meantime, combine the onion, carrot, daikon, garlic, scallions, ginger, and chile flakes in a medium mixing bowl and mix it well.

When the cabbage has been brining for 1 hour total, rinse it under cold water to wash off the brine and visible salt from the surface and between the leaves. Drain well, giving the wedges a good shake.

Working with one cabbage piece at a time, use clean hands (or gloves to avoid chile hands) to rub the chile mixture between the cabbage leaves and onto the surface. As they're done, transfer them to a wide,

(cont.)

high-rimmed container (I use a 4-quart Dutch oven here) that'll hold all the cabbage compactly and whose rim will come at least a ½ inch above the cabbage. When you've added the eight pieces of cabbage, spoon any remaining chile mixture on top.

Firmly press on the cabbage so a thin layer of liquid rises to the surface and more or less submerges the cabbage. If there's insufficient liquid, top it off with this quick brine (see page 267). Next, use a sheet of parchment paper to cover the entire surface and press down gently to make sure no cabbage or vegetables are directly exposed to the air.

FERMENT THE KIMCHI

Cover the container with a lid that fits loosely (nothing airtight and nothing ajar—you want just a little bit of airflow so carbon dioxide can escape during the fermentation). Put the container in a warm area out of direct sunlight (see page 267 for tips) and let the kimchi ferment for 7 days.

Once it's fermented, transfer the kimchi to one large or several smaller clean jars, close the lids tightly, and store in the fridge for up to 1 year.

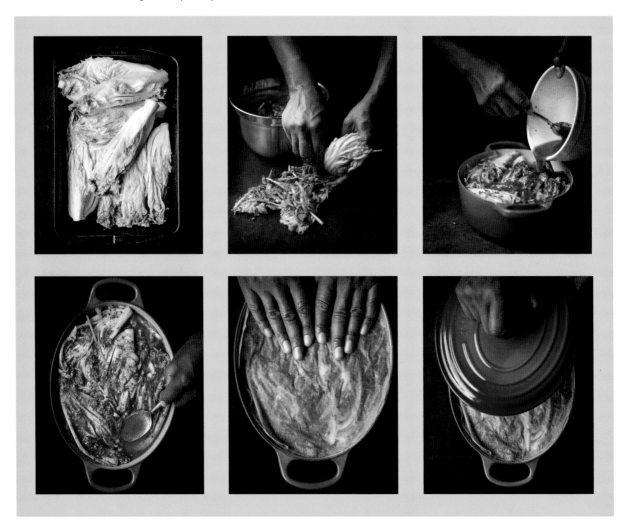

RADISH AND SPRING ONION KIMCHI

Makes about 6 cups

Kimchi is a category, not a single preparation. For example, there is no cabbage here and no chile either. But this take on white kimchi is still a thrill—whole radishes, greens and all, fermented in a savory brine of garlic, ginger, and spring onions. Use scallions when the pretty purple bulbs of spring onions go away.

2 pounds small radishes with unblemished greens, radishes quartered

2 bunches slim spring onions, trimmed and thinly sliced
8 medium garlic cloves, peeled

4-inch knob ginger, peeled and thinly sliced against the grain
1 tablespoon kosher salt

PREP THE KIMCHI
Quarter the radishes, keeping the greens attached as best you can. It's okay if some pieces of radish don't have greens attached. Put the radishes and spring onions in a medium mixing bowl. Combine the garlic, ginger, salt, and ½ cup of water in a blender and puree until completely smooth. Pour the blended mixture over the radishes and onions in the bowl, toss to coat well, and let it all sit at room temperature for 30 minutes so the salt starts to soften the radishes and draw out their juices.

Transfer the mixture to a clean 2-quart glass jar (or divide it evenly between two 1-quart jars). Firmly press the radish mixture so a thin layer of liquid rises to the surface to submerge it by at least 1 inch. If there's insufficient liquid, top it off with this quick brine (see page 267).

FERMENT THE KIMCHI
Cover the jar loosely with a lid (nothing airtight and nothing ajar—you want just a little bit of airflow so carbon dioxide can escape during the fermentation). Put the container in a warm area out of direct sunlight (see page 267 for tips) and let the kimchi ferment for 5 days.

Once it's fermented, close the lid tightly and keep in the fridge for up to 6 months.

ICY FERMENTED PINEAPPLE

Makes about 6 cups

The sweet-tart, tropical flavors of pineapple make a particularly refreshing flaky ice. But a week fermenting in a simple brine transforms these straightforward pleasures into a sophisticated treat with notes of lychee, passion fruit, and a bit of funk. A flurry on top of gingery sautéed peaches (page 355) makes a stunner of a light summer dessert.

To choose a pineapple that's good and ripe, look for fruits that have a yellow or golden (not a green) hue to their skin, that are heavy for their size, and that smell fragrant when you give them a close sniff.

1 ripe pineapple, top and bottom trimmed off to reveal the flesh

2¼ teaspoons kosher salt
½ cup maple syrup

1 juicy lime

PREP THE PINEAPPLE
Stand the pineapple on a cutting board and use a chef's knife to carve off the skin. Carve off the brown eyes, quarter the pineapple, and cut the flesh from the core. Next, cut the flesh into 1-inch pieces and transfer to a clean 2-quart jar. Discard the core.

Combine 3 cups of cold water and 2 teaspoons of the salt in a medium mixing bowl, stir well to dissolve the salt, and pour enough of the salty water into the jar to cover the pineapple by 2 to 3 inches, discarding any extra. Press a small piece of parchment paper onto the surface to make sure no pineapple is directly exposed to the air.

FERMENT THE PINEAPPLE
Cover the jar with a lid that fits loosely (nothing airtight and nothing ajar—you want just a little bit of airflow so carbon dioxide can escape during the fermentation). Put the jar in a warm area out of direct sunlight (see page 267 for tips) and let the pineapple ferment for 7 days. The liquid will look cloudy and the pineapple's color will have faded slightly.

MAKE THE ICY PINEAPPLE
After the 7 days of fermenting, drain the pineapple well. Combine the pineapple, maple syrup, and the remaining ¼ teaspoon of salt in a blender. Use a Microplane to grate the lime's zest into the blender, then halve the lime and squeeze the juice into the blender. Blend on high speed until as smooth as possible, about 2 minutes.

Pour the puree into a glass or ceramic container that'll hold the amount in a depth of about 1½ inches (a 9 x 12-inch baking dish works well). Cover and freeze until frozen through, about 4 hours or up to 2 days.

Thirty minutes before you're ready to serve, take the mixture from the freezer and use the tines of a fork to scrape it into fairly fine, flaky shaved ice. Return the ice to the freezer for about 30 minutes more, so it's nice and firm. Serve immediately or cover and keep in the freezer for up to 2 weeks.

PIKLIZ

Makes about 8 cups

Pikliz is the most iconic Haitian condiment, a fiery, crunchy cabbage relish that's in practically every family's fridge and a common sight on the beaches of Haiti, where men sell grilled seafood on makeshift grills and scoop homemade pikliz from plastic bottles that once held soda. We serve it with almost everything: fried green plantains (page 83) and taro root fritters (page 87), lobster (page 208), and whole fish (page 212). Yet all that fruity heat (eight Scotch bonnet chiles!), acidic punch, and cabbage crunch will excite everyone's table, whether you're grilling chicken or scrambling eggs.

As a chef, I'm tempted to speed up prep and cut all these vegetables with a mandoline. But I actually recommend cutting everything by hand, like the Haitian women in my life do. It takes a little longer but gives the pikliz a rustic, more dynamic quality when each bite has a slightly different shape and flavor. In other words, my mom cuts everything by hand and so should you!

½ medium head green cabbage, quartered, cored, and thinly sliced (about 6 cups)

1 large white onion, cut into thin half-moon slices

¼ cup kosher salt

2 medium carrots, peeled and julienned or cut into thin rounds

8 Scotch bonnet or habanero chiles, stemmed, halved, and thinly sliced

2 large shallots, cut into thin half-moons

1 cup distilled white vinegar

1 cup lime juice (from 8 to 10 juicy limes)

MAKE THE PICKLE

Combine the cabbage, onion, and salt in a large bowl, toss well, and let sit for 10 minutes so the cabbage and onion soften a bit. Add the carrots, chiles, and shallots, and toss well. Add the vinegar and lime juice and mix well. Let sit for 10 minutes more, then give it one more good mix.

Transfer the mixture to a narrow 2- to 3-quart container with an airtight lid and use a big spoon to press down on the mixture (it's okay if it's still not totally submerged in liquid). Cover and refrigerate for at least 18 hours, mixing once halfway through. It keeps in the container in the fridge indefinitely but it's best within 6 months.

QUICK-PICKLED RED ONIONS

Makes about 4 cups

A brief tumble with salt and another with vinegar turns red onions into this bright, crisp, pink pickle that brings a pop of acidity to elevate asparagus salad (page 39), watermelon-tomato soup (page 152), or your simplest dishes.

4 cups sliced (¼-inch half-moons) red onions (about 2 medium)

1½ teaspoons kosher salt

1½ cups red wine vinegar, plus more if necessary

MAKE THE PICKLE

Combine the onions and salt in a medium mixing bowl, toss well, and set aside for 15 minutes so the salt has a chance to pull out some of the water from the onions. Add the vinegar, stir and toss well, and set aside for 15 minutes more.

Stir once more and transfer to a 1-quart jar, topping it off with more vinegar if necessary to submerge the onions. Let them pickle for at least 4 hours at room temperature or even better, cover and refrigerate for 12 hours before eating.

The onions keep in the fridge for up to 3 months.

CHILE AND LIME–PICKLED RHUBARB

Makes 4 cups

When rhubarb's here, you know spring is, too. Yet that's only one reason I'm so into it. I also love the crisp texture, gorgeous pink color, and unique, invigorating tartness. This bold pickle helps preserve the vegetable past its short season, with ginger, chiles, and mint keeping the flavors fun. Use it to brighten beets (page 52), stir it into yogurt sauces, or add olive oil to turn it into a quick vinaigrette for crisp greens.

1 pound rhubarb, trimmed and cut into ¼-inch-thick slices

3-inch knob ginger, peeled and cut into thin matchsticks

3 large mint sprigs

2 small moderately spicy fresh red chiles, such as Fresnos, thinly sliced

¾ cup red wine vinegar

¾ cup coconut sugar, finely chopped palm sugar, or date syrup

½ teaspoon kosher salt

¾ cup lime juice (from 6 to 8 juicy limes)

MAKE THE PICKLE

Combine the rhubarb, ginger, mint, and chiles in a medium mixing bowl and stir well.

Combine the vinegar, coconut sugar, and salt in a small pot and set it over high heat. Bring the mixture to a boil, then immediately turn off the heat, stirring to help the last of the sugar dissolve. Pour the hot liquid over the rhubarb mixture, add the lime juice, and stir well. Let it cool to room temperature.

Transfer to a narrow jar or container, so the rhubarb is just submerged in the liquid. Cover tightly and refrigerate for 12 hours before using.

The pickles keep in the fridge for up to 3 months.

PRESERVED LEMONS

Makes 4 lemons

From North Africa to the Middle East to South Asia, preserved lemons enliven dishes with brightness and super-pronounced lemon flavor. High-quality brands exist—Les Moulins Mahjoub, for instance—but making them yourself is a breeze, plenty of salt and lemon juice transforming the entire fruit into a dynamic dish enhancer. Sliver the peel and use it to perk up dressings, soft-boiled eggs with asparagus (page 109), and crispy skinned fish (page 191).

   And while most recipes call for the peel alone, the flesh and liquid have tons of flavor, too. I even add chopped whole preserved lemons to chicken stews, and make them into dressings with olive oil. You could even spoon them into dips like hummus (page 143) and ranch (page 148).

4 large lemons, washed
   especially well
1 cup kosher salt

6 fresh or dried bay leaves
6 small dried red chiles

6 tablespoons lemon juice
   (from about 2 juicy lemons)

PREP THE LEMONS

Trim off the nub at each end of the lemons. One by one, stand the lemons upright and use a sharp knife to almost cut them in half lengthwise, stopping about ½ inch from the bottom. Rotate the lemon and make another similar cut, as if you were quartering the lemon, but again stopping about ½ inch from the bottom.

   Put ¼ cup of the salt at the bottom of a clean 1-quart mason jar. Working over a bowl and one at a time, sprinkle about ½ tablespoon of salt into each lemon, gently pulling the quarters apart without breaking the lemons into pieces. The salt should cover any exposed lemon flesh. Once they're salted, add the lemons to the jar along with any salt loose in the bowl, pressing on them so they release some juice and tucking the bay leaves and chiles between the lemons. Top with the remaining salt, then pour in the lemon juice.

CURE THE LEMONS

Close the jar tightly, shake well, and let the lemons cure at room temperature for 3 days, each day giving the jar a flip and a good shake.

   After the third day, top up the liquid in the jar with water if necessary to completely submerge the lemons. Close tightly again, shake well, and refrigerate for at least 3 weeks before using. Now it's ready to use and keeps in the fridge for up to 6 months.

   For the recipes in this book, briefly rinse the lemons to remove excess salt, scrape out the flesh, and use only the peel.

BREAD-AND-BUTTER SQUASH PICKLES

Makes about 3½ cups

Summer squash, crisp onions, and fresh turmeric root step in to freshen up this classic American pickle. Sweet and sour, seasoned with mustard seeds and cloves, the gorgeous pickle provides bracing, golden relief to any rich and fatty situation, like my BBQ ribs (page 253).

2 cups thin half-moons zucchini (about ½ pound)

2 cups thin half-moons yellow summer squash (about ½ pound)

1 tablespoon kosher salt

1 cup apple cider vinegar

¼ cup maple syrup

1 tablespoon yellow mustard seeds

½ medium yellow onion, cut into thin half-moons

4 inches fresh turmeric, peeled, halved lengthwise, and thinly sliced, or 1 teaspoon powdered

9 whole cloves

6 medium garlic cloves, thinly sliced

MAKE THE PICKLE

Combine the zucchini, summer squash, and salt in a medium heatproof mixing bowl, toss really well, and let sit for 10 minutes so the vegetables soften and release water (to absorb more flavor from the pickling liquid later).

When they have softened, combine the remaining ingredients in a small pot and bring to a boil over high heat. Boil for 30 seconds to mellow the onion and garlic, then turn off the heat. Let the mixture cool for 2 minutes, then immediately pour it over the zucchini and squash. Toss well, and let it pickle, uncovered and stirring halfway through, for at least 2 hours before using.

To store them longer, transfer to a 1-quart jar, cover, and store in the fridge for up to 3 months.

VIETNAMESE-STYLE PICKLES

Makes about 3 cups

My go at do chua, the carrot-and-daikon pickle common on the Vietnamese table, brings the same sweet, tart crunch that makes them such a delight with grilled meat (page 244) and crispy-skin fish (page 191), along with tons of fresh herbs. I use a mandoline to slice the vegetables extra thin, which is pretty and gives them a great texture.

4 medium carrots, peeled and very thinly sliced

1 medium yellow onion, cut into very thin half-moon slices

A 6-inch piece daikon radish, peeled, quartered, and very thinly sliced

2 small moderately spicy fresh chiles, such as jalapeños, Fresnos, or a mixture, very thinly sliced

2 tablespoons kosher salt

2 cups unseasoned rice vinegar

¾ cup honey

MAKE THE PICKLE

Combine the vegetables and chiles in a large heatproof mixing bowl, add the salt, and toss really well. Let sit for 10 minutes.

Combine the vinegar, honey, and 1 cup water in a small pot and stir well. Set the pot over high heat, bring to a boil, and immediately turn off the heat. Pour the liquid into the bowl with the vegetables, stir well, and let it fully cool.

Transfer to a narrow container in which the liquid will submerge the vegetables. Cover and refrigerate for at least 4 hours or up to 6 months.

QUICK-PICKLED CUCUMBERS

Makes about 6 cups

Fabulous for cutting the richness of rendang-style short ribs (page 262) and for eating out of hand, these have just the right balance of tang and salt. I like Persian cucumbers for this pickle, but other crunchy, thin-skinned varieties, like English or Japanese, work, too. Just be sure to halve them and scoop out their seeds before slicing.

8 large Persian cucumbers, thinly sliced

2 medium shallots, cut into thin half-moon slices

2 moderately spicy fresh red chiles, such as Fresnos, thinly sliced

2 teaspoons kosher salt

1½ cups unseasoned rice vinegar

MAKE THE PICKLE

In a medium mixing bowl, combine the cucumbers, shallots, and chiles, sprinkle on the salt, and toss well. Set aside for 5 minutes. Pour on the vinegar, mix well, and let pickle for at least 1 hour, stirring once halfway through.

For longer storage, transfer to a narrow container in which the liquid will submerge the vegetables, cover with an airtight lid, and keep in the fridge for up to 3 months.

11

Purees, Sauces, Dressings, Oils, Butters, and Milks

Three Vegetable Purees

These three silky purees make luscious accompaniments to savory meat dishes, perfect for sopping up rich curries (page 260 and 262) and adding creaminess to a lean cut of beef (page 257). They're dead-simple: you simmer vegetables with aromatics until they're so tender they begin to fall apart, then you whiz them in the blender and you're ready to serve.

PARSNIP-ALMOND PUREE

Makes about 4 cups

½ cup extra-virgin olive oil
5 garlic cloves, peeled
1 large shallot, roughly chopped

2½ teaspoons kosher salt
4 cups peeled, chopped (about 1 inch) parsnips (about 4 large)

½ cup nut milk, homemade (page 321) or store-bought
⅓ cup raw almonds

MAKE THE PUREE

Heat the oil in a medium pot over medium heat until shimmery. Add the garlic, shallots, and salt and cook, stirring occasionally, until the shallots soften and brown at the edges, about 2 minutes. Add the parsnips, nut milk, and almonds along with 2 cups of water.

Increase the heat to high, bring the liquid to a boil, and reduce the heat to maintain a moderate simmer. Cook until the parsnips are so tender they start to fall apart and the nut milk has evaporated and only the translucent oil remains, about 20 minutes. Let cool slightly, then blend the mixture on high until silky smooth with little flecks of almond skin, about 3 minutes. Keep warm to serve.

Fully cooled, it keeps in an airtight container in the fridge for up to 3 days.

CAULIFLOWER-CASHEW PUREE

Makes about 5 cups

6 cups cauliflower (small florets and roughly chopped stems), from 1 small head

1 cup raw cashews
⅔ cup nut or seed milk, homemade (page 329) or store-bought

4 large garlic cloves, smashed and peeled
1 tablespoon kosher salt

MAKE THE PUREE

Combine the ingredients in a medium pot along with 2 cups of water, set over high heat, and bring it to a simmer. Adjust the heat to maintain a moderate simmer and cook until the cauliflower is completely tender and the liquid has completely evaporated, about 30 minutes. Let it cool slightly, then puree in a blender on high, occasionally stopping to scrape the puree down the sides and toward the blade if necessary, until silky smooth, about 3 minutes. Keep warm to serve.

Fully cooled, the puree keeps in an airtight container in the fridge for up to 3 days.

CARROT-COCONUT MILK PUREE

Makes about 3 cups

4 cups peeled, chopped (about ½ inch) carrots (4 to 6 large)
½ cup well-shaken coconut milk

½ cup extra-virgin olive oil
2½ teaspoons kosher salt
5 garlic cloves, peeled

1-inch knob ginger, peeled and roughly chopped against the grain

MAKE THE PUREE

Combine all the ingredients along with 1 cup of water in a medium-large pot. Set it over high heat, bring to a boil, and reduce the heat to maintain a moderate simmer. Cook, stirring occasionally, until the carrots are so tender they start to fall apart and the coconut milk has completely evaporated and only the translucent oil remains, 35 to 40 minutes.

Let it cool slightly, then transfer the mixture to a blender and blend on high speed, stopping and stirring if necessary, until silky smooth, 1 to 2 minutes. Keep warm to serve.

The puree keeps in an airtight container in the fridge for up to 3 days.

EPIS

Makes about 4 cups

Don't let the list of ingredients throw you. A quick spin in a food processor turns them into epis, an all-purpose Haitian seasoning used to marinate meat and fish, enliven meatloaf (page 238), and flavor stews, like this stunner made with beef (page 254). Use it to give anything a Haitian kick.

½ cup extra-virgin olive oil

3 tablespoon white wine vinegar

3 tablespoons lime juice (from 2 juicy limes)

3 tablespoons fresh thyme

2 tablespoons kosher salt

10 garlic cloves, peeled

4 whole cloves

3 large shallots, roughly chopped

2 celery stalks, roughly chopped

1 medium green bell pepper, stemmed, seeded, and roughly chopped

1 medium white onion, roughly chopped

1 medium parsley bunch, bottoms trimmed, roughly chopped

1 small cilantro bunch, bottoms trimmed, roughly chopped

1 bunch scallions, trimmed and roughly chopped

3 Scotch bonnet or habanero chiles, stemmed

MAKE THE EPIS

Combine all the ingredients in a large mixing bowl and toss really well. Working in batches if necessary, process in a food processor or pulse in a blender into a chunky puree (the consistency should be similar to that of chunky pesto).

The epis keeps in an airtight container in the fridge for up to 7 days and in the freezer (in small portions, for ease of use) for up to 1 month.

RED CURRY PASTE

Makes about 2 cups

Your new secret weapon in the kitchen, this blended paste of lemongrass and galangal, dried chiles and cilantro, and spices ignites the flavor of many dishes in this book, including whole fish (page 211), duck curry (page 217), curried watermelon (page 180), or peach curry (page 206).

Note: Even my blended version of curry paste takes some effort, but the good news is it makes more than what you'll need for any one recipe and freezes quite well. I suggest freezing in tablespoon portions: Scoop 1-tablespoon mounds of the paste onto a wax paper–lined plate, put them in the freezer until fully frozen, then transfer them to an airtight container and freeze for up to 3 months.

40 small dried red chiles, stemmed

¼ cup plus 1 tablespoon black peppercorns

1 tablespoon cumin seeds

1 tablespoon coriander seeds

3 tablespoons turmeric powder

6-inch knob ginger, peeled and thinly sliced against the grain

1 cup roughly chopped shallots

½ cup roughly chopped cilantro stems

3 large stalks lemongrass, trimmed (see page 15), bruised, then thinly sliced

3-inch knob fresh galangal, peeled and thinly sliced against the grain

MAKE THE CURRY PASTE

Combine the chiles, peppercorns, cumin, and coriander in a medium skillet, set it over high heat, and toast, shaking the pan and tossing the spices every 30 seconds or so, until the spices are very fragrant and toasty, about 2 minutes. Let cool slightly on a plate, then grind in a spice grinder to a fairly fine powder. Transfer the mixture to a medium mixing bowl, add the turmeric, and stir well.

Combine the ginger, shallots, and cilantro stems in a blender and alternate between blending and

stopping to scrape down the sides and stir until a semi-smooth mixture comes together. Add the lemongrass and galangal, then blend again, stirring and scraping as necessary, until you have a stiff, crumbly paste. Depending on your blender, it could take as long as 5 minutes. You might need to add a little water to help blend—if so, add a tablespoon at a time and up to 4 tablespoons total. Be patient—you'll get there!

Transfer the blended mixture to the bowl with the spices and stir really well.

The curry paste keeps in an airtight container in the fridge for up to 1 week and in the freezer (see Note) up to 3 months.

AROMATIC CHILE PASTE

Makes about 1¾ cups

With this rich, fragrant paste at the ready, you'll have the ammunition to spice up nearly anything on your table. It's naturally sweet from garlic and shallots, hot from the one-two punch of both fresh and dried chiles, and loosely held together by vibrant red oil infused with all those savory, aromatic flavors. It enlivens soups and stews, marinades for fish and meat, dips (page 139) and quick sautés (page 179) and grilled vegetables (page 58). Or simply set some on the table so guests can apply it as a finishing touch.

1¼ cups avocado oil

16 large garlic cloves, thinly sliced

2 cups sliced (about ¼ inch) shallots (about 4 large)

2 teaspoons kosher salt

1 cup small dried red chiles (about 65)

7 fresh red Thai chiles, stemmed and halved

MAKE THE PASTE

Heat ¼ cup of the oil in a wide, heavy skillet over medium heat until shimmery. Add the garlic, shallots, and salt, and cook, stirring occasionally, until they're golden brown and fully soft, 10 to 12 minutes.

Add the dried and fresh chiles along with the remaining 1 cup of oil. Wait for the oil to get hot and the dried chiles to puff slightly, then cook, stirring occasionally, until the dried chiles turn a brighter shade of red but before they turn brown, about 2 minutes. Turn off the heat and let the mixture cool to warm. Transfer to a blender and puree until fairly smooth, 1 to 2 minutes.

The paste keeps in an airtight container in the fridge for up to 2 months. Stir well before using.

XO SAUCE

Makes about 2 cups

Born in Hong Kong in the high-flying '80s, this oily, funky, chewy sauce takes its name from fancy booze, even though it doesn't contain any. The "XO" in the title is a nod to "extra old" cognac, meant to indicate luxury in the form of crazy-expensive dried scallops that provide an umami punch to the classic. In their place, I look to dried tomatoes, which when teamed up with dried shrimp create a similar alchemy.

You can buy the sauce (though jarred versions are typically packed with additives and soy oil), but I highly recommend making your own for use with clams (page 183) and charred red cabbage (page 74) or otherwise unadorned chicken, pork, or fish.

1 cup dried shrimp

1 cup avocado oil

¼ cup sun-dried tomatoes, finely chopped

8 large cloves garlic, finely chopped

5 fresh Thai chiles, thinly sliced

3 small dried red chiles, stemmed and snipped into thin slices with scissors

1 large shallot, finely chopped

1-inch knob ginger, peeled and finely chopped

1½ teaspoons kosher salt

2 tablespoons coconut aminos

1 tablespoon honey

MAKE THE SAUCE

Put the shrimp in a small mixing bowl, add enough hot water to cover, and soak the shrimp for 20 minutes. Drain well, then finely chop.

Combine the shrimp, oil, tomatoes, garlic, fresh and dried chiles, shallot, ginger, and salt in a large, heavy skillet and stir well. Set the skillet over medium heat and let the oil heat up. Once it reaches a rapid

bubble as the moisture escapes the aromatics (you'll also see a little white foam on the surface), start stirring occasionally and cook until the ingredients have softened and everything turns brown a bit at the edges, about 10 minutes. Be careful not to let anything get too dark.

Stir in the coconut aminos and honey, lower the heat to medium-low, and keep cooking until the foam disappears and the ingredients below the oil are golden brown, shriveled, and a little chewy, about 15 minutes more.

Let the sauce cool (it'll turn a mahogany color when it does). It keeps in an airtight container in the fridge for up to 3 months.

HARISSA

Makes about 2 cups

To make my version of harissa, I look to the mild heat and dried-fruit quality of dried Mexican chiles to echo the chiles traditionally used to give the deservedly famous North African condiment its deep, complex flavor. Use the spice paste in a dead-simple dressing for asparagus (page 39), along with olives and preserved lemon for roasted fish (page 191), or for punching up cashew hummus (page 140).

4 dried ancho chiles
4 dried chipotle chiles
4 dried New Mexico chiles
4 dried pasilla chiles
1 tablespoon coriander seeds

1 tablespoon cumin seeds
½ cup extra-virgin olive oil, plus extra for storage
5 large garlic cloves, peeled
1 teaspoon smoked paprika

1 tablespoon kosher salt
2 tablespoons date syrup or honey
2 tablespoons sherry vinegar

MAKE THE HARISSA

Pull the stems off the chiles and discard them. Cut a slit in the side of each dried chile, open it up like a book, and scrape out the seeds. (I just toss the seeds into my jar of red chile flakes to use another day.) Brittle dried chiles may crumble a bit, which is just fine.

Put the dried chiles in a medium skillet and set over high heat. When the pan starts to heat up (you'll start to smell the chiles), start tossing the chiles every 30 seconds or so until they're toasty, turn a shade or so darker, and puff up slightly, about 3 minutes. Soak the chiles in a bowl of hot water for 15 minutes to soften them.

In the meantime, combine the coriander and cumin in the skillet, set it over high heat, and toast, shaking the pan and tossing the spices every 30 seconds or so, until the spices are very fragrant and toasty, about 2 minutes. Let cool slightly.

When the chiles are soft, drain them well, discarding the soaking water, then transfer the chiles to a blender. Add the toasted spices, the ½ cup of olive oil, and the remaining ingredients, then blend, occasionally stopping to stir and scrape the mixture down the sides and toward the blades if necessary, to make thick paste that's as smooth as possible, about 2 minutes. Super smooth is great and so is slightly coarse.

Transfer the harissa to a narrow container with an airtight lid and pour in just enough extra olive oil to cover with a thin layer of oil to help it last longer. It keeps covered in the fridge for up to 1 month.

SPICY CASHEW DRESSING

Makes about 2½ cups

Thick enough to serve as a dip and creamy enough to dress dark, hearty greens, this tangy, coconut-y mixture, with just a little bit of heat from curry paste, is my legume-less rendering of the peanut sauce that comes with Thai satay.

1 cup unsalted roasted cashews

1 cup well-shaken coconut milk

2 medium shallots, roughly chopped

4-inch knob ginger, peeled and roughly sliced against the grain

3 tablespoons coconut aminos

2 tablespoons unseasoned rice vinegar

2 tablespoons red curry paste, homemade (page 297) or store-bought

MAKE THE DRESSING

Combine all the ingredients in a blender and blend on high speed to a super-smooth, thick puree, about 2 minutes.

The dressing keeps in an airtight container in the fridge for up to 1 week.

VIETNAMESE-STYLE CHILE-LIME SAUCE

Makes about 2½ cups

My version of nuoc cham, the Vietnamese dipping sauce, is even more intensely flavored than the classic, packing a wallop of acid and salty, funk, and heat. I often treat it as a dressing, too, for just about everything, from salads to fish and meat. It leaves a big impression, especially considering it takes mere minutes to make.

1 cup fish sauce
½ cup unseasoned rice vinegar
⅓ cup honey

¼ cup lime juice (from about 2 juicy limes)
8 fresh Thai chiles, thinly sliced

6 medium garlic cloves, finely chopped

MAKE THE DRESSING
Combine all the ingredients in a container with an airtight lid along with ½ cup of warm water and stir well.
   The dressing keeps covered in the fridge for up to 1 month.

GINGER-SCALLION SAUCE

Makes about 2 cups

Pouring smoking hot oil over chopped ginger and scallions scalds them, coaxing out a delicate sweetness and floral quality that makes this Chinese condiment so craveable. It's tough to think of something it *doesn't* improve—eggs or duck legs (page 220), grilled chicken or grilled broccoli (page 61). The method is so easy that, even at home, I sometimes take the time to get fancy with the ginger, cutting it into teeny, tiny cubes, á la brunoise.

3 bunches scallions, trimmed and thinly sliced	4-inch knob ginger, peeled and very finely chopped	1 teaspoon kosher salt
		¾ cup avocado oil

MAKE THE SAUCE

Combine the scallions, ginger, and salt in a medium heatproof mixing bowl and stir well.

Heat the oil in a small skillet over high heat just until it smokes, about 3 minutes. Immediately pour the oil over the ginger and scallions. You'll hear the oil sizzle and pop as it scalds the mixture and see the scallions turn bright green. Stir well, then flatten the scallions and ginger so they're covered by the thin layer of oil that rises to the top.

Refrigerate the bowl, uncovered, so it cools quickly, then use it or keep it covered in the fridge for up to 1 week.

LEMONGRASS–BLACK PEPPER DRESSING

Makes about 2¼ cups

My recipe for this classic Vietnamese marinade doubles as a spirited sauce. Use it to infuse pork, chicken, and high-fat fish like salmon or black cod with flavor, and also to finish those same proteins, roasted or grilled.

1 cup fish sauce

1 cup honey

4 large stalks lemongrass, trimmed (see page 15), bruised, and finely chopped

4 large garlic cloves, very finely chopped

1 large shallot, very finely chopped

1 tablespoon coarsely ground black peppercorns

4 fresh Thai chiles, thinly sliced

MAKE THE DRESSING

Combine all the ingredients in a container with an airtight lid and stir well. The dressing keeps covered in the fridge for up to 1 month.

JALAPEÑO OIL

Makes about 1¼ cups

Jalapeño chiles are just barely cooked in oil then blended for a condiment that you'll dream about. More flavorful than hot, the grassy flavor of these green chiles is on full display, adding dimension to sautéed greens, eggs, guacamole (page 144), grilled lobster (page 208), and even chicken soup (page 164). Once you have it in your fridge, I bet you'll expand this list.

1 cup avocado oil

3 large jalapeño chiles, stemmed and halved lengthwise

½ teaspoon kosher salt

MAKE THE OIL

Combine the oil, chiles, and salt in a medium saucepan, set it over medium-high heat, and wait until bubbles form around the chiles. Reduce the heat to medium-low and let the chiles sizzle just until they turn a brighter shade of green, about 2 minutes. Turn off the heat and let the mixture cool.

Transfer to a blender, making sure to scrape any salt that has collected in the bottom of the pan into the blender as well. Puree until as smooth as possible, about 1 minute.

The oil keeps in an airtight container in the fridge for up to 3 weeks.

TOASTED CHILE OIL

Makes 1½ cups

Make this and there's no going back to bottled. And anyway, it takes three ingredients and less than ten minutes, plus the process fills your kitchen with the chiles' glorious perfume. Drizzle it into bowls of soup (coconut based ones, page 163, for example) or hearty salads (say, the cucumbers on page 32), mix it into sauces and marinades, and just get creative!

1½ cups avocado oil

1½ cups dried small red chiles (about 1½ ounces), stemmed

1 teaspoon kosher salt

MAKE THE OIL

Combine the oil, chiles, and salt in a small pot and set it over medium heat. Once the oil is hot, after 3 to 5 minutes, start stirring every 30 seconds or so until the chiles turn a bright shade of red but before the oil sizzles, about 2 minutes more. Immediately remove the pot from the heat and let the oil cool slightly. Transfer to a blender and blend on high speed until as smooth as possible, about 2 minutes.

The oil keeps in an airtight container in the fridge for up to 6 months. Stir well before using, because the oil and chile solids tend to separate.

SLOW-ROASTED CHERRY TOMATOES

Makes about 1½ cups

A low oven concentrates the goodness of hot-weather beauties, leaving you with wrinkly, slightly chewy flavor bombs—the sweetness, acidity, and umami of tomatoes times ten. Whatever they touch gets better. Think tomatoes on tomatoes in a salad (page 47) or fish, roasted chicken, and vegetable sides invigorated with little explosions of summer. Top-notch tomatoes are amazing here, but the method even helps less-than-perfect specimens reach closer to their full potential.

2 pints cherry tomatoes, halved

8 large garlic cloves, thinly sliced

3 tablespoons extra-virgin olive oil

1 tablespoon kosher salt

1 teaspoon coconut sugar

Handful basil leaves

MAKE THE TOMATOES

Preheat the oven to 350°F.

Combine all the ingredients in a large mixing bowl and toss gently but well. Spread the mixture on a sheet pan in a single layer, flipping the tomatoes cut-sides up, and keeping everything concentrated in the middle of the pan (any at the edges of the pan risk burning). Roast until the tomatoes shrivel, brown at the edges, and are no longer juicy, anywhere from 40 minutes to 1 hour, depending on how juicy the tomatoes were to start.

Let the tomatoes cool completely and discard the basil. They keep in an airtight container in the fridge for up to 1 week.

AFRICAN PEPPER SAUCE

Makes about 2 cups

Pepper sauce is a West African condiment used in many parts of the continent, with plenty of local variations (dried shrimp in Nigeria, smoked fish in Ivory Coast, just to name a few). I make mine by roasting tomatoes, onions, bell peppers, and chiles to concentrate their flavors and natural sugars then whizzing them in the blender. This sauce gets its bold heat and depth from Scotch bonnets (or habaneros) and ginger and works great with everything from roasted vegetables, birds, and fish, like crispy-skin salmon and sweet plantains (page 205).

2 medium tomatoes (about ¾ pound total), cored and cut into sixths

2 Scotch bonnet or habanero chiles, stemmed

2-inch knob ginger, peeled and thinly sliced against the grain

1 medium red bell pepper, stemmed, seeded, and cut into 2-inch pieces

1 medium red onion, cut into eighths

6 large garlic cloves, peeled

1 tablespoon kosher salt

½ cup avocado oil

MAKE THE SAUCE

Preheat the oven to 450°F. Combine all the vegetables and aromatics in a large baking dish or sheet pan (it should fit the vegetables in a crowded, more or less single layer). Season with the salt and evenly drizzle with the oil. Roast until the tomatoes have shriveled slightly, the onion is tender, and everything is browned at the edges, about 25 minutes.

Let the mixture cool slightly, then puree it, including the oil, in a blender until smooth, 1 to 2 minutes. It keeps in an airtight container in the fridge for up to 5 days.

KOREAN BARBECUE–STYLE SAUCE

Makes about 3 cups

Dates provide body and sweetness and Korean chile flakes bring their distinctive smoky, faintly sweet character to this great sauce that channels ssämjang, the condiment I can't get enough of when eating Korean barbecue. Rib eyes (page 258) love it and so does any rich meat, fish, and even root vegetables.

2 tablespoons avocado oil

10 scallions, trimmed, greens thinly sliced, whites roughly chopped, separated

8 garlic cloves, roughly chopped, plus 3 more, minced

1 cup pitted Medjool dates

1 cup coconut aminos

½ cup unseasoned rice vinegar

3 tablespoons honey

2 tablespoons fish sauce

2 tablespoons gochugaru (Korean chile flakes)

2 tablespoons toasted sesame oil

1 tablespoon mushroom powder, homemade (page 326) or the Nom Nom Paleo brand

1 teaspoon kosher salt

2-inch knob ginger, peeled and roughly sliced against the grain

1 medium shallot, minced

MAKE THE SAUCE

Heat the avocado oil in a medium saucepan over medium heat until shimmery. Add the scallion whites and chopped garlic and cook, stirring occasionally, until lightly browned, about 2 minutes. Add the dates and cook, stirring, for 1 minute more, to soften them a bit.

Add the coconut aminos, vinegar, honey, fish sauce, chile flakes, sesame oil, mushroom powder, salt, ginger, and 1 cup of water, raise the heat, and bring to a lively simmer. Cook, stirring occasionally, until the dates fall apart to make a chunky, thick, and saucy mixture, about 8 minutes.

Let the mixture cool slightly, then puree it in a blender until very smooth and thick. Transfer to a bowl and let cool to room temperature. Stir in the shallot, scallion greens, and minced garlic and serve.

The sauce keeps in an airtight container in the fridge for up to 1 week. Serve at room temperature.

TAMARIND BBQ SAUCE

Makes about 2 cups

Slather this tangy BBQ sauce on ribs and chicken just before they're done, applying some high heat to let it set up on the flesh and char to bring an element of bitter to balance the sticky sweetness. Even vegetables take well to it. My favorite? Toss some of the sauce with grilled beets for a killer side.

2 tablespoons avocado oil

12 large garlic cloves, roughly chopped

3-inch knob ginger, peeled and thinly sliced against grain

1 teaspoon black peppercorns

2 teaspoons kosher salt

1 cup all-natural ketchup

¾ cup Tamarind Water (page 327)

¼ cup coconut aminos

¼ cup coconut sugar

1 dried chipotle chile, stemmed

MAKE THE SAUCE

Heat the oil in a medium skillet over medium heat until shimmery. Add the garlic, ginger, black peppercorns, and salt, and cook, stirring occasionally, until the garlic is golden, 3 to 5 minutes.

Add the ketchup, tamarind water, coconut aminos, coconut sugar, and chipotle, stir well, and let it come to a simmer. Cook, stirring occasionally, until the chipotle has softened, about 3 minutes. Transfer the mixture to a blender and blend on high speed until smooth, about 1 minute.

The sauce keeps in an airtight container in the fridge for up to 3 weeks.

PRUNE CHAR SIU SAUCE

Makes about 2½ cups

Prunes give my soy-free riff on Chinese BBQ sauce hoisin vibes with a deep, complex sweetness. Perfect for roasted or grilled pork, it's quite special painted onto ultra-tender duck legs (page 220), then broiled until sticky and charred.

1 cup pitted prunes
1 tablespoon avocado oil
8 large garlic cloves, peeled
1½ teaspoons kosher salt
½ cup coconut aminos
¼ cup honey

¼ cup apple cider vinegar
2 tablespoons blackstrap molasses
1 tablespoon hot smoked paprika
1 teaspoon toasted sesame oil

1 teaspoon Eight Spice (page 326), or Chinese five-spice powder plus 1 crumbled small dried red chile
1 teaspoon ground white pepper

MAKE THE SAUCE

Put the prunes in a small mixing bowl, pour in 1 cup of hot water, and let them soak for 20 minutes or so to soften them.

Heat the avocado oil in a small pot over medium heat until shimmery. Add the garlic and salt and cook, stirring frequently, until golden and slightly softened, 1 to 2 minutes. Take the pot off the heat, add the remaining ingredients along with the prunes and their soaking liquid, and stir well. Return the pot to medium heat, bring to a simmer, and cook for about 3 minutes to bring the flavors together.

Transfer the mixture to a blender and blend on high speed to a smooth, BBQ sauce consistency, about 2 minutes.

The sauce keeps in an airtight container in the fridge for up to 10 days.

GINGERED MANGO CHUTNEY

Makes about 3 cups

Any fans of the jarred stuff will go nuts for the golden, fruity product you can make yourself in 15 minutes with ripe mangoes, ginger, cinnamon, and chiles.

¾ cup maple syrup

4 cups peeled and diced (about 1 inch) ripe mango (about 4)

3 large garlic cloves, very thinly sliced

Three 3-inch cinnamon sticks

2 moderately spicy fresh red chiles, like Fresnos, very thinly sliced

3-inch knob ginger, peeled and julienned (1½ x ⅛ inch)

½ cup unseasoned rice vinegar

1 teaspoon kosher salt

MAKE THE CHUTNEY

Heat the maple syrup in a medium saucepan over medium-high heat until it starts to bubble. Adjust the heat to cook at a lively simmer and stir frequently until it turns a shade or so darker and reduces by about one third (it'll cling to a spoon rather than dribbling right off), about 3 minutes.

Stir in the mango, garlic, cinnamon, chiles, and ginger and let the syrup come to a simmer. Reduce the heat to cook at a moderate simmer, stirring occasionally, until the mango is spoon-tender and turns a slightly deeper, darker yellow, about 10 minutes. Stir in the vinegar and salt and keep cooking, stirring occasionally, until there's no more liquid left in the pan, about 2 minutes more.

The chutney keeps in an airtight container in the fridge for up to 2 weeks.

MY RED MOLE

Makes about 9 cups

There is not one mole, but many. This storied category of Mexican sauce takes innumerable forms depending on its region of origin and the cooks who make it. Its color can range green to yellow, brick red to chocolate brown to midnight black. Its composition can be fairly simple or remarkably complex. This one was formulated by a Haitian man with the help of an Indian woman (thank you, Kumi!) who grew up adoring Mexican food in Tucson, Arizona. It's admittedly one of the most time-consuming recipes in this book—thank you to Claudette, a Mexican friend, for helping me streamline it *a bit*—a labor of love that loves you back.

Part of the magic of this mole, and the types of moles it's modeled after, is the way its many ingredients—the chiles and spices and fruit and nuts and seeds—all come together to make something harmonious and sublime, with no ingredient shining more than the others. Instead, they converge to make a velvety and rich, bittersweet and tangy, delicately spicy and warmly spiced sauce that you'll want to eat with everything.

Note: Piloncillo (also called panela) is a minimally processed sweetener made from the juice of sugarcane cooked to concentrate the sweetness and then left to harden often as discs or conical blocks. Common in Latin American cooking, it has a complex flavor that's worth seeking out in order to make this mole. Look for it in Latin American markets or online.

For Frying and Soaking the Chiles
6 dried New Mexico chiles
3 dried guajillo chiles
2 dried ancho chiles
2 dried chipotle chiles
1 cup avocado oil

For Frying the Aromatics, Fruit, and Nuts
5 garlic cloves, peeled
2 large yellow onions, chopped into 1-inch pieces

2 medium tomatoes (about ¾ pound), cored and cut into 1-inch pieces
2 very ripe bananas (dark yellow and brown) or damn-that's-ripe plantains (see page 18), peeled and cut into 1-inch-thick slices
⅓ cup unsulphured dried sweet cherries
⅓ cup raisins
¼ cup raw hazelnuts
¼ cup raw pecans
¼ cup raw pepitas (hulled pumpkin seeds)
4 fresh or dried bay leaves

2 star anise
1½-inch piece cinnamon stick
1 tablespoon dried thyme
1 tablespoon dried oregano, preferably Mexican

For Finishing the Mole
4 cups chicken stock, salted homemade or store-bought
3 tablespoons kosher salt
¼ cup finely chopped piloncillo or coconut sugar
3 ounces dark chocolate, roughly chopped

FRY AND SOAK THE CHILES

Pull the stems off the chiles and discard them. Cut a slit in the side of each New Mexico, guajillo, and ancho chile, open it up like a book, and scrape out the seeds into a bowl, setting the bowl and chiles aside.

In a large Dutch oven, heat the oil over medium heat until just shimmery. Working in a few batches to avoid crowding and frying similar-size chiles in the same batch, fry the chiles until they puff and get shiny,

(cont.)

about 30 seconds per batch. As they're done, use a medium strainer to scoop out the chiles and transfer them to a large bowl, keeping the oil in the pot. When they're all fried and in the bowl, pour in 4 cups of warm water and set aside to let the chiles soften, about 20 minutes.

FRY THE AROMATICS, FRUIT, AND NUTS

In the meantime, to the large pot still over medium heat, add the garlic, onions, tomatoes, bananas, cherries, raisins, hazelnuts, pecans, pepitas, bay leaves, and the reserved chile seeds. Cook, stirring occasionally, until the onions have shriveled a bit and turned golden with brown at the edges and the nuts and seeds are deep golden brown and toasty, 8 to 10 minutes. Add the star anise and cinnamon, turn off the heat, and stir for a minute or so, until they toast a bit. Transfer the mixture to a medium bowl.

Scoop out the chiles, reserving the chile soaking liquid, and transfer them to a blender along with 1 cup of the soaking liquid. Blend on high speed to a super-smooth paste, stopping, stirring, and scraping the sides as needed to get it all smooth, 2 to 3 minutes. Be patient. Getting them super smooth is important for the rich, velvety texture of the finished mole. Transfer the chile mixture back to the pot. Add the onion mixture, including the oil, to the blender, then add the thyme, oregano, and 1 cup of the chile soaking liquid and blend—again, stopping, stirring, and scraping the sides as well as gradually adding more water as necessary—until super smooth, 2 to 3 minutes. Transfer to the pot with the chile puree.

FINISH THE MOLE

Stir well, return the pot to medium heat, and cook (it'll steam, sizzle, and pop as it fries, so consider partially covering the pot), stirring frequently, until the mixture turns about two shades darker to a dark-chocolate brown and thickens to the texture of a slightly loose paste, about 15 minutes.

Add the chicken stock, salt, piloncillo and any remaining chile soaking water and let it come to a simmer. Partially cover the pot (it'll splatter as it thickens) and cook at a moderate simmer, stirring every 10 minutes or so, until it's rich and reduced, thick but still velvety and saucy, about 30 minutes. Turn off the heat, add the chocolate, and stir until completely melted and well combined. Just before serving, bring it back up to simmer for a moment.

The mole keeps in an airtight container in the fridge for up to 3 days.

STRAWBERRY JAM

Makes about 3 cups

A relatively brief simmer in maple syrup turns high-season strawberries into tender, concentrated red jewels. A splash of lemon ensures they keep the bright flavor that makes the fruit such a delight. Keep this distillation of the season on hand for nut butter toasts and endless desserts, from topping custards (page 363) to swirling into homemade ice cream (page 348).

2 pounds strawberries, hulled and halved

1 cup maple syrup
2 tablespoons lemon juice

½ teaspoon kosher salt

MAKE THE JAM

Combine all the ingredients in a medium, heavy pot, such as a 5- to 6-quart Dutch oven. Bring to a lively simmer over medium-high heat and cook, stirring every 3 minutes or so, until the strawberries collapse and are super tender and all the strawberry juices have reduced to a thick, shiny glaze, 18 to 20 minutes. Test by running a flexible spatula across the bottom of the pot. If it takes a few seconds for the sauce to fill in the space left by the spatula, the jam is ready. Let it cool completely.

The jam keeps in an airtight container in the fridge for up to 2 weeks.

Nut and Seed Butters

Nut and seed butters are my perfect food. High in protein and good fats, toasty and rich, they're just the thing for a quick, guilt-free treat, whether you pair it with honey or jam or, as I definitely never do, take down unembellished spoonfuls as a midnight snack. I love making them at home, which is both rewarding and economical (those alt nut butters can be pricey!).

The options are endless, but the three in this section should get you going and are just the thing for the recipes in this book. Nutty and rich, sunflower seed butter is chunky after you fold in whole seeds at the end. Pecans buddy up with a little honey. And cashews come alive with the heat of chiles, channeling one of my favorite treats as a kid: the Scotch bonnet–spiked peanut butter that relatives would bring from Haiti when they came to visit my family in Queens, and that we could barely wait to spread over crisp cassava crackers and top with guava jelly. (Of course, omit the chiles and you have an all-purpose version.)

Blending Tips: The process is a cinch in a high-wattage blender, like a Vitamix, but you can totally make these butters in a standard, low-wattage blender (say, 500 watts at minimum). It just takes a little patience and elbow grease.

Follow the following recipes, then blend on high speed until the nut or seed mixture looks like a coarse crumble that the blades can no longer catch because it's stuck to the sides of the jar. Stop the blender, then use a flexible spatula to push the mixture down the sides toward the blade. Repeat this process—blending, stopping, and scraping the sides—until the crumble turns into a dry paste, then a grainy puree, and finally a mixture that catches in the blades without your assistance. Now, blend until the mixture becomes a silky, smooth, very thick liquid, loose enough to very slowly drip off the spatula. The whole process should take about 10 minutes.

SPICY CASHEW BUTTER

Makes about 2 cups

1 pound raw cashews
(about 3 cups), roasted (see
page 26) and cooled

6 tablespoons avocado oil
1 teaspoon kosher salt

2 Scotch bonnet or
habanero chiles

MAKE THE CASHEW BUTTER
Combine the ingredients and blend on high speed until the cashews have formed a smooth butter, about 3 minutes, nonstop, in a high-wattage blender, like a Vitamix, or about 10 minutes in a standard blender (see Blending Tips, page 317).

The butter keeps in an airtight container in the fridge for up to 1 month.

HONEY PECAN BUTTER

Makes about 2 cups

1 pound shelled raw pecans
(about 4 cups), roasted (see
page 26) and cooled

2 tablespoons avocado oil
1 tablespoon honey

½ teaspoon kosher salt

MAKE THE PECAN BUTTER
Combine the ingredients and blend on high speed until the pecans have formed a smooth butter, about 3 minutes, nonstop, in a high-wattage blender, like a Vitamix, or about 10 minutes in a standard blender (see Blending Tips, page 317).

The butter keeps in an airtight container in the fridge for up to 1 month.

CRUNCHY SUNFLOWER SEED BUTTER

Makes about 2 cups

1 pound hulled raw sunflower
seeds (about 3 cups), roasted
(see page 26) and cooled

2 tablespoons avocado oil
2 tablespoons maple syrup

1 teaspoon kosher salt

MAKE THE SUNFLOWER BUTTER
Put 2 cups of the sunflower seeds in a blender (for a smooth version, add all the seeds) with the remaining ingredients and blend on high speed until the sunflower seeds have formed a smooth butter, about 3 minutes, nonstop, in a high-wattage blender, like a Vitamix, or about 10 minutes in a standard blender (see Blending Tips, page 317). Transfer to a container with an airtight lid and stir in the remaining sunflower seeds.

The butter keeps in the fridge for up to 1 month.

Nut and Seed Milks

We may have reached peak alternative milk, but so many of the brands that pack grocery store shelves use thickeners or highly processed oil for texture. Thank goodness making your own is a cinch. The method is more or less the same for nuts, seeds, and coconut flakes: Soak them overnight (in the case of most nuts and seeds), blend them with a date for sweetness and a sprinkle of salt, and strain them through what might be the best-named kitchen tool ever—the nut bag.

They're all jammed with nutrients and flaunt the particular character of the main ingredient. Hemp milk is creamy and grassy; sunflower seed milk is nutty and earthy; pumpkin seed milk is subtly sweet, nutty, and a gorgeous pale green color; and hazelnut milk is buttery and nutty with a little lovely viscosity. The coconut milk is much lighter than the kind you want to use for cooking, but just right for when you want the fruit's flavor without its richness.

NUT AND SEED MILKS

Makes about 3 cups

For Pecan, Hazelnut, Sunflower, and Pumpkin Seed Milk

1 cup raw, unsalted nuts or seeds	1 pitted Medjool date or 1 tablespoon sweetener (maple syrup, date syrup, or coconut sugar)	1 teaspoon flaky sea salt

SOAK THE NUTS OR SEEDS

Combine the nuts or seeds with 3 cups of water in a jar or container (it's okay if the nuts or seeds float). Cover and let them soak in the fridge for at least 12 hours or up to 2 days.

MAKE THE MILK

Once the nuts or seeds have soaked, drain them and put them in a blender along with 3 cups of fresh water. Add the date and salt and blend on high speed until as smooth as possible, about 2 minutes.

Put the nut bag in a large bowl or other container and pour the mixture into the nut bag. Give the top of the bag a loose twist to close it, then firmly knead the mixture to force the milk into the bowl. Keep at it until no more milk comes out. Discard the solids.

The milk keeps in an airtight container in the fridge for up to 4 days. It may separate, so give it a good shake or stir before using.

For Coconut Milk

1 cup unsweetened coconut flakes	1 pitted Medjool date or 1 tablespoon sweetener (maple syrup, date syrup, or coconut sugar)	1 teaspoon flaky sea salt

MAKE THE MILK

Combine everything in a blender with 3 cups of water and blend on high speed until as smooth as possible, about 2 minutes. Put the nut bag in a large bowl or other container and pour the mixture into the nut bag. Give the top of the bag a loose twist to close it, then firmly knead the mixture to force the milk into the bowl. Keep at it until no more milk comes out. Discard the solids.

The milk keeps in an airtight container in the fridge for up to 4 days. It may separate, so give it a good shake or stir before using.

For Hemp Milk

1 cup hulled raw hemp seeds	1 pitted Medjool date or 1 tablespoon sweetener (maple syrup, date syrup, or coconut sugar)	1 teaspoon flaky sea salt

MAKE THE MILK

Combine everything in a blender with 3 cups of water and blend on high speed until as smooth as possible, about 2 minutes. There's no need to strain.

The milk keeps in an airtight container in the fridge for up to 4 days. It may separate, so give it a good shake or stir before using.

12

Mixes and Blends

SUNFLOWER SEED FURIKAKE

Makes about 1½ cups

Furikake is a Japanese seasoning blend, made in seemingly endless varieties but often including nori seaweed and sesame seeds, that's sprinkled onto bowls of rice, vegetable dishes, and much more. This one gets nutty crunch from sunflower seeds, depth from crispy garlic, and a little heat from dried chiles. Sprinkle it over asparagus salad (page 39) or anything nori-friendly that can use a lift.

2 tablespoons avocado oil

5 garlic cloves, thinly sliced

2 nori sheets

½ cup raw sesame seeds, toasted (see page 26)

½ cup unsalted roasted sunflower seeds

1½ teaspoons flaky sea salt

2 small dried red chiles, crumbled

MAKE THE FURIKAKE

Set a small strainer over a small heatproof bowl. Combine the oil and garlic in a small skillet, set it over medium heat, and wait for the garlic to sizzle. Reduce the heat to medium-low and slowly fry the garlic just until it's light golden brown and completely crisp, about 5 minutes. Immediately pour the mixture into the strainer. Reserve the crispy garlic for the furikake. Reserve the tasty garlicky oil for another purpose.

Stack the nori sheets shiny-sides down. Use kitchen scissors to cut into long strips along the indentations. Stack those strips and snip them crosswise into ⅛-inch-wide strips. Combine the nori in a medium bowl with the crispy garlic, sesame seeds, sunflower seeds, salt, and chiles. Stir really well.

The furikake keeps in an airtight container in the pantry for up to 1 month.

GARAM MASALA

Makes about ½ cup

You can absolutely buy garam masala, the warming spice mixture from the Indian subcontinent whose composition varies from region to region. But there's nothing like making it yourself—buying whole spices (who knows when that supermarket mix was ground?) and toasting them in a pan so their aromas fill your kitchen. It does wonders in a slow simmer of meat or vegetables, makes a great rub for pork chops about to hit the grill, and ignites the hazelnuts for creamy tomato soup (page 155).

3 tablespoons coriander seeds

1 tablespoon cumin seeds

1 tablespoon black peppercorns

10 green cardamom pods

8 dried bay leaves

8 small dried red chiles

6 whole cloves

MAKE THE SPICE MIXTURE

Combine the coriander, cumin, peppercorns, cardamom, bay leaves, chiles, and cloves in a medium skillet, set it over high heat, and toast, shaking the pan and tossing the spices every 30 seconds or so, until the spices are very fragrant and toasty, about 2 minutes.

Let cool slightly on a plate, then working in batches if necessary, grind in a spice grinder to a fine powder. The garam masala keeps in an airtight container in the pantry for up to 6 months.

JAPANESE CURRY SPICE

Makes a scant ½ cup

This spice mixture is designed to evoke the curry popular in Japan, which after the typical centuries-long game of culinary telephone, turned out sweeter, milder, and no less awesome than the versions from the Indian subcontinent on which it was based.

I can't say it enough: Toast and grind whole spices and see the difference for yourself. What might seem like work is actually a pleasure and the result is unlike any curry powder you'd buy at the store. Use it to make Japanese-style curry or to flavor virtually any other rich stew. Just two tablespoons raise the bar on a simple honey glaze for sweet potatoes (page 96) that get broiled until bubbly and charred.

1½ tablespoons black peppercorns
1 tablespoon coriander seeds
1 tablespoon cumin seeds
2 teaspoons whole cloves

1½ teaspoons fennel seeds
6 green cardamom pods
4 dried bay leaves

1 dried chipotle chile
1 tablespoon ground turmeric
1 teaspoon cocoa powder

MAKE THE SPICE MIXTURE

Heat a medium skillet over medium heat, add the peppercorns, coriander, cumin, cloves, fennel, cardamom, bay leaves, and chipotle and toast, tossing every 30 seconds or so, until very fragrant and a shade darker, about 3 minutes. Let cool slightly.

Transfer the mixture to a spice grinder, then working in batches if necessary, grind to a fine powder. Transfer to a small bowl, add the turmeric and cocoa powder, and stir well.

The curry spice keeps in an airtight container in the pantry for up to 6 months, but the sooner you use it, the better it is.

SMOKY CHILE SALT

Makes about ½ cup

A great finishing salt, this mix brings the smoky quality of chipotle and the fierce heat of small dried chiles. Sprinkle it on fried chicken (page 226) and grilled foods, or mix it with sugar and serve it with fruit (page 360).

20 small dried red chiles, stemmed

8 dried chipotle chiles, stemmed

¼ cup flaky sea salt

MAKE THE CHILE SALT

Working in batches if necessary, grind everything in a spice grinder and grind to a fine powder.

The chile salt keeps in an airtight container in the pantry for up to 6 months.

EIGHT SPICE

Makes about ⅔ cup

When you start toasting your own spices, you tend to go overboard. So it was probably during an over-enthusiastic moment that I added a couple more spices to Chinese five spice. Forgive me, but I do love the zing from dried chile and the extra dimension from nutmeg and allspice. Try it in my take on breakfast sausage (page 120) or in a char siu-style sauce you can slather on duck (page 311), pork, or anything, really.

Twelve 3-inch cinnamon sticks
2 tablespoons coriander seeds
2 tablespoons allspice berries

2 tablespoons fennel seeds
2 teaspoons whole cloves
8 star anise

6 small dried red chiles
2 small nutmegs, lightly crushed under the flat of a knife blade

MAKE THE SPICE MIXTURE

Combine all the ingredients in a large pan, set it over high heat, and toast, stirring frequently as the spices heat up, until fragrant and toasty, about 3 minutes. Let cool slightly. Working in batches if necessary, grind in a spice grinder to a fine powder.

   The eight spice keeps in an airtight container in the pantry for up to 6 months.

MUSHROOM POWDER

Makes about 2 cups

Michelle Tam, my friend and the powerhouse behind Nom Nom Paleo, makes a fantastic umami-boosting product called Magic Mushroom Powder. It's available at most Whole Foods markets and online, so grab some and use it to season everything from roasted vegetables, roast chicken, soups, stews, and meatloaf (page 238), and steak sauce (page 309). If you can't find it, don't worry: Michelle has graciously let me share the not-so-secret recipe, which you'll find here with a few tweaks.

1½ ounces dried sliced porcini mushrooms

1½ teaspoons black peppercorns
1 cup kosher salt

1½ tablespoons red pepper flakes
1 tablespoon dried thyme

MAKE THE POWDER

Preheat the oven to 350°F. Spread the dried mushrooms in a medium sheet pan in a single layer and toast in the oven until dry and crisp, about 8 minutes. Let cool slightly.

   Working in batches if necessary, grind the mushrooms and peppercorns into a fine powder in a spice grinder. Transfer the mixture to a medium bowl and combine with the remaining ingredients. Stir well to make sure everything is evenly dispersed.

   The mushroom powder keeps in an airtight container in the pantry for up to 6 months.

TAMARIND WATER

Makes about 6 cups

To extract the pleasures of the tamarind pod for recipes in this book, you must soak the pulp in hot water to help dislodge straggling fibers and other bits. When you strain them off, you have a tangy, fruity liquid that you can use to glaze ribs (page 310), stew beef (page 260), steam mussels (page 184), and turn into a refreshing drink (page 339).

One 14-ounce block seedless tamarind pulp (also labeled tamarind paste)

MAKE THE TAMARIND WATER

Put the pulp in a large mixing bowl and add 5 cups of hot tap water. Let the tamarind soak and soften for 30 minutes. Every 5 minutes or so, use a whisk or sturdy spoon to break up large chunks and stir vigorously since the tamarind flesh sticks to the pod and fibers and dislodging it takes a bit of force.

Set a fine-mesh strainer over a medium mixing bowl. Pour the mixture into the strainer, then stir, press, and smash the solids to extract as much liquid and pulp as possible. Return the remaining solids to the mixing bowl and add 1¼ cups of hot tap water and vigorously stir it (I like to use a whisk) to get the last bits of pulp off the pods and fibers. Strain the mixture again through the strainer into the bowl and this time discard the solids.

The tamarind water will keep in an airtight container in the fridge for up to 3 weeks and in the freezer (in 1-cup portions for ease of use) for up to 3 months. Stir well before each use.

PALEO-FRIENDLY FLOUR BLEND

Makes about 8 cups

Gluten-free and Paleo-friendly baking can be a little tricky. Luckily, this quick mix is a quick fix that can go cup for cup with wheat flour in most cakes and muffins. With almond flour for body, coconut flour for structure, and tapioca flour to fill the spaces in between, this blend is lower carb, higher protein, and full of nutrients.

Because it's part of several recipes in this book, I recommend this big batch to make baking that much easier. When you cook, keep in mind that these flours have different properties than wheat flour. For instance, inserting a knife into the center might be a great test for traditional baked goods, but not for those baked with this flour blend, as even if the knife came out clean they would not be sufficiently cooked. Instead, I use a thermometer. At 200°F, you're good.

| 4 cups extra-fine almond flour | 2⅔ cups tapioca flour | 1⅓ cups coconut flour |

MAKE THE BLEND

Sift the ingredients through a fine-mesh strainer into a large mixing bowl, breaking up any clumps, and stir very well. The flour blend keeps in an airtight container in the pantry for up to 6 months.

13

Smoothies, Coolers, Shrubs, and Haitian Hot Chocolate

SPICY PINEAPPLE-TURMERIC SMOOTHIE

Serve 2 to 4

A bright, vitamin C–packed smoothie, it has a touch of zing and tastes like the tropics.

3½ cups pineapple chunks (about 1 inch)

1 cup fresh orange juice

½ cup well-shaken coconut milk

3-inch knob fresh turmeric, peeled and thinly sliced against the grain

1 medium ripe banana, peeled

2 Medjool dates, pitted

½ small hot fresh red chile, such as Thai

2 cups ice cubes

MAKE THE SMOOTHIE

Combine everything but the ice in a blender, add the ice, and blend on high speed until as smooth as possible, 1 to 2 minutes. Serve right away.

RED BERRY, GOJI BERRY, AND HEMP SEED SMOOTHIE

Serves 2 to 4

This one has got a strawberries-and-cream thing going, and a big hit of protein and good stuff from hemp seeds, and the superfood extraordinaire—dried goji berries.

1 pound red berries, such as hulled strawberries and raspberries
½ cup dried goji berries

1 cup pineapple chunks (about 1 inch)
1 cup fresh orange juice

1 cup hulled raw hemp seeds
¼ cup maple syrup
2 cups ice cubes

MAKE THE SMOOTHIE
Combine all the ingredients but the ice in a blender, add the ice, and blend on high speed until as smooth as possible, 1 to 2 minutes. Serve right away.

PEACH LASSI WITH HONEY AND CARDAMOM

Serves 2 to 4

This refreshing, yogurt-based drink from the Indian subcontinent takes different forms, from salty to sweet, and the familiar mango flavor is just one of many. I love to use juicy summer peaches with fragrant cardamom and almond-milk yogurt, which is just the thing for breakfast, a midday pick-me-up, or a cooling dessert.

2 large ripe peaches, pitted and quartered

1 cup plain alternative milk yogurt, such as coconut, cashew, or almond

½ cup any nut or seed milk, homemade (page 321) or store-bought

3 tablespoons honey

4 green cardamom pods

1 juicy lime

2 cups ice cubes

MAKE THE SMOOTHIE

Combine the peaches, yogurt, nut milk, honey, and cardamom in a blender. Use a Microplane to grate the lime zest into the blender, then halve the lime and squeeze in the juice. Add the ice, then blend on high speed until smooth and creamy, 1 to 2 minutes.

Serve right away.

BLUEBERRY–BLUE ALGAE SMOOTHIE WITH GINGER AND LIME

Serves 2 to 4

They say to eat your colors. Well, blue spirulina powder may be the most perfect blue found in nature, a unique color as cool as its special health properties. The algae (yes, it's algae!) is packed with vitamins, minerals, and essential fatty acids. It makes an unstoppable team with antioxidant-monster blueberries, gets a protein boost from almonds, and has an unexpected zing from ginger and lime.

1 juicy lime

1 pint blueberries, plus more
   for garnish

1 cup raw almonds

1 cup alternative milk of choice,
   such as almond, coconut, or
   hemp (page 321)

3 tablespoons maple syrup

2 teaspoons blue spirulina
   powder, plus more for garnish

1 ripe banana, peeled

¼ teaspoon flaky sea salt

3-inch knob ginger, peeled and
   roughly sliced against the
   grain

3 cups ice cubes

MAKE THE SMOOTHIE

Use a Microplane to grate about half the lime's zest into a blender, then halve the lime and squeeze in one half's worth of juice. Reserve the other half for another time.

   Add all the remaining ingredients but the ice to the blender, then add the ice and blend on high speed until super smooth, 1 to 2 minutes. Garnish with additional blueberries and spirulina, if you like. Serve right away.

MY FAVORITE GREEN SMOOTHIE

Serves 2 to 4

I'm a big fan of greens in my smoothies, because let's be real: As much as I love kale salad, chomping through one can occasionally make you feel like a cow. Here, three types of greens are pureed with avocado for creaminess and enough sweet-tart pineapple and grapes to make you forget you're basically drinking salad.

1 cup packed stemmed hearty greens, such as kale, collards, or Swiss chard

2 cups packed mature spinach, stem bottoms trimmed

½ small bunch parsley

1 cup coconut water

1 large ripe Hass avocado, pitted

2 cups green grapes, frozen

1 cup pineapple chunks (about 1 inch)

Large handful mint leaves

Juice of 1 lime

3 cups ice cubes

MAKE THE SMOOTHIE

Combine the greens, spinach, parsley, and coconut water in a blender and blend on high speed until as smooth as possible, about 1 minute. Scoop in the avocado flesh; add the grapes, pineapple, mint, lime juice, and then the ice; and blend on high speed until as smooth as possible, about 1 minute more. Serve right away.

SUPER PROTEIN SMOOTHIE WITH GINGER

Serves 2 to 4

Bananas, nuts, and seeds join forces to bring you a tasty smoothie to supercharge your day. Naturally sweet and irresistibly nutty, it's also a breeze to throw together, because hemp milk, made from the highest protein plant of them all, is also the easiest alt milk to make.

3 cups hemp milk, homemade (page 321) or store-bought

Heaping ¼ cup sunflower seed butter, homemade (page 319) or store-bought

2 medium ripe bananas, peeled

6 Medjool dates, pitted

2-inch knob ginger, peeled and roughly sliced against the grain

2 cups ice cubes

One 3-inch cinnamon stick

MAKE THE SMOOTHIE

Combine the hemp milk, sunflower butter, banana, dates, and ginger in a blender, add the ice, and blend until as smooth as possible, 1 to 2 minutes.

Pour into large glasses and use a Microplane to grate on cinnamon to taste. Serve right away.

COCONUT LEMONADE

Serves 6

Working in a kitchen is an incredible thrill. It's also really, really hot. This drink was born on the line, during a momentary lull in the dinner rush, when hours of cooking made me desperate for an ice-cold drink that was hydrating, refreshing, and bright. I came up with this lemonade made with nutty coconut water and creamy coconut milk, with a touch of maple syrup and sea salt to balance things out. The result is round, not too sweet, and just ever so tart, an excellent option to swig after you've spent the evening cooking for friends and then to set out on the table in an ice-filled pitcher.

2 cups coconut water
1 cup well-shaken coconut milk

1 cup lemon juice (from 6 to 8 juicy lemons)
1 cup maple syrup

½ teaspoon kosher salt
6 thin lemon slices
Small handful mint leaves

MAKE THE LEMONADE
Combine the coconut water, coconut milk, lemon juice, maple syrup, salt, and 2 cups of water in a large bowl and whisk to combine. Transfer the lemonade to an ice-filled pitcher, give it a stir, and let sit for 5 minutes to chill.

Stir once more, then pour into six tall ice-filled glasses. Garnish with the lemon slices and mint, then serve.

CITRUS COOLER WITH CUCUMBERS AND HERBS

Serves 8

The juice and fragrant zest of lime, lemon, and orange team up with muddled grassy cucumbers and herbs in this refreshing drink.

For the Syrup

1 cup maple syrup

½ cup orange juice (from about 2 juicy oranges), plus finely grated zest of 2 oranges

¼ cup plus 2 tablespoons lime juice (from about 3 juicy limes), plus finely grated zest of 2 limes

¼ cup lemon juice (from 2 or 3 juicy lemons), plus finely grated zest of 2 lemons

For the Cooler

1 Persian cucumber, cut into 8 pieces

Handful of mixed basil and mint leaves

6 cups club soda, sparkling water, or seltzer

MAKE THE SYRUP

Combine the maple syrup, citrus juices, and citrus zests in a medium saucepan, set over high heat, and bring to a simmer. Immediately turn off the heat, then let the mixture cool completely.

The syrup keeps in an airtight container in the fridge for up to 2 weeks.

MAKE THE COOLER

Divide the cucumber and herbs among eight tall glasses and use a muddler (or handle of a wooden spoon) to bruise the herbs and crush the cucumber pieces to releases their juices. To each glass, add ice, ¼ cup of the citrus syrup, and ¾ cup of the club soda. Stir well and serve.

HIBISCUS COOLER WITH SPICE SYRUP AND LIME

Serves 8

The stunning red color comes from an infusion of dried hibiscus. The tropical flower, whose trees shade the hilltops of Haiti, contributes its unique tartness to refreshing drinks across the globe, from Thailand to Mexico. I round out that acidity with maple syrup infused with warm spices like cinnamon, ginger, black pepper, and star anise.

For the Spice Syrup
1 cup maple syrup
2-inch knob ginger, unpeeled and roughly chopped
1½ teaspoons black peppercorns

Three 3-inch cinnamon sticks
1½ teaspoons coriander seeds
5 star anise

For the Hibiscus Infusion
1½ cups dried hibiscus flowers

For the Cooler
2 juicy limes, quartered
Club soda, sparkling water, or seltzer, for topping off

MAKE THE SPICE SYRUP
Combine all the syrup ingredients and 1½ cups of water in a small saucepan and bring to a simmer over medium heat. Simmer vigorously for 5 minutes to infuse the liquids with spice flavor. Strain the syrup through a mesh strainer into a bowl, discarding the solids. Let the syrup cool completely.

MAKE THE HIBISCUS INFUSION
Put the hibiscus in a large mixing bowl. Bring 6 cups of water to a boil and pour the water over the hibiscus. Let steep for 30 minutes. Strain the liquid through a mesh strainer into another large mixing bowl, pressing firmly on the hibiscus to extract as much liquid as possible then discard the hibiscus. Let cool completely. Add the spice syrup and whisk well to combine, then transfer to a pitcher to serve.

MAKE THE COOLER
Fill eight tall glasses with ice. Pour in the cooler, squeeze in the juice from the lime quarters, and top with a splash (say, 2 tablespoons) of soda. Stir and serve.

TAMARIND COOLER WITH SPARKLING APPLE CIDER

Serves 8

Tangy tamarind, caramel-y maple, and sparkling apple cider gives this drink all the fall vibes.

For the Tamarind Syrup
1 cup Tamarind Water (page 327)
1 cup maple syrup

For the Cooler
4 juicy limes, halved
24 or so thin apple slices
   (optional)

4 cups sparkling apple cider
2 cups sparkling water, club
   soda, or seltzer
8 lime twists, for garnish
   (optional)

MAKE THE SYRUP

Combine the tamarind water and maple syrup in a small saucepan, bring to a boil over high heat, then immediately turn off the heat. Let cool fully.

   The syrup keeps in an airtight container in the fridge for up to 3 weeks.

MAKE THE COOLER

Fill eight tall glasses with ice cubes. To each glass, squeeze in half a lime, add a few apple slices (if using), pour in ¼ cup of the tamarind syrup, top with ½ cup of the sparkling apple cider and ¼ cup of the sparkling water, and stir well. Garnish with the lime twists (if using).

GINGER SHRUB WITH CARROT AND ORANGE

Serves 8

Shrubs, loosely defined, are drinks made with a syrup made from vinegar and fruit. Here, the fruit component is swapped for ginger, whose sweet tingle updates the classic duo of carrot and orange, making it brighter—and even more like drinking straight sunshine.

For the Ginger Shrub
1 cup unpeeled, thinly sliced (against the grain) ginger (about 4 ounces)
1 cup white wine vinegar
1 cup maple syrup

For the Drinks
Small handful basil leaves (optional)
4 cups carrot juice
4 cups fresh orange juice

Club soda, sparkling water, or seltzer, for topping off
Slim carrot spears for garnish (optional)

MAKE THE SHRUB
Combine all the ingredients in a blender and puree until as smooth as possible. Transfer to a medium pot and bring to a simmer over medium-high heat. Reduce the heat to maintain a gentle simmer and cook for 2 minutes to fully infuse the ginger flavor.

Turn off the heat and let the shrub cool for about 5 minutes. Strain it through a fine-mesh strainer into a medium mixing bowl, pressing the solids firmly with the back of a spoon to extract as much liquid as possible. Discard the solids and let the shrub cool fully.

The shrub keeps in an airtight container in the fridge for up to 2 weeks.

MAKE THE DRINKS
Fill eight tall glasses with ice. To each glass, add a few basil leaves (if using) and pour in ¼ cup of the ginger shrub, ½ cup of the carrot juice, and ½ cup of the orange juice. Stir well, then finish with a splash (say, 2 tablespoons) of soda and garnish with carrot spears (if using).

RED BERRY SHRUB WITH COCONUT VINEGAR

Serves 8

Big red berry flavor takes so well to the tropical spark of coconut vinegar. Its subtle nuttiness and rousing acidity makes for an especially invigorating drink.

For the Red Berry Shrub
3 cups fresh red berries, such as hulled strawberries and raspberries, plus extra for garnish

1 cup plus 2 tablespoons maple syrup
¾ cup coconut vinegar

For the Drinks
½ cup or so fresh red berries (optional)
5⅓ cups unsweetened coconut-flavored sparkling water, such as LaCroix
8 small rosemary sprigs (optional)

MAKE THE SHRUB

Combine all the shrub ingredients in a blender and puree on high speed until as smooth as possible. Transfer to a small saucepan, bring to a boil over high heat, then immediately turn off the heat. Pour the mixture through a medium-mesh strainer set over a medium mixing bowl to strain out the seeds.

Chill the shrub in the fridge until cold. It keeps in an airtight container for up to 2 weeks.

MAKE THE DRINKS

Fill eight tall glasses with ice and a few berries (if using). To each glass, add ⅓ cup of the berry shrub and ⅔ cup of the soda and stir well. Garnish with the rosemary sprigs (if using) and serve.

BANANA SHRUB WITH PASSION FRUIT AND LIME

Serves 8

Cooked banana evokes warmth and comfort, but pureed with bright vinegar for a cold drink, the familiar turns remarkable. Lime and passion fruit turn this shrub into a super-tropical, super-refreshing drink.

For the Banana Shrub
1 very-ripe banana (yellow with some black spots), peeled and cut into 1-inch pieces
1¼ cups maple syrup
1 cup coconut vinegar

For the Drinks
24 thin, round slices of lime
½ cup lime juice (from 4 or 5 juicy limes)
6 cups sparkling water, club soda, or seltzer

4 passion fruits, halved
Small handful mint leaves

MAKE THE SHRUB

Put all the shrub ingredients in a small saucepan with ½ cup water and bring to a boil over high heat. Reduce the heat to cook at a lively simmer until the banana turns pale brown and gets soft enough to smash with barely any pressure, about 3 minutes.

Turn off the heat, then spoon off and discard any foam from the surface. Transfer to a blender and puree on high until completely smooth, about 30 seconds.

The shrub keeps in an airtight container in the fridge for up to 2 weeks.

MAKE THE DRINKS

Fill eight tall glasses with ice. To each glass, add three of the lime slices and pour in ¼ cup of banana shrub, 1 tablespoon of the lime juice, and ¾ cup of the sparkling water. Stir well, scoop the flesh from half a passion fruit into each glass, and garnish with a few mint leaves.

HAITIAN HOT CHOCOLATE

Serves 4

Once in a while, on dark, cold winter mornings before Catholic grade school, my sister and I would trudge into the kitchen wearing our uniforms only to be greeted by a smell that saved our spirits from those grim early hours. Before my mom zipped off to work, she handed us mugs of hot chocolate made in the Haitian style with cinnamon, star anise, and vanilla, spices that filled our relatives' suitcases when they visited from home. We'd alternate between tongue-scalding sips and bites of margarine-slathered white toast (hey, it was the '80s!) that we'd dunk in the hot drink.

A mugful still brightens the darkest winter day, even with store-bought spices.

2½ cups well-shaken coconut milk

1½ tablespoons coconut sugar

1 teaspoon virgin coconut oil

½ teaspoon vanilla extract

7 star anise

Four 3-inch cinnamon sticks

5 ounces chopped dark chocolate

¼ teaspoon flaky sea salt

MAKE THE DRINK

Combine the coconut milk, coconut sugar, coconut oil, vanilla, star anise, cinnamon, and 1½ cups water in a medium saucepan. Set the pan over medium-low heat, bring to a gentle simmer, and cook for 2 minutes to infuse the flavor of the spices. Add the chocolate and salt, then use a flexible spatula to stir and scrape until the chocolate has completely melted.

Serve warm in mugs.

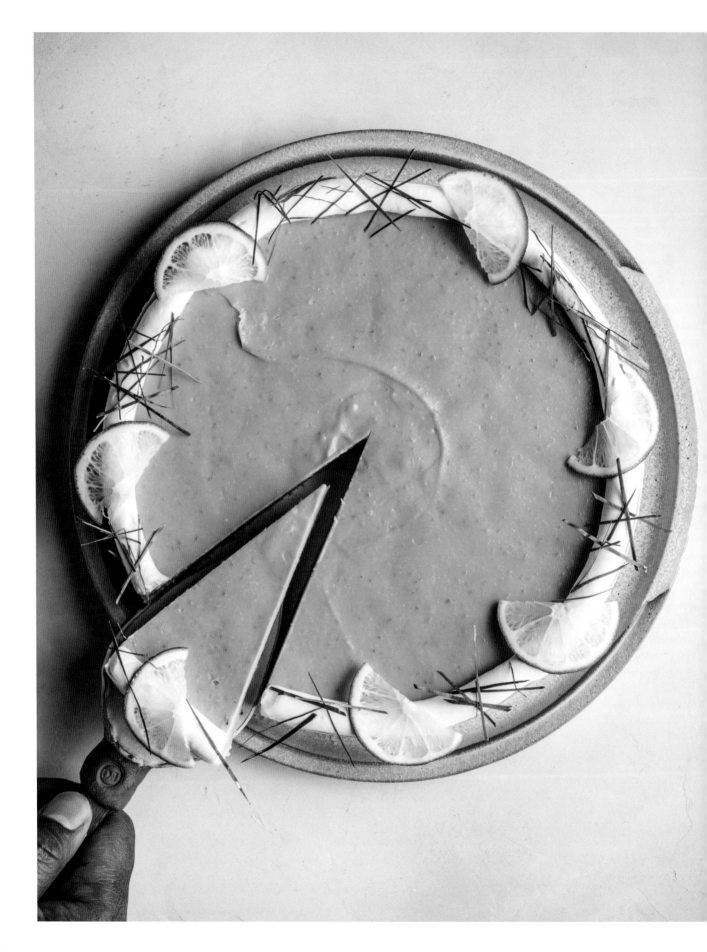

14

Desserts and Sweets

Ice Cream, Sherbet, and Sorbet

Any ice cream lover will covet these dairy-free flavors, made with coconut cream and roasted cashews to re-create the lush texture of the standard scoop. Old classics like vanilla and strawberry (swirled with jam for even more fruit flavor) join modern ones like chocolate chip cookie dough and chocolate brownie (given a little Mexican twist with cinnamon). My Turkish coffee–inspired flavor, with brewed beans tinged with cardamom, very well might become a new classic in your house. A sherbet and a sorbet feature lively flavors like citrus and bright aromatics for a light ending to any meal.

Note: I worked hard to make sure these ice creams are simple—you soak cashews, you blend, you let the ice cream machine do its thing, then you freeze. Behind the straightforward process, however, is a carefully calibrated ratio of protein, fat, and sugar. To maintain this ratio, these recipes do ask for extra precision, so please weigh the palm sugar and cashews, rather than using volume measures. Also note that if you're planning to churn Very Vanilla Ice Cream in order to make Chocolate Chip Cookie Dough or Jammy Strawberry Ice Cream, feel free to omit the vanilla beans.

VERY VANILLA ICE CREAM

Makes about 3 pints

6 ounces raw cashews, roasted (see page 26) and cooled

2⅔ cups well-shaken coconut cream, at room temperature

8 ounces palm sugar, finely chopped

¼ cup virgin coconut oil

3 tablespoons vanilla extract

2 teaspoons kosher salt

2 vanilla beans, tips trimmed, split lengthwise

SOAK THE CASHEWS

Combine the cashews and 1¼ cups of water in a narrow jar (it's okay if they float) and let the nuts soak in the fridge overnight.

MAKE THE ICE CREAM

Drain the cashews well and then put them in a blender along with the coconut cream, palm sugar, coconut oil, vanilla extract, and salt. Use a small knife to scrape the vanilla bean seeds into the blender, saving the pods for another use (when steeped, they'll still provide great vanilla flavor). Blend the mixture on high speed until completely smooth, 3 to 5 minutes. Transfer to a large metal mixing bowl, stir well, and let cool in the fridge, whisking halfway through, until it's no longer warm (that long blending will have heated it a bit), about 1 hour.

Transfer the cold mixture to an ice cream maker and churn (in batches if necessary) until solid but still creamy, 30 to 40 minutes depending on your machine. Transfer to a container (preferably glass) with an airtight lid, cover with parchment paper pressed against the surface of the ice cream, and freeze until frozen, about 6 hours or overnight. Then it's ready to eat. Covered, it keeps in the freezer for up to 2 weeks.

Chocolate Chip Cookie Dough

¾ cup smooth nut butter, homemade (page 317) or store-bought

¾ cup dark chocolate chips
¼ cup plus 2 tablespoons coconut sugar

1 large egg, lightly beaten

MAKE THE COOKIE DOUGH

Preheat the oven to 350°F. Combine the nut butter, chocolate chips, coconut sugar, and egg in a medium bowl and stir until well combined. Transfer the mixture to a large baking dish and press into an even, ½-inch-thick layer. Bake until it's tender and puffy, like a soft-baked cookie, but still a little crumbly, about 10 minutes. Let cool completely, remove the cookie dough from the pan, and crumble into bite-size pieces. The cookie dough keeps in an airtight container at room temperature for up to 1 day.

MAKE THE ICE CREAM

Churn a batch of Very Vanilla Ice Cream (page 347). While it's churning, pop a large mixing bowl in the freezer, so it gets nice and cold.

Transfer the ice cream to the frozen bowl and fold in the cookie dough until well distributed. Transfer to a container (preferably glass) with an airtight lid, cover with parchment paper pressed against the surface of the ice cream, and freeze until frozen, about 6 hours or overnight. Then it's ready to eat. Covered, it keeps in the freezer for up to 2 weeks.

Jammy Strawberry Ice Cream

2 cups strawberry jam, homemade (page 316) or store-bought, well stirred to loosen

MAKE THE ICE CREAM

Churn a batch of Very Vanilla Ice Cream (page 347). While it's churning, pop a large mixing bowl in the freezer so it gets nice and cold.

Transfer the ice cream to the frozen bowl and fold in the strawberry jam until the ice cream is evenly light pink with well-distributed berry pieces. Transfer to a container (preferably glass) with an airtight lid, cover with parchment paper pressed against the surface of the ice cream, and freeze until frozen, about 6 hours or overnight. Then it's ready to eat. Covered, it keeps in the freezer for up to 2 weeks.

CINNAMON-CHOCOLATE ICE CREAM WITH BROWNIE BITS

Makes about 3 pints

6 ounces raw cashews, roasted (see page 26) and cooled

4 cups chopped (about ¼ inch) baked brownies, homemade (page 381) or store-bought

2⅔ cups well-shaken coconut cream, at room temperature

8 ounces palm sugar, finely chopped

1 ounce Dutch-process cocoa powder

¼ cup virgin coconut oil

¼ cup vanilla extract

2 teaspoons kosher salt

¾ teaspoon freshly ground cinnamon

TOAST AND SOAK THE CASHEWS

Combine the cashews and 1¼ cups of water in a narrow jar (it's okay if they float) and let the nuts soak in the fridge overnight.

MAKE THE ICE CREAM

Preheat the oven to 350°F. Spread the brownie pieces on a large baking dish and bake until they're dry all the way through, about 10 minutes. Let them cool completely.

Drain the cashews well and then put them in a blender along with the coconut cream, palm sugar, cocoa powder, coconut oil, vanilla, salt, and cinnamon. Blend on high speed until completely smooth, 3 to 5 minutes.

Transfer to a large metal mixing bowl, stir well, and let it cool in the fridge, whisking halfway through, until no longer warm (that long blending will have heated it a bit), about 1 hour. Transfer the cold mixture to an ice cream maker and churn (in batches if necessary) until solid but still creamy, 30 to 40 minutes depending on your machine. While it's churning, pop a large mixing bowl in the freezer so it gets nice and cold.

Transfer the ice cream to the frozen bowl and fold in the brownie bits until well distributed. Transfer to a container (preferably glass) with an airtight lid, cover with parchment paper pressed against the surface of the ice cream, and freeze until frozen, about 6 hours or overnight. Then it's ready to eat. Covered, it keeps in the freezer for up to 2 weeks.

CARDAMOM-COFFEE ICE CREAM

Makes about 3 pints

6 ounces raw cashews, roasted (see page 26) and cooled

2⅔ cups well-shaken coconut cream, at room temperature

8 ounces palm sugar, finely chopped

1½ ounces whole coffee beans

¼ cup virgin coconut oil

¼ cup vanilla extract

2 teaspoons kosher salt

18 green cardamom pods

TOAST AND SOAK THE CASHEWS

Combine the cashews and 1¼ cups of water in a narrow jar (it's okay if they float) and let the nuts soak in the fridge overnight.

MAKE THE ICE CREAM

Drain the cashews well and then put them in a blender along with the remaining ingredients and blend on high speed until smooth (tiny flecks of coffee beans are fine), 3 to 5 minutes. Pour the mixture through a fine-mesh strainer into a large metal mixing bowl, stir well, and let it cool in the fridge, whisking halfway through, until no longer warm (that long blending will have heated it a bit), about 1 hour.

Transfer the cold mixture to an ice cream maker and churn (in batches if necessary) until solid but still creamy, 30 to 40 minutes depending on your machine. Transfer to a container (preferably glass) with an airtight lid, cover with parchment paper pressed against the surface of the ice cream, and freeze until frozen, about 6 hours or overnight. Then it's ready to eat. Covered, it keeps in the freezer for up to 2 weeks.

ORANGE-GINGER SHERBET

Makes about 3 pints

2⅔ cups fresh orange juice, plus the finely grated zest of 2 oranges

8 ounces palm sugar, finely chopped

1⅓ cups well-shaken coconut cream, at room temp

4-inch knob ginger, peeled and thinly sliced against the grain

1 teaspoon kosher salt

MAKE THE SHERBET

Combine everything in a blender, then blend on high speed until completely smooth, 2 to 3 minutes. Transfer to a large metal mixing bowl, stir well, and let it cool in the fridge, whisking halfway through, until chilled, for 30 minutes or so.

Transfer the cold mixture to an ice cream maker and churn (in batches if necessary) until solid but still slushy, 30 to 40 minutes depending on your machine. Transfer the sherbet to a container (preferably glass) with an airtight lid, cover with parchment paper pressed against the surface of the sherbet, and freeze until frozen, about 6 hours or overnight. Then it's ready to eat. Covered, it keeps in the freezer for up to 2 weeks.

MINTY LIME AND JALAPEÑO SORBET

Makes about 3 pints

13 ounces palm sugar, finely chopped

1 cup lime juice (from about 8 juicy limes), plus the finely grated zest of 8 limes

2 cups loosely packed mint leaves

1 teaspoon kosher salt

1 small jalapeño chile

MAKE THE SORBET

Combine the palm sugar and 3½ cups of water in a small pot, set over high heat, and bring to a boil. Adjust the heat and simmer until a thin syrup forms that just barely coats a spoon, about 3 minutes. Pour the syrup into a medium mixing bowl (preferably metal) and put it in the fridge to cool completely.

Combine the cooled syrup with the remaining ingredients in a blender and blend until smooth, about 1 minute.

Transfer the cold mixture to an ice cream maker and churn (in batches if necessary) until solid but still slushy, 30 to 40 minutes depending on your machine. Transfer the sorbet to a container (preferably glass) with an airtight lid, cover with parchment paper pressed against the surface of the sorbet, and freeze until frozen, about 6 hours or overnight. Then it's ready to eat. Covered, it keeps in the freezer for up to 2 weeks.

MILKSHAKES

Each makes 2 (10-ounce) milkshakes

A blender and some trimmings turn ice cream into decadent treats. Keep extra fudge sauce and coconut caramel on hand for drizzling over scoops of ice cream and other sweets. Don't feel like making the ice creams on pages 347 to 350? Then just grab a good dairy-free pint from the store.

DOUBLE-CHOCOLATE MILKSHAKE

2 cups Cinnamon-Chocolate Ice Cream (page 348) or store-bought chocolate

2 tablespoons Fudge Sauce (page 354)

½ cup nut or seed milk, homemade (page 321) or store-bought
Tiny pinch flaky sea salt

MAKE THE MILKSHAKE
Combine all the ingredients in a blender and blend on high speed until smooth. Serve immediately.

VIETNAMESE COFFEE–STYLE MILKSHAKE

2 cups vanilla ice cream, homemade (page 347) or store-bought

½ cup cold-brew coffee or cold coffee

2 tablespoons coconut caramel (page 370)

½ cup nut or seed milk, homemade (page 321) or store-bought

Tiny pinch flaky sea salt

MAKE THE MILKSHAKE

Combine all the ingredients in a blender and blend on high speed until smooth. Serve immediately.

FUDGY VANILLA MILKSHAKE

2 cups vanilla ice cream, homemade (page 347) or store-bought

½ cup nut or seed milk, homemade (page 321) or store-bought

Tiny pinch flaky sea salt

2 tablespoons Fudge Sauce (page 354)

MAKE THE MILKSHAKE

Blend the ice cream, milk, and salt on high speed until smooth. Drizzle the fudge sauce all over the insides of two serving glasses. Pour in the milkshake and serve immediately.

GRASSHOPPER MILKSHAKE

2 cups vanilla ice cream, homemade (page 347) or store-bought

½ cup packed mint leaves

2 tablespoons dark chocolate chips

½ cup nut or seed milk, homemade (page 321) or store-bought

Tiny pinch flaky sea salt

MAKE THE MILKSHAKE

Combine all the ingredients in a blender and blend on high speed until smooth with little flecks of chocolate; serve immediately.

JAMMY STRAWBERRY MILKSHAKE

2 cups strawberry ice cream,
  homemade (page 348) or
  store-bought

2 tablespoons strawberry jam,
  homemade (page 316) or
  store-bought

½ cup nut or seed milk,
  homemade (page 321) or
  store-bought

Tiny pinch flaky sea salt

MAKE THE MILKSHAKE

Combine all the ingredients in a blender and blend on high speed until smooth. Serve immediately.

DATE SHAKE

2 cups vanilla ice cream,
  homemade (page 347) or
  store-bought

½ cup nut or seed milk ,
  homemade (page 321) or
  store-bought

4 Medjool dates, pitted

½-inch piece cinnamon stick,
  freshly grated

Tiny pinch flaky sea salt

MAKE THE SHAKE

Combine all the ingredients in a blender and blend on high speed until smooth. Serve immediately.

FUDGE SAUCE

Makes 1½ cups

½ cup well-shaken coconut cream

½ cup coconut sugar

1½ teaspoons virgin coconut oil

½ teaspoon vanilla extract

¼ teaspoon flaky sea salt

¼ cup plus 2 tablespoons
  Dutch-process cocoa powder

3 heaping tablespoons dark
  chocolate chips

MAKE THE SAUCE

Combine the coconut cream, sugar, oil, vanilla, and salt in a small saucepan. Stir well and bring to a simmer over medium-low heat. While whisking, pour in the cocoa powder in a slow, steady stream and keep whisking until smooth with no clumps of cocoa powder. Turn off the heat and whisk in the chocolate chips until melted and smooth. Serve warm.

   The fudge sauce keeps in an airtight container in the fridge for up to 2 weeks. Before serving, reheat in a small saucepan over low heat with a teaspoon of water or coconut milk to loosen.

SAUTÉED PEACHES WITH GINGER AND ICY FERMENTED PINEAPPLE

Serves 6

Juicy, fragrant summer peaches get glazed with caramelized maple syrup, ginger, and cinnamon, then topped with funky shaved ice made from fermented pineapple. Make the shaved ice ahead and this impressive dessert comes together in minutes.

2 teaspoons virgin coconut oil

6 medium ripe peaches, pitted and each cut into 8 wedges

5-inch knob ginger, peeled, halved lengthwise, and thinly sliced

Four 3-inch cinnamon sticks

¼ cup plus 2 tablespoons maple syrup

2 teaspoons vanilla extract

½ teaspoon kosher salt

Icy Fermented Pineapple (page 282)

MAKE THE DISH

Melt the coconut oil in a medium skillet over medium heat, then add the peaches, ginger, and cinnamon. Increase the heat to medium-high and cook until the peaches begin to caramelize with a bit of golden brown on their cut sides, 3 to 4 minutes.

Reduce the heat to medium, slide the pan off the heat, and add the maple syrup and vanilla. Return the pan to the heat and continue cooking, stirring occasionally and tossing the peaches in the syrup, until the peaches are tender but still hold their shape and the liquid has reduced to a tight glaze that clings to the peaches, about 4 minutes. Season with the salt and stir gently but well. Let it all cool to room temperature.

Divide the peaches among six bowls and top with the icy fermented pineapple.

SHAVED COCONUT ICE WITH SUMMER FRUITS

Serves 4 to 6

Throughout much of Asia, the refreshing base for various desserts isn't ice cream but shaved ice, scraped to a divine fluff, dressed with bright syrups, and decked out with fruits and candied vegetables. You don't need a special machine (though of course, they exist), just a fork to rake across a mixture of frozen coconut water and milk. Topped with a mix of local and tropical summer fruits, this after-dinner treat is as striking and tasty as it is easy to make. For maximum refreshment, serve this treat in frozen bowls, so it stays cold longer.

For the Coconut Shaved Ice
1½ cups well-shaken coconut milk
1½ cups coconut water
½ cup maple syrup
1½ tablespoons lime juice (from 1 juicy lime)
½ teaspoon flaky sea salt

For the Pickled Cherries
½ cup coconut sugar or finely chopped palm sugar
3 tablespoons unseasoned rice vinegar
½ small jalapeño, thinly sliced
2 cups halved, pitted sweet cherries

For the Dish
3 cups assorted summer fruits (sliced nectarines, diced Champagne mango, diced pineapple, young coconut meat, grapes)
Pinch flaky sea salt

MAKE THE COCONUT SHAVED ICE
Combine all the coconut shaved ice ingredients in a medium mixing bowl and whisk well. Transfer to a glass or ceramic container that'll hold the amount in a depth of about 1½ inches (a 9 x 12-inch baking dish works well).

Freeze, uncovered, until frozen solid, at least 6 hours. Use the tines of a fork to scrape the mixture until it has the fluffy texture of shaved ice, then give it all a stir with the fork, since the coconut milk sometimes separates during freezing. Put the shaved ice back in the freezer to refreeze for at least 30 minutes or until you're ready to serve.

The shaved ice keeps, covered, in the freezer for up to 7 days.

PICKLE THE CHERRIES
Combine all the pickled cherries ingredients in a medium saucepan and cook over medium heat at a lively simmer until the cherries are so tender they collapse and the liquid reduces to a syrup that's a little thicker than maple, 10 to 15 minutes. Cool to room temperature. The cherries keep in an airtight container in the fridge for up to 1 week.

MAKE THE DISH
Scoop the coconut shaved ice into bowls, spoon on the mixed fruit, and top with the pickled cherries and their syrup. Sprinkle on the salt and serve right away.

FROZEN MAKRUT LIME AND AVOCADO PIE

Serves 12

I remember the first time I was offered an avocado dessert. I stared at that slice of frozen chocolate-avocado pie, extremely dubious that the main ingredient in guacamole could succeed in a sweet setting. My later travels through Southeast Asia, where the fatty fruit ends up in sweet shakes and plenty of desserts, revealed how unwarranted that skepticism had been. It's amazing, really, how its flavor fades into the background and its creamy richness becomes a luscious vehicle for other flavors. Like in this pie, where avocado helps power bright lime for a revivifying frozen treat with a nutty cashew-and-coconut crust.

For the Crust
1½ cups raw cashews
½ cup unsweetened coconut flakes
5 large Medjool dates, pitted
½ teaspoon flaky sea salt

For the Filling
4 or 5 juicy limes

4 large ripe Hass avocados, pitted and flesh scooped from the skins
1 cup maple syrup
½ cup plain coconut yogurt
½ cup melted virgin coconut oil
½ teaspoon flaky sea salt
3 large fresh or frozen makrut lime leaves, center ribs removed, finely chopped

For Serving
½ cup plain coconut yogurt
1 tablespoon maple syrup
7 or so thin half-moon lime slices
5 large makrut lime leaves, center ribs removed, cut into very thin strips

MAKE THE CRUST

Preheat the oven to 350°F. Pulse the cashews in a food processor or blender into a crumbly meal, like slightly coarse bread crumbs. Combine the cashew crumbs and coconut flakes in a medium ovenproof skillet or baking dish, stir well, and bake, stirring halfway through, until the mixture is fragrant and goes from white to beige, about 6 minutes. Let cool to room temperature.

In the meantime, puree the dates in a blender into a smooth paste. Add the date puree and salt to the cashew-coconut mixture and stir until a crumbly dough forms. Press the dough in an even, packed layer onto the bottom of a 9-inch nonstick springform pan. Refrigerate the crust while you make the filling.

MAKE THE FILLING

Use a Microplane to grate the zest of 4 of the limes. Halve the limes and squeeze enough juice to give you ½ cup. Put the zest and juice in a blender along with the remaining filling ingredients and puree on high speed until super smooth and creamy. Pour the filling into the pan, over the crust, and smooth the top using an offset spatula. Give the pan a few firm, short taps on the counter to help the filling release any air bubbles. Smooth the surface again if necessary. Put the pan pie in the freezer, uncovered, until fully frozen, at least 12 hours or up to 3 days.

SERVE THE PIE

Remove the frozen pie from its pan and let it sit at room temperature for 15 minutes, so it softens just enough to slice. In a small bowl, combine the coconut yogurt and maple syrup and stir until nice and smooth. Either dollop it on individual pie slices later or get fancy and transfer it to a piping bag and pipe a ring around the pie's edge. Garnish with the lime slices and sprinkle with the makrut lime leaves to serve.

Keep any unserved pie in the freezer, so it doesn't melt.

A BIG FRUIT PLATE WITH SALTY CHILE SUGAR

Serves 6

In Southeast Asia, people often enjoy fresh fruit and vegetables dipped in a mixture of salt, sugar, and chile. I love it, too, as a way to serve a low-key, low-effort summer dessert to friends, as the sun sets and the grill cools off from dinner. The bounty in the photo showcases just some of your options and offers a way to go all out if you like. Buy what looks best (I veer toward sweet-tart fruits and crunchy, mild vegetables), cut it into two-bite pieces, and have everyone dip into this blend of salt, smoky chiles, coconut sugar, and a bit of lime zest to take it from tasty to terrific.

1 lime
2 tablespoons Smoky Chile Salt
  (page 325)

2 tablespoons coconut sugar

Fresh fruit to generously serve
  6 people

MAKE THE DISH

Use a Microplane to zest the lime onto a small plate, reserving the remaining lime for another use. Leave the zest uncovered on the counter for about 20 minutes while you cut all that beautiful fruit into party-friendly, two-bite pieces. This allows the zest to dry a bit, so it doesn't clump when you add it to the salt mixture.

Combine the chile salt and coconut sugar in a small bowl. When the lime has dried a bit, add it to the bowl and stir well.

Arrange the sliced fruits on a platter. Serve with the salty chile sugar for dipping.

VANILLA CUSTARD WITH BERRIES AND BASIL

Serves 4

Vanilla-infused coconut milk sets into a delicate custard thanks to the algae extract agar-agar (available online and at natural-food stores), giving you the creamy pleasure without the dairy or the fuss of tempering eggs. Berries, both fresh and concentrated in the form of jam, offer tart and textural contrast.

For the Custard
2¾ cups well-shaken coconut milk
¼ cup finely chopped palm sugar or coconut sugar
1 teaspoon vanilla extract
½ teaspoon powdered agar-agar

For Serving
4 cups mixed berries (strawberries, raspberries, blueberries, and blackberries)
¼ cup strawberry jam, homemade (page 316) or store-bought
1 tablespoon extra-virgin olive oil
Small handful basil leaves

MAKE THE CUSTARD

Combine the coconut milk, palm sugar, and vanilla in a blender and blend on medium-high until smooth. Then, while the blender is running, gradually sprinkle in the agar-agar and wait a few seconds after it's all added, to be sure it's well dispersed. Pour the mixture into a small pot and bring to a boil over medium heat. Agar-agar needs to boil to activate; as soon as the entire surface comes to a boil, it's ready.

Remove from the heat and divide the mixture among four cereal bowls. Cool briefly, 10 minutes or so, then carefully transfer the custards to the refrigerator so they can set and chill a bit, about 1 hour.

Covered, they keep in the fridge for up to 2 days.

SERVE THE DISH

Hull the strawberries and halve any large berries. Stir 1 tablespoon of warm water into the jam to loosen it. Remove the chilled custards from the fridge. Spoon on the strawberry jam and top with the berries. Drizzle on the olive oil and sprinkle on the basil. Serve right away.

COCONUT RICOTTA WITH CHERRIES, BLACK PEPPER, AND BASIL

Serves 4

Here's a cool one: Coconut milk set up with agar-agar, the plant-based gelatin substitute, transforms into soft, ricotta-like curds with a few pulses in the food processor. Fresh summer cherries and simmered, spiced cherries keep things interesting; pistachios offer crunch; and black pepper adds a sneaky surprise.

For the Coconut Ricotta
2¾ cups well-shaken coconut milk
¼ cup finely chopped palm sugar or coconut sugar
⅛ teaspoon kosher salt
1 teaspoon powdered agar-agar

For the Spiced Cherries
2 cups pitted, whole sweet cherries, such as Rainier, black, or bing
½ cup honey
4 star anise
Two 3-inch cinnamon sticks
⅛ teaspoon kosher salt

For Serving
1 cup halved, pitted cherries
¾ cup unsalted roasted pistachios
2 tablespoons extra-virgin olive oil
½ teaspoon black peppercorns, very coarsely cracked
Small handful basil leaves

MAKE THE COCONUT RICOTTA

Combine the coconut milk, sugar, and salt in the blender. Blend for a few seconds, then with the blender still running, sprinkle in the agar-agar and blend for a few seconds more to combine well. Pour the mixture into a small saucepan and set it over high heat. As soon as it reaches a boil, turn off the heat. Transfer the mixture to a small bowl, let it cool for about 2 minutes, then chill completely in the refrigerator until set, about 1 hour.

Gently pulse the mixture in a food processor, in batches if necessary, to create a ricotta-like texture with small, soft curds. It keeps in an airtight container in the fridge for up to 4 days.

MAKE THE SPICED CHERRIES

Combine all the ingredients for the spiced cherries in a small saucepan and cook over medium heat at a lively simmer, until the cherries are so tender they collapse and the liquid reduces to a syrup that's a little thicker than maple, 20 to 25 minutes. Cool to room temperature.

It keeps in an airtight container in the fridge for up to 3 days.

SERVE THE DISH

Spoon the coconut ricotta onto a serving platter or into four individual bowls. Spoon on the spiced cherries and their syrup, then scatter on the halved cherries and pistachios. Drizzle with the oil, then sprinkle on the crushed black pepper and the basil. Serve right away.

WARM COCONUT MILK SOUP WITH BANANA, APPLE, AND WINTER SQUASH

Serves 4 to 6

Warm soup for dessert might strike you as odd, but it's not to Southeast Asian diners. In Thailand, for instance, even on the most sweltering nights, I've eaten coconut milk soups—sweet, a little salty, and scented with vanilla-y pandan leaf—adorned with various fruits and vegetables for the most satisfying end to an evening. Back home, I tend to reserve this rendition for colder nights when the season has brought winter squash and apples into my kitchen.

For the Banana Custard
Splash of virgin coconut oil

1 ripe banana, peeled

2¾ cups well-shaken coconut milk

¼ cup finely chopped palm sugar or coconut sugar

¼ teaspoon kosher salt

½ teaspoon powdered agar-agar

For the Dish
½ teaspoon kosher salt, plus a pinch more for blanching

1 cup cubed (¼ to ½ inch) butternut squash

1 cup cubed (¼ to ½ inch), peeled taro root

3 cups well-shaken coconut milk

3 inches fresh or frozen pandan leaf (optional)

2 tablespoons finely chopped palm sugar or coconut sugar

1 green apple, unpeeled, cored, and diced (¼ to ½ inch)

1 ripe banana, peeled and sliced

Raw sesame seeds, toasted (see page 26)

MAKE THE BANANA CUSTARD

Preheat the oven to 350°F. Rub the coconut oil on a small ovenproof pan, add the banana, and roast until the banana's light golden and tender (you'll be able to cut it with a spoon using very little no pressure), 8 to 10 minutes. Transfer the banana to a blender and blend with the coconut milk, sugar, and salt on high speed until smooth, about 1 minute. With the blender still running, sprinkle in the agar-agar and blend for a few more seconds. Pour the mixture into a medium saucepan and bring to a boil over medium heat. Agar-agar needs to boil to activate; as soon as the entire surface comes to a boil, it's ready.

Remove from the heat, divide the mixture among small soup bowls, and let it cool to room temperature so it sets to a custard-like texture.

Covered, it keeps in the fridge for up to 2 days. Let it come to room temperature before serving.

MAKE THE DISH

Bring a medium pot of water to a boil and season it with a pinch of salt. Line a plate with a clean kitchen towel. Add the butternut squash and cook until it's bright orange and just tender through, about 1 minute. Use a mesh skimmer to scoop out the squash and transfer it to the plate. Repeat with the taro root, transferring it to the same plate. Set aside.

Combine the coconut milk and pandan leaf (if using) in a medium pot, set over medium heat, and bring to a simmer. Continue to simmer, stirring occasionally, until it thickens just enough to coat a spoon (a bit thinner than melted ice cream), about 10 minutes. Stir in the sugar and the ½ teaspoon salt and simmer until they fully dissolve, about 2 minutes more. Discard the pandan leaf (if using).

Add the butternut squash, taro, and apple to the coconut milk. Simmer gently just until they're heated through, 1 to 2 minutes. Add the banana and simmer for 1 minute more.

To serve, divide the coconut milk mixture among the bowls of banana custard. Sprinkle with the sesame seeds and serve right away.

BERRY AND ALMOND CLAFOUTIS

Serves 12

Because it takes approximately five minutes of active time, this dessert is ideal for days when time is short and berries are fat. The easy batter in my almond flour–based version bakes to a really cool texture, not so much the cakey custard you'd get in the French countryside as a baked crème brûlée. Use whichever berries look best in the market, though I have a soft spot for the Oregon-born marionberry or its tart cousin, the blackberry. Frozen berries work in the clafoutis, too. Just thaw them first and drain on towels overnight in the fridge to remove excess liquid.

Served for brunch, lunch, or dessert, it's extra lovely topped with fresh berries tossed with a little maple, dolloped with tangy almond yogurt, and scattered with freeze-dried berries for crunch.

For the Clafoutis

2 tablespoons melted virgin coconut oil, plus 1½ teaspoons for greasing the pan

2 tablespoons coconut sugar

1 cup well-shaken coconut milk

¼ cup extra-fine almond flour

½ cup maple syrup

¼ cup tapioca flour

1 teaspoon almond extract

1 teaspoon vanilla extract

¼ teaspoon kosher salt

3 large eggs plus 1 yolk

1 pint marionberries or blackberries

For Serving

1 cup mixed berries, large ones halved

1 teaspoon maple syrup

Tiny pinch kosher salt

1 cup plain almond-milk yogurt, liquid poured off, stirred well

Small handful freeze-dried berries, such as strawberries or raspberries

MAKE THE CLAFOUTIS

Preheat the oven to 375°F. Rub the bottom and sides of a medium, heavy skillet (an 8- or 9-inch cast iron works great) with the 1½ teaspoons of coconut oil and sprinkle the coconut sugar all over the bottom. This will help the clafoutis release from the pan after baking.

Combine the coconut milk and almond flour in a blender and blend until smooth and no longer grainy from the almond flour, about 1 minute. Add the maple syrup, the tapioca flour, the almond and vanilla extracts, the salt, the eggs and yolk, and the remaining 2 tablespoons of coconut oil and blend until smooth, about 30 seconds. Pour the batter into the skillet and scatter on the berries.

Bake until puffy at the edges, golden brown all over, and set in the center (the tip of a small knife will come out clean), 35 to 40 minutes. Let it rest and cool for at least 20 minutes before serving. It will deflate and a lip will form around its edge, giving it the silhouette of a pie.

SERVE THE DISH

In a small bowl, combine the berries, maple syrup, and salt, and stir gently but well. Stir the almond yogurt until it's nice and smooth. Either dollop it on individual slices later or get fancy and transfer it to a piping bag and pipe small dots all over the clafoutis. Next spoon on the berry-syrup mixture. Finally, sprinkle on freeze-dried berries, crushing any large pieces in your hand as you go.

Serve slices warm or room temp. Store any leftovers in the fridge for up to 3 days. Gently warm in the oven to serve.

CHOCOLATY BANANA BREAD WITH WALNUTS AND CARAMEL

Makes 16 slices

Walnuts, nut butter, and almond flour make this fragrant banana bread a good source of energy-giving protein. Chocolate chips and coconut caramel make it a great source of sweet indulgence.

For the Coconut Caramel
1¾ cups well-shaken coconut milk
3 tablespoons coconut sugar
¼ teaspoon flaky sea salt

For the Banana Bread
1 cup extra-fine almond flour
¼ cup coconut flour
3 tablespoons tapioca flour
1 teaspoon baking soda

¼ teaspoon kosher salt
¼ cup plus 2 tablespoons melted virgin coconut oil, plus more for greasing the pan
¾ cup coconut sugar
2 large eggs
2 teaspoons vanilla extract
¼ cup plus 2 tablespoons smooth almond or cashew butter

1 overripe banana (mostly brown with black patches), mashed
1 cup raw walnuts, roasted (see page 26) and roughly chopped
1 cup dark chocolate chips
½ teaspoon flaky sea salt

MAKE THE COCONUT CARAMEL
Combine all the coconut caramel ingredients in a deep medium saucepan and set over medium heat. Bring to a lively simmer and cook, stirring occasionally and more frequently as it thickens, until it reduces to about ½ cup (it'll look very thick, creamy, and almost gelatinous, and bubble very rapidly), about 20 minutes.

MAKE THE BANANA BREAD
Preheat the oven to 350°F. In a medium mixing bowl, combine the flours, baking soda, and kosher salt and stir well, breaking up any almond flour clumps as you go. In a large bowl, combine the coconut oil, sugar, eggs, and vanilla and whisk until the sugar dissolves and the mixture is a single color and smooth. It's ready when the mixture slowly and steadily falls back into the bowl when you lift the whisk.

Whisk in the almond butter and banana until well combined. Working in two batches, fold the flour mixture into the wet ingredients, completely incorporating the first batch before adding the second. Finally, fold in the walnuts and chocolate chips.

Line the bottom and sides of an 8-inch square baking pan with parchment paper, then grease the paper with coconut oil. Spread the batter evenly into the pan and dollop large spoonfuls of the caramel here and there on the top. Bake until a knife inserted in the center comes out clean and the caramel topping is golden and begins to bubble, about 25 minutes. As the bread comes out of the oven, sprinkle it with the flaky salt. Cool slightly, then remove the loaf from the pan and transfer to a cutting board. Cut into 16 slices.

The slices keep in an airtight container at room temperature for up to 4 days.

APPLE BUNDT CAKE WITH CIDER CARAMEL

Serves 12

Moist, apple-studded spiced Bundt cake wears a crown of cider-coconut caramel that drips prettily off the sides.

For the Cake
3 cups Paleo-Friendly Flour Blend (page 327)
1½ teaspoons baking powder
1 teaspoon kosher salt
½ teaspoon freshly ground cinnamon

¾ cup avocado oil
1½ cups coconut sugar
3 large eggs
1½ tablespoons vanilla extract
2 cups unpeeled, cored, and diced (about ¼ inch) apple
1 tablespoon virgin coconut oil

For the Caramel
2 cups apple cider
½ cup maple syrup
½ cup well-shaken coconut milk
Two 3-inch cinnamon sticks
1 apple, cored and sliced thin
½ teaspoon apple cider vinegar

MAKE THE CAKE

Preheat the oven to 325°F and move an oven rack to the center position. In a medium mixing bowl, combine the flour blend, baking powder, salt, and cinnamon.

In a large bowl, combine the avocado oil and sugar and whisk until the sugar dissolves. Whisk in the eggs, one at a time, completely incorporating each egg before adding the next. Add the vanilla and continue whisking until the mixture is shiny, thickened, and completely smooth, about 2 minutes. As you lift the whisk from the bowl, the mixture should slowly and steadily fall back into the bowl forming ribbons.

Working in two batches, add the flour mixture to the bowl with wet ingredients and fold it in, completely incorporating the first batch before adding the second. Finish by adding the diced apples and giving everything a few final good stirs to make sure all is mixed.

Grease a nonstick 9-inch Bundt pan with the coconut oil. Fill the pan with the batter, smooth the top with a spatula, and bake on the center rack until the cake registers 200°F in the center (temperature is the best way to tell when cakes made with my Paleo-friendly flour blend are ready), 50 to 55 minutes.

MAKE THE CARAMEL AND SERVE

While the cake cooks, combine the cider, maple syrup, coconut milk, and cinnamon in a medium saucepan, set over medium-high heat, and bring to a lively simmer. Cook, stirring occasionally and more frequently as it thickens, until you have a golden brown, creamy sauce that very heavily coats a spoon, 15 to 18 minutes. When the sauce is ready, discard the cinnamon sticks, then add the apple cider vinegar, fold in the sliced apples, and simmer until they just start to soften, about 1 minute more. Keep in a warm place until the cake is ready.

Remove the cake from the oven and run a butter knife around the edges to ensure it releases from the pan. Grab a plate or cutting board that's slightly larger than the pan and invert it onto the pan. Protecting your hands from the hot pan with oven mitts or a kitchen towel, firmly grab the sides of both the pan and plate and swiftly invert the pan onto the plate. Let the plate rest on the counter for a few seconds, then carefully remove the pan, slowly lifting from one side, then the other, to expose the cake.

Let the cake rest for at least 15 minutes. Grab the caramel sauce and spoon the sliced apples (not the caramel just yet) on top of the cake. Drizzle the caramel sauce over the cake to serve.

Leftovers keep in an airtight container at room temperature for up to 4 days.

HAITIAN SPICED PINEAPPLE UPSIDE-DOWN CAKE

Serves 12

Mom often made pineapple upside-down cake, the most famous of Haitian desserts, augmenting a boxed mix with various spices and extracts brought from Haiti by visiting relatives and popping a can of pineapple (and some freakishly red maraschino cherries) for the topping.

Mom was busy with a demanding job and two kids. I have a little more time on my hands, so I look to fresh pineapple, caramelizing it with maple syrup and spices then tiling it onto the bottom of the pan before baking the cake. Believe me, it's worth the effort. When you haul the cake from the oven, the heady perfume of vanilla, almond, cinnamon, and star anise fills the room. When you flip the cake and lift the pan, the pineapple slices glisten like jewels and stun your friends waiting at the table.

For the Pineapple Topping
¾ cup virgin coconut oil, plus more for greasing the pan

1 ripe pineapple

½ cup coconut sugar

½ cup maple syrup

Three 3-inch cinnamon sticks

5 star anise

For the Cake
2¾ cups Paleo-Friendly Flour Blend (page 327)

1 tablespoon plus 1 teaspoon baking powder

1 teaspoon kosher salt

One 1-inch piece cinnamon stick

2 cups coconut sugar

¾ cup melted virgin coconut oil

5 large eggs

½ cup well-shaken coconut milk

2 tablespoons vanilla extract

2 teaspoons almond extract

1 lime, for zesting

MAKE THE TOPPING
Trace the outside of an 11-inch pan onto a piece of parchment paper to make a rough circle about 1 inch bigger than the pan, then cut out the circle. You want the parchment to be just a tad bigger than the base of the pan so it has a little lip to contain the topping. Tuck the parchment into the base of the pan and rub it and the sides of the pan with a little coconut oil.

Carve off the brown eyes, quarter the pineapple, and cut off and discard the core (see page 376). Cut the quarters crosswise into ⅛-inch-thick slices.

Set a mesh strainer over a large heatproof bowl. Combine the remaining coconut oil, coconut sugar, maple syrup, cinnamon sticks, and star anise in a large saucepan and bring to a simmer over medium heat. Add the pineapple and simmer until it releases its juices and they reduce into a rich syrup and the pineapple is very golden, translucent, and tender, about 10 minutes. Pour the mixture through the strainer. Reserve the pineapple, discard the whole spices, and pour the strained liquid back into the saucepan. Continue reducing the liquid until it's as thick as molasses, about 8 minutes more. Set the liquid aside.

Starting from the dead center of the parchment, lay down once piece of pineapple, then shingle the remaining pineapple slices into a spiral, overlapping each slice over the last in an outward circular pattern, until you cover the entire base of the pan. Set aside while you prep the cake batter.

MAKE THE CAKE
Preheat the oven to 350°F and move an oven rack to the center position. In a medium mixing bowl, combine the flour blend, baking powder, and salt and stir well. Use a Microplane to grate in the cinnamon. In a large mixing bowl, whisk together the coconut sugar and coconut oil until combined. Whisk in the eggs one

(cont.)

at a time, fully incorporating each one before adding the next. Whisk in the coconut milk, vanilla extract, and almond extract until the mixture is well combined, thick, and creamy. As you lift the whisk from the bowl, the mixture should slowly and steadily fall back into the bowl. Use a Microplane to grate in the lime zest. Working in two batches, add the flour to the bowl with the wet ingredients and fold it in, completely incorporating the first batch before adding the second.

Pour the reserved caramelized sauce evenly over the shingled pineapple. Next, pour the cake batter evenly over the sauce. Bake the cake on the center rack until golden brown and a thermometer reads 200°F when inserted in the center (temperature is the best way to tell when cakes made with my Paleo-friendly flour blend are ready), about 35 minutes.

When the cake is done, run a knife around the edges to make sure it releases from the pan. Grab a plate or lightweight cutting board that's slightly larger than the pan and invert the plate onto the pan. Protecting your hands from the hot pan with oven mitts or a kitchen towel, firmly grab the sides of both the pan and the plate and swiftly invert the pan onto the plate. Let the plate rest on the counter for a few seconds, then carefully remove the pan, slowly lifting from one side, then the other, to expose the cake. If any pineapple pieces have stuck to the pan, use a small spatula to gently dislodge them and use them to cover any of the cake's bald spots.

Let the cake rest for at least 15 minutes before serving. Leftovers keep in an airtight container at room temperature for up to 4 days.

MAPLE-GLAZED DATE CAKE WITH GINGER AND ROSEMARY

Serves 12 to 16

The mild sweetness makes this skillet cake great for a morning treat, while the gooey date topping means it will satisfy at any celebration. Ginger and rosemary, the unlikely and dynamic duo I discovered at Jean-Georges, add a note of intrigue.

For the Date Topping
¼ cup virgin coconut oil

1 pound Medjool dates, pitted and quartered

1 tablespoon roughly chopped fresh rosemary leaves, plus some small leaves for garnish

½ cup maple syrup

For the Cake Batter
8 large eggs, yolks and whites separated

½ cup virgin coconut oil

3 cups Paleo-Friendly Flour Blend (page 327)

1 cup honey

2 tablespoons finely chopped ginger

2 teaspoons vanilla extract

2 teaspoons baking powder

½ teaspoon kosher salt

1 teaspoon cream of tartar

For the Maple Glaze
¾ cup plus 2 tablespoons coconut milk

¼ cup maple syrup

¼ teaspoon flaky sea salt

MAKE THE DATE TOPPING

Warm the coconut oil over medium heat in an 11-inch heavy skillet (I like cast iron here). Add the dates and rosemary and give everything a quick stir. Cook until the dates start to soften and the rosemary smells fragrant, about 1 minute. Stir in the maple syrup and simmer gently until it reduces by half and the dates are soft but still hold their shape, 2 to 3 minutes. You will notice the bubbles get smaller and turn golden. Be careful not to reduce the syrup too much—this will become the cake topping, so you want a thin layer of sauce covering the entire bottom of the pan. Keep warm while you make the cake batter.

MAKE THE CAKE BATTER AND BAKE

Preheat the oven to 350°F and move an oven rack to the center position. In a large mixing bowl, combine the egg yolks, coconut oil, flour blend, honey, ginger, vanilla, baking powder, and kosher salt. Whisk to combine.

In a separate large mixing bowl (or the bowl of a stand mixer with the whisk attachment), whip the egg whites with an electric hand mixer on medium speed or a whisk and some elbow grease until frothy, about 2 minutes. Sprinkle in the cream of tartar and whip on high speed until soft peaks form, about 2 minutes more.

One third at a time, fold the egg whites into the flour mixture with a flexible spatula (gently, so you maintain the air you whipped into them), making sure the batter is a single uniform color with no streaks of white before the next addition.

Pour and scrape the prepared cake batter into the skillet with the topping, spreading it evenly over the date mixture. Bake on the center rack until the cake registers 200°F in the center (temperature is the best way to tell when cakes made with my Paleo-friendly flour blend are ready), about 30 minutes.

(cont.)

MAKE THE MAPLE GLAZE AND SERVE

While the cake bakes, bring the coconut milk to a lively simmer in a small saucepan over high heat. Cook, stirring occasionally, until the coconut milk thickens to a creamy, saucy consistency (it'll just barely coat a spoon), about 8 minutes. Whisk in the maple syrup and salt and keep simmering, stirring occasionally, until the sauce thickens to about ⅓ cup (it'll have the consistency of melted ice cream), about 5 minutes more. The glaze thickens as it cools, so be careful not to let it thicken too much. Turn off the heat and keep warm until the cake is ready.

Once the cake is ready, run a knife around the edges to make sure it releases from the pan. Grab a large plate or lightweight cutting board that's slightly larger than the pan and invert the plate onto the pan. Protecting your hands from the hot pan with oven mitts or a kitchen towel, firmly grab the sides of both the pan and plate and swiftly invert the pan onto the plate.

Let the plate rest on the counter for a few seconds, then carefully remove the pan, slowly lifting from one side, then the other, to expose the cake. If any dates have stuck to the pan, dislodge them and use them to cover any of the cake's bald spots. Drizzle the warm maple caramel to glaze the cake, garnish with the small rosemary leaves, and serve.

The cake is best warm from the oven, but keeps, covered, at room temperature for up to 5 days. It reheats well and the slices toast nicely, too.

CHOCOLATE CHUNK BROWNIES WITH CACAO CARAMEL

Makes 16 brownies

The secrets to these are underbaking them, so they're tender and fudgy, and adding cacao powder, the raw and minimally processed analogue to the more common cocoa powder. Since cacao powder is not treated with high heat, it retains more of its nutrients, but I also love its big flavor. It makes these brownies super chocolaty, a decadent dessert taken just to the happy side of over-the-top by cacao-spiked caramel. I like the brownies best warm from the oven, drizzled with the caramel, and beside a cold glass of nut milk.

For the Brownies
¾ cup virgin coconut oil, plus extra for greasing the pan

1½ cups coconut sugar

3 large eggs

1½ tablespoons vanilla extract

¾ cup Paleo-Friendly Flour Blend (page 327)

¾ cup cacao powder

¼ teaspoon kosher salt

7 ounces dark chocolate chunks or chips

For the Cacao Caramel
1¾ cups well-shaken coconut milk

2 tablespoons maple syrup

1 teaspoon cacao powder

¼ teaspoon flaky sea salt

MAKE THE BROWNIES

Preheat the oven to 350°F and move an oven rack to the top position. Line an 8-inch square baking pan with a piece of parchment paper cut about 1 inch longer than the pan so there's a bit of overhang. Grease the parchment paper with a bit of the coconut oil.

Heat the coconut oil in a small pan or microwave it until it's melted and hot. Combine the coconut oil and sugar in a medium mixing bowl and whisk well until it's a single color (the sugar won't completely dissolve and that's just fine). Add the eggs and whisk vigorously to get some air in there until it's thick, creamy, and glossy, like the caramel for caramel apples. When this texture is reached, beat for 1 minute more. This is how to get a crackly top on the brownies and create different textures. Stir in the vanilla. Sift in the flour blend, cacao powder, and kosher salt by adding them to a fine-mesh strainer, holding it over the bowl, and gently tapping it with your palm. Crush and sift in any clumps that get caught in the strainer. Use a flexible spatula to fold in the flour and cacao powder just until you have a thick, creamy batter with no pockets of flour.

Pour the batter into the baking pan and evenly sprinkle on the chocolate chunks. Bake on the top rack until the brownies have a crackly surface and fudgy middle that barely holds together straight out of the oven (if you insert a thermometer into the center, at a slight angle and without touching the pan, it'll register 180°F when the brownies are ready), about 18 minutes. Let the brownies cool to warm in the pan.

MAKE THE CACAO CARAMEL

In the meantime, bring the coconut milk to a lively simmer in a medium saucepan over high heat. Cook, whisking if it threatens to boil over, until it has reduced by half, about 10 minutes. Whisk in the maple syrup, cacao powder, and flaky salt and keep simmering, stirring occasionally, until it's as thick as molasses, 5 to 7 minutes more. Keep the caramel in a warm place until ready to serve.

When the brownies have cooled to warm, use the parchment paper to lift them out of the pan and transfer them to a cutting board, then cut into 16 pieces. Serve the warm brownies drizzled with the cacao caramel.

Fully cooled, the brownies keep in an airtight container at room temperature for up to 4 days.

CHOCOLATE AND NUT-BUTTER TART WITH SEA SALT AND CHIPOTLE

Serves 12 to 16

This pretty tart looks as impressive as it is easy to make. Assemble it, refrigerate it overnight, then bring it to the table and take your bow.

For the Crust

2 cups raw pecans, plus ¼ cup roasted (see page 26) and roughly chopped

6 tablespoons extra-fine almond flour

1 tablespoon cacao powder

6 tablespoons melted virgin coconut oil

3 tablespoons date syrup or maple syrup

¼ teaspoon flaky sea salt

For the Nut-Butter Filling

⅓ cup date syrup or maple syrup

2 tablespoons coconut sugar

⅔ cup melted virgin coconut oil

1 cup smooth sunflower seed butter (see page 319)

1 teaspoon vanilla extract

For the Ganache

6 ounces dark chocolate chunks

¾ cup well-shaken coconut milk

One 1-inch piece cinnamon stick

For Serving

1 teaspoon flaky sea salt

¼ teaspoon chipotle chile powder

MAKE THE CRUST

Preheat the oven to 350°F. Pulse the 2 cups of raw pecans in a food processor or blender into a crumbly meal, like slightly coarse bread crumbs. In a medium bowl, combine the pecan crumbs with the remaining ingredients and mix until they form a dark, crumbly dough.

Put the dough in a 9½-inch fluted tart pan with a removable bottom and press it in an even, packed layer onto the bottom and halfway up the sides of the pan. Using a fork, prick all over the bottom layer of the tart crust.

Transfer the tart pan to the center rack of the oven. Bake the tart crust until toasty and lightly crisp to the touch, like a soft-baked cookie, 12 to 15 minutes. Let the tart crust cool fully while you make the filling.

MAKE THE NUT-BUTTER FILLING

Pour the date syrup into a blender, then add the remaining filling ingredients and puree on high until super smooth. Carefully pour the filling into the tart crust and refrigerate until the filling has set (it'll be firm to the touch), about 1 hour.

MAKE THE GANACHE

Remove the tart crust from the fridge and put it on a nice flat surface since you're going to be making ganache and pouring it in so it comes to the rim of the pan. Put the chocolate in a medium mixing bowl. Pour the coconut milk into a small saucepan and use a Microplane to grate in the cinnamon. Set the pot over medium heat, let it come to a simmer, and immediately pour it over the chocolate. Stir until the chocolate has completely melted and the mixture is smooth and silky, then immediately pour it into the tart crust.

Let the ganache set for about 5 minutes so it doesn't shift or spill on the way to the fridge, then carefully transfer the tart to the fridge to chill for at least 12 hours or up to 24 hours.

SERVE THE TART
Remove the tart from the fridge and carefully ease it out of its pan. Sprinkle the edge of the tart with the roasted pecans, then sprinkle on the flaky salt and chipotle to serve.

Leftovers keep in an airtight container in the fridge for up to 3 days.

FROZEN YOGURT POPS

Makes about 30 popsicles

A low-effort, high-impact dessert, these popsicles were created with both flavor and health in mind, with super-foods snuck into each frozen treat. The base makes enough for 30 popsicles, so you'll need to buy enough molds. The following recipes make enough for 15, so choose two flavors, pull out a blender, and they'll be assembled in no time.

For the Base

3½ cups plain alternative yogurt, well stirred

3½ cups well-shaken coconut milk

½ cup maple syrup

MAKE THE BASE

Whisk together all the base ingredients in a large bowl until well mixed.

For the Popsicles

Sliced fruit, for garnish

2 Fruit Flavors (see the next page), one full batch of each

MAKE THE POPSICLES

If using sliced fruit to decorate the popsicles, put a few pieces in each mold, gently pressing the fruit against the sides so it sticks. Fill each mold about ⅔ of the way with the base, then fill the remaining ⅓ of each mold with a fruit flavor. Cover the molds with the lids, insert sticks, and freeze until fully frozen, about 8 hours or up to 1 month.

To serve, let the popsicles sit at room temperature for 5 to 10 minutes to make unmolding them easy.

For the red berry–lime flavor (enough for 15)

4¼ cups mixed red berries, such as hulled strawberries and raspberries

½ cup plus 2 tablespoons maple syrup

½ teaspoon kosher salt

3 limes, for zesting

MAKE THE FLAVOR

Combine the berries, maple syrup, and salt in a blender, then use a Microplane to grate in the zest of the limes. Puree until as smooth as possible, then strain through a fine-mesh strainer into a bowl, discarding the solids.

For the turmeric-peach flavor (enough for 15)

3 large ripe peaches, halved and pitted

¾ cup finely chopped palm sugar or coconut sugar

1½-inch knob ginger, peeled and roughly chopped against the grain

¾-inch knob turmeric, peeled and roughly chopped

1½ tablespoons lime juice (from 1 juicy lime)

¼ teaspoon kosher salt

MAKE THE FLAVOR

Combine all the ingredients in the blender along with 1 cup of water and puree until as smooth as possible.

For the kiwi-mint flavor (enough for 15)

3 ripe kiwis, peeled and roughly chopped

¾ cup lightly packed spinach leaves

30 mint leaves

¾ cup well-shaken coconut milk

½ cup plus 1 tablespoon maple syrup

¼ teaspoon kosher salt

MAKE THE FLAVOR

Combine all the ingredients in a blender and puree until as smooth as possible.

For the chocolate-avocado flavor (enough for 15)

1 large ripe Hass avocado, pitted

¾ cup well-shaken coconut milk

2 tablespoons cacao powder

½ cup maple syrup

½ teaspoon kosher salt

MAKE THE FLAVOR

Scoop the avocado flesh into a blender, then add the remaining ingredients along with ¾ cup of water. Puree until as smooth as possible.

For the hibiscus-blackberry flavor (enough for 15)

2 cups blackberries

1 cup hibiscus infusion (see page 338)

¼ cup plus 2 tablespoons finely chopped palm sugar or coconut sugar

2 tablespoons lemon juice

½ teaspoon kosher salt

MAKE THE FLAVOR

Combine all the ingredients in a blender and puree until as smooth as possible. Strain through a fine-mesh strainer into a bowl, discarding the solids.

Acknowledgments

It took me three years to fill the pages of this book, but many more to get to page one. So many people deserve credit for getting me there—for inspiring my love of cooking, fueling my curiosity, and teaching me to appreciate food not just for its flavor but also for its history.

Thank you, Mom and Dad, for always making sure a delicious dinner was on the table, from humble weekday meals to holiday feasts. For showing me what hard work is, which not only helped me succeed in professional kitchens but also inspired me to work so much that I had virtually no time to cook complicated dishes at home—that's how so much of the food in this book was born. And for making sure we always knew where we came from. Thank you to my sister, Jessica, who I adore and with whom I made my very first cake, which was so bad we buried it outside.

Thank you, Greg Brainin. You took me in twenty years ago, fresh out of CIA. You taught me how to cook crisp-skinned chicken and lobster with tapioca, how to season, how to sear, how to use acid and heat, how to "make the hits." And you took me back in with no questions after I disappeared when things got dark. Your early forgiveness solidified my sobriety. I am forever grateful.

Thank you, Jean-Georges, for teaching me that food can be healthy *and* taste luxurious, that shopping at farmers markets immediately ups your game, and that the entire world of flavor can star in the foods we eat every day.

Thank you to my other culinary mentors, Marcus Samuelsson and Andy Ricker. Marcus, as a young cook I revered you—a black man doing fine dining—and saved up to eat at Aquavit. Today, I'm honored to call you a friend. Uncle Andy, thank you for your honest advice and endless patience, for the many meals in Chiang Mai and for your friendship.

Thank you to the team at *Top Chef*—Padma, Tom, Gail, my fellow cheftestants, the producers, and the crew—for welcoming me, for giving me the opportunity to travel and cook and learn all over the world, and for letting me do my thing.

A huge thank you to all my teammates and colleagues who helped inspire these recipes through meals and conversations shared and kitchen collaborations had over the years. These recipes reflect some of my favorite moments with you: Jami Flatt, Jonathan Rendon, Erin Koroll, Varanya Geyoonsawat, Brandon Bellerose, Matt Lavoie, Taylor Stark, Khamla Vongsakoun, Andrea Eubanks, Brea Currey, Tyler Malek, Mei Lin, Julie Bauer, Michael Solomonov, Jamie Freedman, Sam Saltos, Ryan Lowder, and Pichet Ong.

And immense gratitude to the entire team that helped me actually create these recipe—to shop for and test and shoot these recipes—Laura Russell, Kevyn Allard, Kaja Taft, Michelle Tam, Lauren Chandler, Sam Taminosian, Michael Toomin, George Howard, Sofia Kraft, Tyler Hansen, Pauline Zuniga, Dominic, Amezcua, Zach Wolf, and Alex Castellano.

Thank you, Eva, for your images, which simultaneously ground and lift this book. Thank you for the stunning work that captures the rich potency of this bold food. Between pandemic downtime and a fussy writer, this book just kept growing, as did its art. I cherished every work day tucked away with you as the years passed from proposal to final cover shoot.

Thank you to Kim and Karen, my agent and my publisher, for believing in this project. And the team at Harper Wave—Rebecca Raskin, Bonni Leon-Berman, Nate Knaebel, Yelena Nesbit, Sophia Lauriello, Penny Makras, Brian Perrin, and Laura Cole. Thank you all for supporting the book I truly wanted to make.

And thank you to my beloved coauthor, JJ. You are literally the best. If you weren't such a bad cook, we might have written a different book, but I think these long recipes will give hope to home cooks, and my hope is that they will be as excited as you were while cooking through them. I will miss your neurotic texts and Jersey sass, which I just don't get enough of in the PNW.

And to my closest family and dearest friends, thank you for your undying support, through thick and thin—Tia (I know you wish corn soup was in this book), Arthur, Kristopher, Steve, Natalie, Vlad, Richard, Warner, Shorty, Ned, Darren, Ben, Peter, Sun, Karen, and Gary.

Index

Note: Page numbers in *italics* refer to illustrations.

Halibut with Summer
Squash and Spiced
Tomatoes, 188, 189
Quick-Seared Tuna with
Blistered Tomatoes
and Tarragon-Mustard
Vinaigrette, 172, 173
Roasted Eggplant with
Dried Tomato Relish,
76, 77
Slow-Roasted Cherry
Tomatoes, 307, 307
Tomatoes on Tomatoes
with Shallot-Chile
Dressing, 46, 47
Tomato–Hazelnut Milk
Soup with Garam
Masala, 154, 155

trout: Grilled Trout with
Sautéed Spinach and
Vegetable-Packed
Ponzu, 196–97,
197
tuna:
Albacore Tataki with
Avocado and Grilled
Cucumber Vinaigrette,
170, 171
Quick-Seared Tuna with
Blistered Tomatoes
and Tarragon-Mustard
Vinaigrette, 172,
173
turkey:
Mom's (Haitian) Meatloaf,
238, 239

Turkey in Red Mole, 240,
241

V

Vanilla Custard with Berries
and Basil, 362, 363
Very Vanilla Ice Cream, 347
Vietnamese Coffee-Style
Milkshake, 353
Vietnamese-Style Chile-
Lime Sauce, 302, 302
Vietnamese-Style Duck
Curry, 216, 217–19, 218
Vietnamese-Style Pickles, 291

W

Warm Coconut Chia
Pudding with Dried
Mangoes and Cherries,
136, 137
Watermelon-Berry Salad
with Chile Dressing and
Lots of Herbs, 36, 37

X

XO Sauce, 299, 299

HarperCollins books may be purchased for educational, business, or sales promotional use. For information, please email the Special Markets Department at SPsales@harpercollins.com.

FIRST EDITION

Designed by Bonni Leon-Berman

Photography by Eva Kosmas Flores

Library of Congress Cataloging-in-Publication Data

Names: Gourdet, Gregory, author. | Goode, JJ, author.
Title: Everyone's table : global recipes for modern health / Gregory Gourdet and JJ Goode.
Description: First edition. | New York, NY : Harper Wave, [2021] | Includes index. | Identifiers: LCCN 2021002287 (print) | LCCN 2021002288 (ebook) | ISBN 9780062984517 | ISBN 9780062984524 (ebook)
Subjects: LCSH: Cooking. | LCGFT: Cookbooks.
Classification: LCC TX714 .G676 2021 (print) | LCC TX714 (ebook) | DDC 641.5— dc23 LC record available at https://lccn.loc.gov/2021002287
LC ebook record available at https://lccn.loc.gov/2021002288

21 22 23 24 25 TC 10 9 8 7 6 5 4 3 2 1